™

References for the Rest of Us! ®

BESTSELLING BOOK SERIES

Are you intimidated and confused by computers? Do you find that traditional manuals are overloaded with technical details you'll never use? Do your friends and family always call you to fix simple problems on their PCs? Then the *...For Dummies®* computer book series from IDG Books Worldwide is for you.

...For Dummies books are written for those frustrated computer users who know they aren't really dumb but find that PC hardware, software, and indeed the unique vocabulary of computing make them feel helpless. *...For Dummies* books use a lighthearted approach, a down-to-earth style, and even cartoons and humorous icons to dispel computer novices' fears and build their confidence. Lighthearted but not lightweight, these books are a perfect survival guide for anyone forced to use a computer.

> *"I like my copy so much I told friends; now they bought copies."*
> — Irene C., Orwell, Ohio

> *"Quick, concise, nontechnical, and humorous."*
> — Jay A., Elburn, Illinois

> *"Thanks, I needed this book. Now I can sleep at night."*
> — Robin F., British Columbia, Canada

Already, millions of satisfied readers agree. They have made *...For Dummies* books the #1 introductory level computer book series and have written asking for more. So, if you're looking for the most fun and easy way to learn about computers, look to *...For Dummies* books to give you a helping hand.

IDG BOOKS WORLDWIDE ®

Family Tree Maker FOR DUMMIES®

by Matthew L. Helm & April Leigh Helm

IDG Books Worldwide, Inc.
An International Data Group Company

Foster City, CA ◆ Chicago, IL ◆ Indianapolis, IN ◆ New York, NY

Family Tree Maker For Dummies®

Published by
IDG Books Worldwide, Inc.
An International Data Group Company
919 E. Hillsdale Blvd.
Suite 400
Foster City, CA 94404
www.idgbooks.com (IDG Books Worldwide Web site)
www.dummies.com (Dummies Press Web site)

Library of Congress Catalog Card No.: 99-67167

ISBN: 0-7645-0661-7

Printed in the United States of America

10 9 8 7 6 5 4 3 2 1

1B/QZ/RS/ZZ/IN

Distributed in the United States by IDG Books Worldwide, Inc.

Distributed by CDG Books Canada Inc. for Canada; by Transworld Publishers Limited in the United Kingdom; by IDG Norge Books for Norway; by IDG Sweden Books for Sweden; by IDG Books Australia Publishing Corporation Pty. Ltd. for Australia and New Zealand; by TransQuest Publishers Pte Ltd. for Singapore, Malaysia, Thailand, Indonesia, and Hong Kong; by Gotop Information Inc. for Taiwan; by ICG Muse, Inc. for Japan; by Intersoft for South Africa; by Eyrolles for France; by International Thomson Publishing for Germany, Austria and Switzerland; by Distribuidora Cuspide for Argentina; by LR International for Brazil; by Galileo Libros for Chile; by Ediciones ZETA S.C.R. Ltda. for Peru; by WS Computer Publishing Corporation, Inc., for the Philippines; by Contemporanea de Ediciones for Venezuela; by Express Computer Distributors for the Caribbean and West Indies; by Micronesia Media Distributor, Inc. for Micronesia; by Chips Computadoras S.A. de C.V. for Mexico; by Editorial Norma de Panama S.A. for Panama; by American Bookshops for Finland.

For general information on IDG Books Worldwide's books in the U.S., please call our Consumer Customer Service department at 800-762-2974. For reseller information, including discounts and premium sales, please call our Reseller Customer Service department at 800-434-3422.

For information on where to purchase IDG Books Worldwide's books outside the U.S., please contact our International Sales department at 317-596-5530 or fax 317-596-5692.

For consumer information on foreign language translations, please contact our Customer Service department at 1-800-434-3422, fax 317-596-5692, or e-mail rights@idgbooks.com.

For information on licensing foreign or domestic rights, please phone +1-650-655-3109.

For sales inquiries and special prices for bulk quantities, please contact our Sales department at 650-655-3200 or write to the address above.

For information on using IDG Books Worldwide's books in the classroom or for ordering examination copies, please contact our Educational Sales department at 800-434-2086 or fax 317-596-5499.

For press review copies, author interviews, or other publicity information, please contact our Public Relations department at 650-655-3000 or fax 650-655-3299.

For authorization to photocopy items for corporate, personal, or educational use, please contact Copyright Clearance Center, 222 Rosewood Drive, Danvers, MA 01923, or fax 978-750-4470.

About the Authors

Matthew Helm is currently the Executive Vice President and Chief Technology Officer for FamilyToolbox.net, Inc. Also, he is publisher of the Journal of Online Genealogy. He is the creator and maintainer of the award-winning Helm's Genealogy Toolbox, Helm/Helms Family Research Page, and a variety of other Web sites. Matthew has spoken at several genealogical conventions, as well as lectured to various genealogical and historical societies. Matthew holds an A.B. in History and an M.S. in Library and Information Science from the University of Illinois at Urbana-Champaign.

April Leigh Helm is the President of FamilyToolbox.net, Inc. Also, she is the editor and maintainer of the Journal of Online Genealogy. April has lectured on genealogy and other topics for various conventions, conferences, and groups. She holds a B.S. in Journalism and an Ed.M. in Higher Education Administration from the University of Illinois at Urbana-Champaign.

Together, the Helms co-authored *Genealogy Online For Dummies,* 1st and 2nd Editions (IDG Books Worldwide, Inc.).

Although for many years they had collected notes on family members and old photographs, it was not until 1990, while living and working in the Washington, D.C. area, that the Helms began seriously researching their family lines. Upon returning to central Illinois in 1994, the Helms found themselves with limited historical and genealogical resources to continue their research. It was then that they jumped into online genealogy.

Here's a little more information about the genealogical Web sites maintained by the Helms:

- Helm's Genealogy Toolbox (`genealogy.tbox.com`) is a comprehensive listing of genealogical sites that Matthew created and introduced to the public in 1994.

- The Journal of Online Genealogy (`www.onlinegenealogy.com`) is an electronic magazine on the World Wide Web that focuses on the use of online resources and techniques in genealogy and family history. The Helms introduced it in July 1996.

- GenealogyPortal.com (`www.genealogyportal.com`) is a site containing eight separate search engines that index sites of interest to genealogists. It was created as a joint project between Matthew and Stephen Wood, the creator and maintainer of the Genealogy Home Page. They introduced the site in March 1999.

ABOUT IDG BOOKS WORLDWIDE

Welcome to the world of IDG Books Worldwide.

IDG Books Worldwide, Inc., is a subsidiary of International Data Group, the world's largest publisher of computer-related information and the leading global provider of information services on information technology. IDG was founded more than 30 years ago by Patrick J. McGovern and now employs more than 9,000 people worldwide. IDG publishes more than 290 computer publications in over 75 countries. More than 90 million people read one or more IDG publications each month.

Launched in 1990, IDG Books Worldwide is today the #1 publisher of best-selling computer books in the United States. We are proud to have received eight awards from the Computer Press Association in recognition of editorial excellence and three from Computer Currents' First Annual Readers' Choice Awards. Our best-selling *...For Dummies*® series has more than 50 million copies in print with translations in 31 languages. IDG Books Worldwide, through a joint venture with IDG's Hi-Tech Beijing, became the first U.S. publisher to publish a computer book in the People's Republic of China. In record time, IDG Books Worldwide has become the first choice for millions of readers around the world who want to learn how to better manage their businesses.

Our mission is simple: Every one of our books is designed to bring extra value and skill-building instructions to the reader. Our books are written by experts who understand and care about our readers. The knowledge base of our editorial staff comes from years of experience in publishing, education, and journalism — experience we use to produce books to carry us into the new millennium. In short, we care about books, so we attract the best people. We devote special attention to details such as audience, interior design, use of icons, and illustrations. And because we use an efficient process of authoring, editing, and desktop publishing our books electronically, we can spend more time ensuring superior content and less time on the technicalities of making books.

You can count on our commitment to deliver high-quality books at competitive prices on topics you want to read about. At IDG Books Worldwide, we continue in the IDG tradition of delivering quality for more than 30 years. You'll find no better book on a subject than one from IDG Books Worldwide.

John Kilcullen
Chairman and CEO
IDG Books Worldwide, Inc.

Steven Berkowitz
President and Publisher
IDG Books Worldwide, Inc.

**Eighth Annual
Computer Press
Awards ≥1992**

**Ninth Annual
Computer Press
Awards ≥1993**

**Tenth Annual
Computer Press
Awards ≥1994**

**Eleventh Annual
Computer Press
Awards ≥1995**

IDG is the world's leading IT media, research and exposition company. Founded in 1964, IDG had 1997 revenues of $2.05 billion and has more than 9,000 employees worldwide. IDG offers the widest range of media options that reach IT buyers in 75 countries representing 95% of worldwide IT spending. IDG's diverse product and services portfolio spans six key areas including print publishing, online publishing, expositions and conferences, market research, education and training, and global marketing services. More than 90 million people read one or more of IDG's 290 magazines and newspapers, including IDG's leading global brands — Computerworld, PC World, Network World, Macworld and the Channel World family of publications. IDG Books Worldwide is one of the fastest-growing computer book publishers in the world, with more than 700 titles in 36 languages. The "...For Dummies®" series alone has more than 50 million copies in print. IDG offers online users the largest network of technology-specific Web sites around the world through IDG.net (http://www.idg.net), which comprises more than 225 targeted Web sites in 55 countries worldwide. International Data Corporation (IDC) is the world's largest provider of information technology data, analysis and consulting, with research centers in over 41 countries and more than 400 research analysts worldwide. IDG World Expo is a leading producer of more than 168 globally branded conferences and expositions in 35 countries including E3 (Electronic Entertainment Expo), Macworld Expo, ComNet, Windows World Expo, ICE (Internet Commerce Expo), Agenda, DEMO, and Spotlight. IDG's training subsidiary, ExecuTrain, is the world's largest computer training company, with more than 230 locations worldwide and 785 training courses. IDG Marketing Services helps industry-leading IT companies build international brand recognition by developing global integrated marketing programs via IDG's print, online and exposition products worldwide. Further information about the company can be found at www.idg.com. 1/24/99

Dedication

For Brynn Kyleakin (who tried her best to be patient while we wrote this book).

Acknowledgments

We wish to acknowledge the following people, without whom this book wouldn't exist:

Lisa Swayne and Laura Moss, who sought us out to write the book.

Paul Levesque, Kim Darosett, and Dennis Cohen who helped us put everything together.

Our respective parents and ancestors, without whom our own genealogies would not be possible.

Publisher's Acknowledgments

We're proud of this book; please register your comments through our IDG Books Worldwide Online Registration Form located at `http://my2cents.dummies.com`.

Some of the people who helped bring this book to market include the following:

Acquisitions, Editorial, and Media Development

Project Editor: Paul Levesque

Acquisitions Editor: Laura Moss

Copy Editor: Kim Darosett

Technical Editor: Dennis Cohen

Editorial Manager: Leah Cameron

Editorial Assistant: Beth Parlon

Production

Project Coordinator: Maridee V. Ennis

Layout and Graphics: Karl Brandt, Barry Offringa, Michael Sullivan, Brian Torwelle, Mary Jo Weis, Dan Whetstine

Proofreaders: Laura Albert, Laura Bowman, Marianne Santy, Ethel M. Winslow

Indexer: Johnna VanHoose

General and Administrative

IDG Books Worldwide, Inc.: John Kilcullen, CEO; Steven Berkowitz, President and Publisher

IDG Books Technology Publishing Group: Richard Swadley, Senior Vice President and Publisher; Walter Bruce III, Vice President and Associate Publisher; Joseph Wikert, Associate Publisher; Mary Bednarek, Branded Product Development Director; Mary Corder, Editorial Director; Barry Pruett, Publishing Manager; Michelle Baxter, Publishing Manager

IDG Books Consumer Publishing Group: Roland Elgey, Senior Vice President and Publisher; Kathleen A. Welton, Vice President and Publisher; Kevin Thornton, Acquisitions Manager; Kristin A. Cocks, Editorial Director

IDG Books Internet Publishing Group: Brenda McLaughlin, Senior Vice President and Publisher; Diane Graves Steele, Vice President and Associate Publisher; Sofia Marchant, Online Marketing Manager

IDG Books Production for Dummies Press: Debbie Stailey, Associate Director of Production; Cindy L. Phipps, Manager of Project Coordination, Production Proofreading, and Indexing; Tony Augsburger, Manager of Prepress, Reprints, and Systems; Laura Carpenter, Production Control Manager; Shelley Lea, Supervisor of Graphics and Design; Debbie J. Gates, Production Systems Specialist; Robert Springer, Supervisor of Proofreading; Kathie Schutte, Production Supervisor

Dummies Packaging and Book Design: Patty Page, Manager, Promotions Marketing

◆

The publisher would like to give special thanks to Patrick J. McGovern, without whom this book would not have been possible.

◆

Contents at a Glance

Cartoons at a Glance

By Rich Tennant

"According to these reports, I'm related to Pee-Wee Herman."

page 323

page 7

"Perhaps you're right. Maybe he is taking this pedigree business a bit too far."

page 121

page 291

"That's a lovely family tree. Now just remove Donald Trump, Cindy Crawford and Arnold Schwarzenegger."

page 181

Fax: 978-546-7747
E-mail: richtennant@the5thwave.com
World Wide Web: www.the5thwave.com

Table of Contents

Introduction

*I*magine you're preparing for that yearly family reunion. You rush around the house, gathering paper plates and napkins and putting the finishing touches on Grandma's famous potato salad. Then all of a sudden, the phone rings. It's Aunt Betty — and she has a favor to ask you. Knowing that you are the genealogist in the family, she wants you to prepare a chart of the family's ancestors. Hesitantly, you agree.

You look at your watch and discover that you have only a few hours before the event begins. The sweat begins to accumulate on your brow, as you sift through the many folders and boxes that contain the fruits of your research. A photocopy of a census record here, and some notes on a napkin over there. Time is running out, and you just can't seem to get everything together. You think to yourself that there must be a better way to organize this mountain of information.

Well, the good news is that there is a better way! We can hear your sigh of relief. The way to put all this information together is to place it into a genealogical program on your computer. Genealogical programs allow you to put a variety of types of information into one easy location. These programs often include the capability to add pictures, sound clips, and even video clips of those special family members. They even help you produce a book — if you ever have the desire to do so — when your research is detailed enough.

Family Tree Maker is one of these fabulous genealogical programs that can make your life oh-so-much easier. In fact, it is the most popular genealogical program on the market today. And, in case you missed the title of this book, the whole point of our ranting here is to show you some easy steps that will help you organize your information by using Family Tree Maker.

We know that genealogists and family historians often do not have much time to enter all their findings into the computer. After all, every minute that you spend with your genealogical program is time taken away from research, right? One reason that we're writing this book is to show you how to use Family Tree Maker efficiently and how to utilize its features to save time and make your research more fruitful.

Is This Book for You?

It's perfectly natural for you to ask if this book is really for you. We already know it's the book for you. But if you're having any doubts whatsoever, we want you to answer the following questions (out loud please):

- ✔ Do I have an interest in researching the history of my family?
- ✔ Do I need to organize my genealogical research?
- ✔ Do I like using computers with Microsoft Windows?

Hey, wait a minute. Some of you didn't answer the questions out loud. However, we're willing to let this slip just this once. If you answered *yes* to either of the first two questions, then this book is for you. The third question was really kind of a trick question. Really it should have read, "Can you tolerate using Microsoft Windows?" So even if you answered *no* to that third question, we still think this book is for you. After all, sometimes in life you must endure things you don't like, and face it, Windows is here to stay. (And personally, we kind of like Windows. There, we said it. Let the stoning begin.)

Whether you like Windows or merely tolerate it, having some experience with Windows is helpful before you delve too far into the book. You don't have to know how to do lots of tricks, but knowing how to navigate with a mouse and use menus is a definite plus.

Becoming an Official Genealogist

Before going any further, we want to point out that some of you may not be official genealogists. You may be saying to yourself, "How do I become an official genealogist?" Well, it doesn't take years of training or even years of researching your family. All it takes is the following:

- ✔ An interest in finding information about your family history (including digging up all the dirt on the black sheep of the family)
- ✔ Saying the following words, "I'm an official genealogist." You can say this out loud or quietly to yourself, depending on where you're reading this

Conventions Used in This Book

Occasionally, in this book we use certain conventions to make it easier for you to follow along. One convention is bolded text — we use bold text for anything that we want you to type in the program.

Also, we use quite a few command arrows, which look like this: ⇨. For example, when you see this in the text:

Choose File⇨New Family File

it means to open the File menu and then choose New Family File. We use command arrows when you need to choose options from the Family Tree Maker menu bar.

How This Book Is Organized

One key to using this book effectively is to know how we organized it. Two types of readers may be reading this book — those who read books cover to cover and those who read only the parts that they are interested in at the time (skimmers, as we like to call you). And some of you cover-to-cover readers will probably become skimmers after you're comfortable with using Family Tree Maker. So, we have written this book with both audiences in mind. If you need to know about something before performing a function in Family Tree Maker, we try our best to refer you to where you can find that information elsewhere in the book.

Here is the general organization of the book.

Part I: Putting Your House in Order

This portion of the book takes you through the nuts and bolts of Family Tree Maker. It begins with a brief overview of the program, discusses how to enter information about yourself, explains how to enter facts on other relatives and ancestors, shows you how to attach pictures and other multimedia objects, and explains how to correct information that you have entered into the program.

Part II: Your Handy-Dandy Research Partner

One of the things that every genealogist can use is a research partner — someone or something that makes researching much easier. Family Tree Maker has several functions and utilities that fit the bill as a research partner. This part covers the tools that are built into the program, as well as tools that are available on the companion Family Tree Maker Web site.

Part III: Share and Share Alike

One key to being a successful genealogist is finding other researchers who are interested in the same family lines that you are. When you find such a researcher, you'll want to be able to share the information that you have in your Family Tree Maker file and import the other researcher's data into your file. This part explains how you can share information by using files and by posting your information on the Web.

Part IV: The Part of Tens

The Part of Tens is a mainstay in the *For Dummies* series. Each chapter lists ten things that can assist you in using Family Tree Maker. These chapters include ten ways to reduce stress, ten bonuses that come with the deluxe package, ten things that can save you time, and ten ways to avoid calling technical support.

Part V: Appendixes

As you may expect, this part includes all the stuff that we couldn't fit into the rest of the book. You can find details on installing the program and a glossary of terms that you'll find useful while using the program.

Icons Used Throughout the Book

To help you get the most out of this book, we add icons to paragraphs or sections that contain important information. Here are the icons that we use in this book:

This icon points out concepts or terms that are unique to genealogy.

When you see this icon, you'll find advice or shortcuts to make your researching easier.

We walk readers step by step through an example.

Look out! This is something tricky or unusual to watch for.

Your Next Step

Now that you've gotten through the administrivia of the book, you're ready to take the next step. If you don't already own a copy of Family Tree Maker, you may want to consider purchasing one before getting too far into the book. The examples in the book are a lot clearer if you can follow along with your own copy of the program. Also, try to have some information on your family ready to put into the program so that you don't get bored entering our examples (however clever they may be).

So, sit down at your computer, open up your copy of Family Tree Maker, pull out some information on your family, and get started!

Part I
Putting Your House in Order

In this part . . .

You have to start somewhere, so why not start with the basics? This part introduces you to genealogical databases and explains how to enter your own information in Family Tree Maker. Then you find out how to enter information on other members of your family, include pictures in your database, and fix mistakes in your database.

Chapter 1

Getting Started

In This Chapter

▶ Introducing genealogical databases

▶ Finding out what Family Tree Maker can do for you

▶ Locating information to get things underway

▶ Checking out Family Tree Maker's Family Page

• •

*W*e know you're eager to start using Family Tree Maker — after all, that's why you're reading this book. However, we need to cover some preliminary things before we get down to the nitty-gritty.

Before you start inputting information about your ancestors into Family Tree Maker, it's helpful to see what genealogical databases can do for you. So the first part of this chapter looks at how genealogical databases fit into your research plan and how you can use one as a sort of research partner. Then we look at what Family Tree Maker can do for you. We also run through the things that you need to have on hand before entering information into the program, and finally, we give you a quick peek at the major building block of the Family Tree Maker program, the (in)famous Family Page.

Genealogical Databases — Your Ideal Research Partner

If we asked you to describe your ideal research partner, how would you answer? Would your ideal partner be someone who doesn't mind traipsing through archives, courthouses, and cemeteries for hours on end? Would it be someone who never gets tired or complains about how much time you spend on genealogy? Or perhaps it would be someone who can help you figure out what to do next in your research? Unfortunately, very few people meet that complete description — or at least that's been our experience. However, a few computer programs we've discovered meet that description to a tee, provided you install them on a portable computer (in other words, a laptop, a notebook, or a palmtop). So, perhaps a genealogical database qualifies as your ideal research partner. After all, it never tires of working with you (unless the computer battery is running low), and it can assist you in deciding what step to take next in your research.

Genealogical databases are computer software applications that allow you to store information about your family and produce some sort of report(s) detailing your findings. Although individual programs may have lots of bells and whistles that allow you to do a number of semi-unique things, basically all genealogical databases allow you to input information and produce some sort of output.

If you hang around genealogical software users long enough (and we encourage you to do so because they're a happening crowd), you'll probably hear them talk about *lineage-linked databases*. This term sounds pretty fancy, but really, it's not a complicated concept. Lineage-linked databases are programs that organize information based on the family relationship of individuals. For example, say that you have information on a father and son. If you enter that information into a lineage-linked database, the program creates two records (one for each individual) and then links them together as a family unit. These links are what enable the program to eventually produce the family trees that reflect your findings and help guide your future research.

Now you're probably wondering why it's important to know what a lineage-linked database is. It's important for the following reasons:

- ✔ Family Tree Maker is a lineage-linked database.

- ✔ Knowing about lineage-linked databases helps you understand how Family Tree Maker deals with the information that you store in it. (Family Tree Maker likes to know not only the information that you put into it, but also how that information relates to an individual as a member of a family.)

But What Can Genealogical Databases Do for Me?

In *Genealogy Online For Dummies* (IDG Books Worldwide, Inc.), we talk about something we like to call the Helm Online Family Tree Research Cycle. Beyond its impressive name, the Research Cycle is a way of thinking about the steps that you, as a genealogist, go through when you're researching your family. The cycle has five phases (see Figure 1-1): planning, collecting, researching, consolidating, and distilling. Genealogical databases are key to at least three of the five phases.

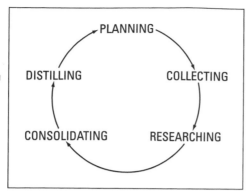

Figure 1-1:
The Helm
Online
Family Tree
Research
Cycle.

To illustrate the phases, we liken them to the steps that you take to plant a tree (plus we like to stay with the family tree motif):

✔ **Planning.** The first step in planting a tree is figuring out what kind of tree you want and finding a good place in your yard for the tree to grow. This step in the cycle is the *planning* phase. You want to select a family that you know enough about to begin a search, as well as think about the resources you want to use to find the information you're looking for.

✔ **Collecting.** After you plan the location for the tree, you go to a nursery and pick out a suitable sapling and materials that you need to ensure that the tree's roots take hold. The second phase of the cycle, *collecting,* is the same — you collect information on the family you're researching by conducting interviews in person, on the phone, or through e-mail, and by finding documents in attics, basements, and other home-front storage areas.

✔ **Researching.** The next step is to actually plant the tree. You dig a hole, place the tree in it, and then cover the roots. Similarly, you spend the *researching* phase of the cycle digging for clues and finding information that can support your family tree. You can use traditional and technological tools to dig — tools like libraries, courthouses, your computer, and the World Wide Web.

✔ **Consolidating.** You've planted the tree and covered its roots. However, to make sure that the tree grows, you spread mulch around it and provide the nourishment that the tree needs to survive. The *consolidating* phase of the cycle is the same in that you take the information you find and place it into your genealogical database. Doing so protects your findings by keeping them in a centralized location and providing an environment in which you can see the fruits of your labor.

✔ **Distilling.** After your tree has taken root and begins to grow, you need to prune the old growth, allowing new growth to appear. Similarly, the *distilling* phase is where you use your genealogical database to generate reports showing the current state of your research. You can use these reports to prune from your database those individuals you've proven don't fit into your family lines — and perhaps find room for new genealogical growth by finding clues to other lines you need to follow.

Now that you know the five phases, you're ready to find out how genealogical databases help you during your research process. In the next few sections, we look at the planning, consolidating, and distilling phases.

Planning

One pitfall that many genealogists encounter on research trips (regardless of whether they're physical or virtual trips) is lost time — they lose a lot of time trying to figure out exactly what to look for at a particular site. We won't ask for a show of hands, but we know that some of you (like at least one of us) sometimes just don't plan your trips very well. You don't identify exactly what you want to accomplish while researching.

Planning is an area where your ideal research partner can help. One of the things that genealogical databases do really well is show you the gaps in your research. In an instant, you can see if you're missing a birth date, marriage date, death date, or some other important detail. You can also quickly determine if you have discrepancies between facts that you need to try to resolve. After you identify these things, you can form a research plan for your next trip and reduce the amount of preparation time that you need after you arrive at your research destination.

Consolidating

After going through the collecting and researching phases, you'll probably have some new information to show for your work. This information may appear in several different forms, from photocopies of original records to notes taken on napkins or typed into your computer's word processor. The next thing you need to do is to store all this wonderful information (in its various forms) in a single location. Genealogical databases help you consolidate information by providing a quick and easy mechanism for typing or attaching your information to an electronic record about a specific individual. The ability to cut and paste information also helps speed up data entry when a piece of information applies to more than one individual.

Distilling

Perhaps the most important thing that a genealogical database can do for you is to give you insight about the status of your research. Most genealogical databases have various reports that show you where holes exist in your research, and provide hints to you regarding which items or family members you need to research next. Genealogical databases can also help validate some of the information that you have discovered.

For example, say that you find something that provides a birth date for an ancestor. You proceed to type that date into your genealogical database. Your genealogical database can validate that birth date by comparing it to the birth dates of the person's parents to ensure that the date is within an acceptable range (that is, that the child was not born before the parents). Although the genealogical database doesn't know the exact birth date of everyone, it can help you avoid silly mistakes that may frustrate you later on.

Family Tree Maker to the Rescue

In the first part of this chapter, we talk about what genealogical databases can do in general. But you're really interested in finding out what Family Tree Maker can do for you, right? Well (drumroll please), here are some of the exciting things it can do:

- ✔ **Store your information.** Family Tree Maker can store all your research details in a couple of different ways. You can type information into the program or attach scanned pictures, sound, or other multimedia.

- ✔ **Generate reports and trees.** You can produce a variety of reports to assist you in your research or to show to other family members at reunions. These reports include Ancestor and Descendant trees, Hourglass and All-in-One reports, Family Group Sheets, Genealogy reports, and Outline Descendant trees. You can even combine these reports and trees to generate a book.

- ✔ **Simplify the research process.** A number of Family Tree Maker utilities can make your research life much easier. You can produce timelines to show when your ancestors lived, keep track of your progress by using a research journal, produce labels to keep your paper files organized, and search for ancestors on CD-ROM and the Internet.

- ✔ **Export information.** Family Tree Maker gives you the ability to export information from your database to share with other researchers and place on the World Wide Web or on CD-ROMs produced by Broderbund (the manufacturer of Family Tree Maker).

A bit about trees, reports, and GEDCOMS

Before you get too far into working with Family Tree Maker, we want to define a few key terms that we use throughout this book:

- **Trees:** By trees, we're referring to the graphical representation of information by Family Tree Maker. Trees are also sometimes referred to as *charts.* In fact, it's probable that we'll slip up and call them charts somewhere along the way. So, if you see charts — the translation is *trees.* As we mention in the definition of reports, trees can really be considered reports. However, we have tried to divide up the chapters so that trees and reports are separated from each other. Why? Because reports and trees have different customizable features, and we want to group like things together. That way they're easier to work with.

- **Reports:** Although you can consider just about any *output* from Family Tree Maker to be a report, for our purposes we define reports as the text-based output from Family Tree Maker. In other words, a report is any output that is not graphically represented and that is not a GEDCOM. The distinction that we're making here really isn't all that

important in the scheme of things. We just mention it because we want to make sure that no one gets confused with our terminology — and, of course, so that we don't get confused, too.

- **GEDCOMs:** GEDCOM is an acronym for Genealogical Data Communication. It is a standard file format that genealogists use to import and export information among genealogical databases. For example, if you want to share your genealogical information with Uncle Bob, and Uncle Bob has a different genealogical program than you do, GEDCOM enables you to send him a file that he can read with his program. If your friends or family ask you for a GEDCOM, you know that they're asking you to export your genealogical data into a file that they can then import into their programs. We cover importing and exporting GEDCOMs in more detail in Chapters 2 and 12.

We try our best to be consistent when using these words. And, there will always be exceptions to these definitions. When that happens, we alert you.

The Stuff You Need to Get Started

Two types of people are probably reading this book right now. Some of you have some information about your family, which you're ready to enter into Family Tree Maker, and some of you are just starting out and need to accumulate some information. Those of you in the first group will most likely want to skip ahead to Chapter 2 to begin entering your information. But if you're a member of the second group of readers, please stick around, because we give you some hints on how to find information about your family that you can then enter into Family Tree Maker.

Interrogating . . . oops, we mean interviewing Aunt Edna

If you don't already have a lot of information on your family, we recommend that you begin with interviewing your relatives. We know you probably do your best to stay away from some of your relatives (we all have some really weird ones), but in the genealogy business, you sometimes just have to bite the bullet and talk to them.

Typically, your relatives will have a lot of information that can help you fill in the gaps in your research. They may know dates and places where particular events occurred, or they may know the location of family letters, Bibles, records, or photographs. Relatives may also know family legends that can give you clues on where to look for your ancestors in this country and in the country that your family emigrated from (assuming that your family emigrated).

Here are some things to keep in mind when interviewing your relatives:

✔ **Make sure that you know what you want to focus on before going to the interview.** Have some questions ready, so you can keep Aunt Edna from wandering all over the place.

✔ **Ask interviewees, ahead of time, whether recording the interviews with a tape recorder or camcorder is okay.** If they don't feel comfortable being taped, be sure to bring some paper to take notes on.

✔ **Placing a time limit on your interviews is a good idea.** A couple of hours is usually enough time to get some useful information without taxing the interviewee or yourself too much.

✔ **If the interview isn't going well, try using some props to liven things up.** Looking at photo albums, Bibles, and other family documents can often jog a person's memory and lead to some very interesting stories.

✔ **Send a thank you note to the interviewee after the interview and offer to share information that you find through your research.** Offering to share your research findings may pique your relatives' interest in what you're doing and prompt them to find more photos and records. And if you're really lucky, your relatives may even be motivated to help you research.

Make sure that you find evidence to back up what your family members tell you. Memories fade, stories get embellished, and people get mixed up. If you have a paper record of some sort that supports what a relative has told you, you'll be better off in the long run.

If you're interested in other ideas of how to interview relatives or what specific questions to ask, you may want to look at the article "A Trip Down Memory Lane" at this Web site address: www.genealogy.com/00000025.html.

Finding enough evidence to put Uncle Ed away

We cannot say this enough: You should always try to prove a fact through a primary source or several secondary sources. *Primary sources* are documents or oral accounts (if the oral account occurred soon after the actual event and was witnessed by the person giving the account), or any other items created at the time that a particular event occurred. *Secondary sources* are documents, oral accounts, or other items that are created some time after an event or are provided by someone who was not an eyewitness to an event.

A good example of a primary source document is a birth certificate. A birth certificate is a primary source document because it's usually prepared within days — if not hours — of a birth and it has signatures of those witnessing the birth. Because the birth certificate is prepared close to the event, the information contained within it is usually considered reliable (although there have been cases in which someone lied about the name of the father or typographical errors occurred when the record was produced by a county clerk). A good example of a secondary source is a newspaper account of an event that was written by someone who did not witness it.

If you have several secondary sources that are in agreement about a fact, they can serve in place of a primary source — at least until you're able to locate some primary sources (if possible).

Of course, some documents are both primary and secondary sources. A death certificate is one such example. It's a primary source for information regarding the death of the individual — such as the death date and cause. However, the individual's birth date and location may be secondary information. Unless the birth and death dates are close together, the birth date and place are secondary sources of information. If the individual who is deceased is older, his or her children probably supplied the information. And obviously the children could not possibly have witnessed the parent's birth. We're not saying that the information is always wrong — we just strongly recommend trying to find a primary source that supplies the birth date and location, or at least find another secondary source that can confirm the death certificate regarding the birth date and location.

A select list of items to bug your relatives about

When you're talking to Aunt Edna or Uncle Ed, ask about certain facts that you can use to populate the pages of Family Tree Maker. Here are some of the things to find out about:

- ✔ Birth dates and places
- ✔ Marriage dates and places
- ✔ Death dates and places, as well as causes of death
- ✔ Names of children
- ✔ Names of parents, grandparents, great-grandparents
- ✔ Physical information such as color of eyes and hair, height, and weight
- ✔ Aliases and nicknames of individuals
- ✔ Titles of family members, such as military, religious, or academic titles
- ✔ Pictures of people and places
- ✔ Historical events that ancestors may have been involved in
- ✔ Residences of ancestors
- ✔ Occupations and locations of companies
- ✔ Baptism, christening, confirmation, and Bar Mitzvah dates and places
- ✔ Attendance at educational institution and graduation dates and places
- ✔ Dates and places of immigration or emigration and naturalization
- ✔ Political office elections and dates of service
- ✔ Military service dates and places

And here are some documents and objects to look for to help you confirm the dates and places of events:

- ✔ Photo albums and loose photographs
- ✔ Diaries
- ✔ Family Bibles
- ✔ Drivers licenses
- ✔ Mortgage papers

- ✓ Insurance papers

- ✓ Permits

- ✓ Vital records (birth, death, marriage, and divorce certificates)

- ✓ Wills and other legal papers

- ✓ Employment and retirement records

- ✓ Enlistment, discharge, and other military records

- ✓ Obituaries and other newspaper articles

- ✓ Letters

- ✓ Naturalization papers and passports

- ✓ Land deeds and titles

- ✓ Membership cards and organizational records

- ✓ Church programs

- ✓ Tax records

- ✓ Pension applications and records

Many more sources of information are available. Some of these sources may require you to contact a governmental institution or library, or to research online. Fellow genealogists in your family may have already collected other sources, so you may want to find out if anyone else has researched the family. After all, you don't want to reinvent the wheel. Of course, make sure that your relative constructed the wheel correctly in the first place.

Taking a Look at the Infamous Family Page

As with any partner in life, you need to be able to recognize "the looks." You know, there's a different look for different needs. And why should it be any different with your research partner? Family Tree Maker has some looks all its own. The one you'll see most often is a warm and inviting look called the Family Page. It's light yellow color is quite appealing, and we haven't seen anyone yet who can resist completing those blank fields. Seriously though, the Family Page is the basic screen that contains a snapshot of an immediate family. Figure 1-2 shows an example of the Family Page.

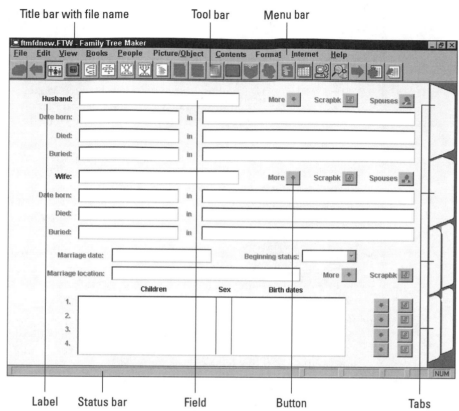

Title bar with file name   Tool bar   Menu bar

Label   Status bar   Field   Button   Tabs

Figure 1-2:
The Family
Page.

The Family Page contains several different elements. Here are short descriptions of these elements so that you know how we refer to them throughout the book:

- **Title bar.** The title bar is the box at the very top of the page (in the default Windows settings, it's the color blue). It contains, as you may have guessed, the title of the current file that you're working in, followed by the words Family Tree Maker. If you're working with several Family Tree Maker files, the title bar is a handy way to remember which file you're working with. The title bar also contains three symbols on the far right that allow you to resize the window on the screen and close the program.

- **Menu bar.** The second line of the screen is the menu bar. This bar contains a number of commands that you can use to perform functions in Family Tree Maker. The default commands include File, Edit, View, Books, People, Picture/Object, Contents, Format, Internet, and Help.

Clicking one of these words produces a pull-down menu, giving you more options. If an option appears in gray (rather than black), you cannot currently perform that function.

✔ **Toolbar.** Beneath the menu bar is a row of buttons with pictures on them, which is commonly known as the toolbar. This amazing toolbar allows you to perform a function within Family Tree Maker with just one click. The default toolbar contains 19 tools, but you can customize it to your liking. If a tool appears in gray, then you cannot perform that function at the current time.

✔ **Labels.** Beneath the toolbar is the main portion of the Family Page — the meat of the page, if you will. The page has a series of bolded text followed by a colon, usually in front of a blank box or a button. This bolded text is a *label*. Labels tell you what kind of information to place into the blank box that follows them. Labels also appear in gray if they aren't currently available.

✔ **Fields.** The blank boxes that we refer to in the preceding bullet are called *fields*. Fields are where you type in the information for each family member. You can move from field to field by clicking inside the next field or by simply pressing the Tab key on your keyboard.

✔ **Buttons.** You may have noticed a few buttons sprinkled throughout the Family Page. These buttons (such as More, Scrapbk, and Spouses) take you directly to other pages of the Family Tree Maker so that you can add information to those pages.

✔ **Tabs.** On the far right side of the Family Page, you should see some objects that look like the tops of file folders. These objects are called *tabs*. Tabs allow you to navigate through the Family Pages of other family members. The first large tab at the top takes you to the page for the parents of the Husband who is displayed on that Family Page, the next tab is for the parents of the Wife, and the four smaller tabs are for the children of the Husband and Wife. (Husband and Wife are Family Tree Maker's default labels for the two main individuals on a Family Page. For information about how to change these labels, see Chapter 2.)

✔ **Status bar.** At the very bottom of the Family Page is the status bar. This area provides you with additional information about the specific individual or report that you're looking for. For example, if your cursor is positioned in the Husband field of the Family Page, the status bar shows you the name of the Husband's parents and the number of children and spouses the husband has.

Chapter 2

Starting with the One You Know Best — You

In This Chapter

▶ Entering facts about yourself in Family Tree Maker

▶ Determining what information to include in your database

▶ Enhancing your file with scanned pictures and records

Despite what your better half or your mother thinks, you are the person who knows the most about yourself. So naturally, we suggest that you start with entering information about yourself in Family Tree Maker. Typically, genealogists begin researching the most current generation of the family and work their way backward in time. So after you enter information about yourself, enter information about your spouse (if you have one) and children (if you have any). Then move on to entering information about your parents, grandparents, and earlier family members.

In this chapter, we guide you through the process of entering your personal information to complete the basic unit in Family Tree Maker — called the Family Page — as well as its accompanying screens that hold specialized data. We also introduce you to the families we use in our examples, the Canine (pronounced kah-neen) and Feline (pronounced fa-lee-nay) families.

Before you begin, you may want to dig out some information on yourself and your family so that you can follow along with our examples. After all, typing in your own information rather than our examples makes this chapter much more fun.

If you have not already installed Family Tree Maker, see Appendix A for instructions on how to do so. In it, we detail all the steps that you need to take before you start entering information.

Completing Your Family Page

The initial page that you see when you first open Family Tree Maker or when you create a new Family File is a blank yellow Family Page (with the exception of opening Version 7.0, which we cover in a minute). Don't panic — this is the only time that you see a blank page upon entry. From now on, when you open Family Tree Maker, it brings up the last database that you were working in. Anyway, the Family Page is where you start building your database.

Before you get to the Family Page in Version 7.0, you see the Start Your Family Tree window. The first one looks like a pedigree chart (or family tree) and collects name information about you, your parents, and their parents. When you supply the information and click Next, a Births window pops up, in which you can supply birth dates and locations for each person named in the preceding window. After you're done with it, you see a Deaths window that collects death dates and locations. And the last window you see asks if you want to run a quick FamilyFinder Search. You can choose to run a search online, on CD-ROMs, or not at all; then click Finish. If you choose to run a search, Family Tree Maker gives you instructions for getting to the Family Page when you're done reviewing your search results. If you choose not to run a search, Family Tree Maker gives you instructions for running a search later and then brings up the Family Page.

The Family Page in Family Tree Maker, as shown in Figure 2-1, contains basic information about vital events (births, marriages, and deaths) in the lives of a particular family's members. In your case, it will contain the vital events of your immediate family after you enter information about yourself. If you aren't familiar with the Family Page and how to *navigate* it (computer lingo for moving around a page or between pages), take a look at the overview of the Family Page in Chapter 1.

The cursor starts out in the Husband field, so if you're female, you need to tab down to the Wife field to begin. Don't worry if you aren't married, these are just Family Tree Maker's default labels.

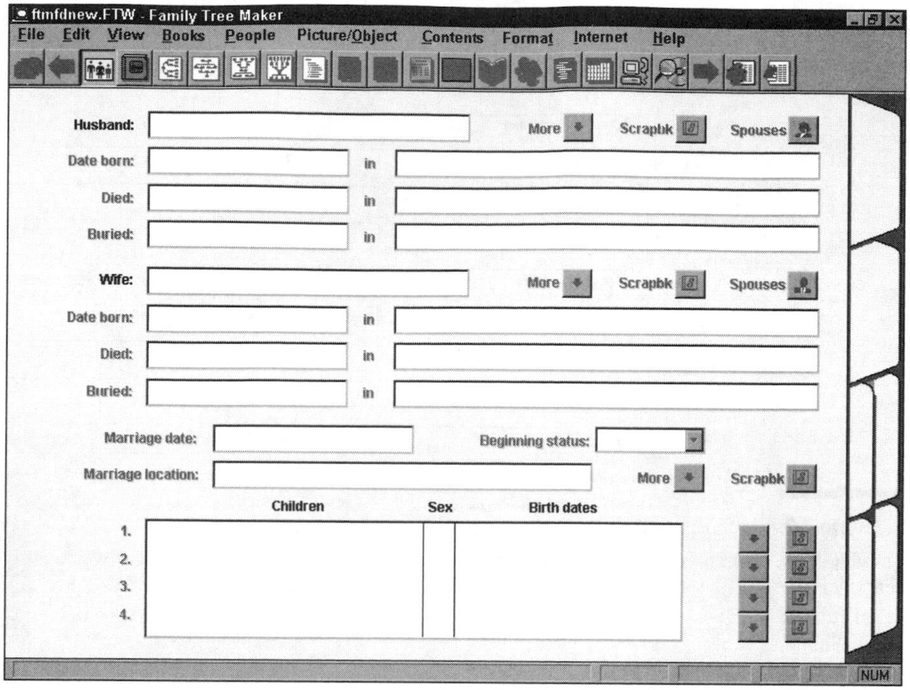

Figure 2-1:
A blank
Family Page
in Family
Tree Maker.

All about you

We recommend that you start building your database by first entering information about yourself, your spouse, your children, and your grandchildren and then work backward through your parents, grandparents, great-grandparents, and so forth. Of course, if you don't have a spouse (or a significant other), children, or grandchildren, then you can proceed directly to entering information about your ancestors after providing details about you.

If you'd like to follow along with our example for completing the Family Page, please refer to Figure 2-2 as you follow these steps:

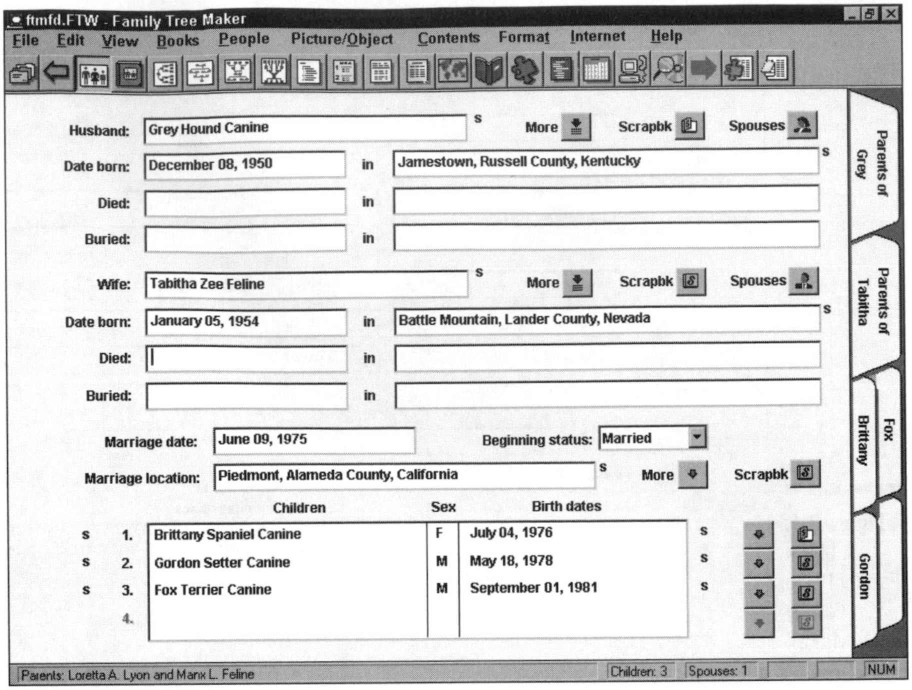

Figure 2-2:
Completed
Family Page
of Tabitha
Feline.

1. Enter your full name.

Using the appropriate field (Husband or Wife) based on your gender or family role, enter your name in this order: first name, middle name, last name. (If you're a married female, enter your maiden name as your last name.) Even if you're unmarried, you need to use one of these two fields for your own information and just leave the spouse field blank.

You may be wondering why we want you to use maiden names for females. The reason is that all references to them before they were married are under their maiden names. When you search through premarriage census and vital records, you'll most likely be looking for females in documents that use their parents' names. If you list the wife by her married name, you won't know under which name to look for her in these records.

In our example, we entered information about a sample person — Tabitha Zee Canine. Canine is Tabitha's married name, and her maiden name is Feline. Moving the cursor to the Wife field of the first Family Page, we entered Tabitha Zee Feline, because we want her information to reflect her maiden name.

When you enter your name, Family Tree Maker automatically creates a Family Page for your parents. When you're ready to enter more detailed information about your parents, you can click the appropriate tab on the right side of the screen to access their Family Page.

2. **Enter your date of birth in the Date Born field.**

You can navigate through the fields by using the Tab key or by clicking with your mouse to move the cursor. Some of the fields (such as the Date Born, Died, and Location fields) are disabled when you first begin. As soon as you type your name, these fields become active so that you can enter information in them.

To complete the Date Born field, enter your birth date, including the month, day, and four-digit year. Tabitha was born on January 5, 1954, so we entered January 05, 1954.

The software has a default format for dates, so you can spell out the date (January 05, 1954) or abbreviate it with numerals (01/05/1954), whichever you prefer. The system automatically converts the date to the spelled-out format (January 05, 1954) unless you change the default format by choosing File➪Preferences➪Dates & Measures and selecting a different Date Format.

By allowing you to change the default format for dates, Family Tree Maker accommodates those of you who prefer to enter dates in another order — day, month, and then year (for example 05 January 1954). The U.S. military and some countries use this format for dates.

Because Family Tree Maker doesn't know whether '54 means 1754, 1854, or 1954, you must use four-digit years for the dates you record in the program. If you inadvertently use only two numerals for the year, the software prompts you to use a four-digit year. For example, if you enter **01/05/54** into a Date Born field, a dialog box appears, asking you to enter a complete year for the date.

Additionally, if you aren't sure about the exact date of an event, Family Tree Maker enables you to approximate a date by using abbreviations for *circa* (Cir) or *about* (Abt). Upon entering either code, the software automatically enters Abt — the default setting — in the field. For example, if you enter **cir. 01/05/1954**, Family Tree Maker converts it to Abt January 05, 1954. The same happens if you enter cir without the period. If you prefer Cir to Abt, you can change the default settings. Simply choose File➪Preferences➪Dates & Measures, and then enter how you want your Date Labels to appear.

3. **Enter your place of birth in the In field.**

Always include as much information as possible in every field, including the town, county or parish, and state in which you were born. If you want, you can also include the country. For our example, Tabitha was born in Battle Mountain, Nevada, so we entered Battle Mountain, Lander County, Nevada, USA.

All the location fields have a *Fastfields* feature. As soon as you begin typing, Family Tree Maker starts guessing what you're entering, based on names of locations that you've entered before. The program remembers up to 50 location names for common use.

4. **While your cursor is in the birthplace field, press Ctrl+S (in other words, press the Ctrl key and the S key simultaneously).**

   You can also get to this screen by choosing View⇨Source from the menu bar. Either way, the Source-Citation dialog box appears.

5. **Cite the evidence that you have for the date and place of birth.**

   We suggest that you get in the habit of entering source citations as you go along. The cursor begins in the Title of Source field. For Tabitha, we typed in Birth Certificate of Tabitha. Then we moved down to the Citation Page field (if your cursor is not already there, you can use your Tab key to move to it). In this field, we entered the certificate number.

   In the citation text field, you type in the information that specifically tells you about the birth. For example, for Tabitha, we typed this: Birth Certificate Number 11-11111 states that Tabitha Zee Feline was born on January 4, 1954, at 11:03 p.m. at the Animal Clinic Hospital located in Battle Mountain, Lander County, Nevada, USA. The attending physician is listed as German Shepherd.

   After you enter the citation text, you may notice that the Footnote field is autofilled with your information. That's fine for right now, so click the OK button. After you click OK, a small *s* appears next to the birthplace field. This notation indicates that a source is defined for that field. If you need to edit the source at any time in the future, you can always click in the birthplace field and press Ctrl+S. We explain more about sources in Chapter 6.

6. **Take a look at the Died and In fields for death information.**

   Because you're entering information about yourself, you obviously don't have a date or place of death. At least we hope this is the case. So for now, just take a look at these fields. Soon enough, you'll be entering information about others, and you'll undoubtedly have some death data to include on different Family Pages.

7. **If you're using Version 7.0, take a look at the Buried and In fields for burial information.**

   As with the death information, if you're entering information about yourself, you shouldn't need to worry about burial information quite yet. But you may need to use this field to complete other Family Pages.

8. **Enter information about your spouse. If you've never had a spouse, skip to Step 10.**

   Enter your spouse's name in the appropriate Husband or Wife field. After the date and place of birth fields are active, tab down and enter your spouse's information in the Date Born and In fields just like you did for yourself. If you're widowed, include information about your spouse's passing in the Died and In fields, as well as the Buried and In fields.

   Tabitha is married to Grey Hound Canine, so we typed his name (in that order) in the Husband field. Then we entered his birth date in the Date Born field and his birthplace in the In field.

   If you've had more than one spouse, Family Tree Maker allows you to enter multiple partners. We cover this feature in detail in "Picking Your Favorite (or Current) Spouse," later in this chapter.

   After you enter your spouse's name, Family Tree Maker automatically creates a Family Page for your spouse's parents. When you're ready to enter more detailed information about your in-laws, you can click the appropriate tab on the right-hand side of the screen to open their Family Page, or you can choose View⇨Index of Individuals, from which you can choose either of the parents by name.

   Don't forget to add sources for each of the items you enter for your spouse. Review Steps 4 and 5 for information about completing a source citation.

9. **Enter your marriage information in the Marriage Date, Beginning Status, and Marriage Location fields.**

   The Marriage Date and Marriage Location fields are disabled until you enter names in both the Husband and Wife fields. After the fields become active and you finish entering the basic information about you and your spouse, tab down to the Marriage Date field and enter the date of your wedding. In the Marriage Location field, enter the town, county or parish, and state where you were married. If you want, you can also include the country.

   For our example, Tabitha and Grey were married June 9, 1975, in Piedmont, California. We entered June 09, 1975 in the Marriage Date field and Piedmont, Alameda County, California, USA in the Marriage Location field.

   The Beginning Status field reflects the relationship status between the persons whose information appears in the Husband and Wife fields. This field starts out blank until you enter information in the other two marriage fields, and then it shows *Married* for the relationship unless you specify otherwise. If the Beginning Status field reflects the wrong status for the relationship, choose a different status from the drop-down list. Your choices are Friends, Married, Other, Partners, Private, Single, and Unknown. Also, the Beginning Status field controls titles for some of the other fields on the Family Page. If you select Friends or Partners for the relationship status of the two people, Family Tree Maker automatically changes the Husband and Wife field labels to Friend or Partner, and the Marriage Date and Marriage Location fields to Meeting Date and Meeting Location.

Because Tabitha and Grey are married, we left the Beginning Status field to its default setting — married.

10. **If you have children, enter information about them in the field at the bottom of your Family Page, as shown in Figure 2-2. Include their names, sex, and birth dates. If you don't have kids, skip this step.**

Family Tree Maker can be a little deceiving when you're entering facts about your children. At first glance, you may think that you can enter information about only one to four children, but this is not the case. To add a fifth or subsequent child to your list, just press Enter after recording the previous child's date of birth; an additional line then appears. (You can also use the scroll bar to add to additional lines — the scroll bar appears after you enter the fourth child's information.)

Enter each child's full name, sex, and date of birth in the appropriate columns. After you enter a child's information, Family Tree Maker automatically creates a Family Page for that child. When you're ready to enter more detailed information about your children (such as their birthplaces, marriage information, and so forth), click the appropriate child's tab on the right side of the screen to open his or her Family Page. Or you can choose View⇨Index of Individuals, from which you can select the child by name.

In our example, Tabitha and Grey have three children: Brittany Spaniel, Gordon Setter, and Fox Terrier, and their dates of birth are July 4, 1976, May 18, 1978, and September 1, 1981, respectively. We entered Brittany Spaniel Canine in the first line of the first column, selected F in the second column to indicate that she's a female, and then entered her birth date in the third column. After we pressed the Enter key, the cursor dropped to the next line, ready for us to enter information about Gordon.

While following the preceding steps, you may have noticed some yellow boxes popping up while your cursor hovered over a field. These boxes are called Bubble Help (or instructional boxes) and are designed to help you fill out a field or to tell you a little about what a particular button does. If these bubbles begin to annoy you at some future date, you can disable them — a process commonly called *bursting the bubble*. You can find all the details on disabling them in Chapter 13.

Proving that you exist

Descartes is credited with the phrase "I think, therefore I am." But most genealogists would correct that to read "I'm in records, therefore I am." To a pure genealogist, a person did not exist or an event did not occur unless a primary or secondary piece of evidence proves that it occurred. Obviously we don't have pieces of paper to document every single second of our lives, but documentation does exist for most of the major events of our lives.

To give you an idea of how to provide evidence to support the occurrence of events in your ancestors' lives, first try to prove that you exist. You do this by providing evidence for the basic fields that you filled out on your Family Page:

✔ **Name:** Seems easy enough, doesn't it? Of course, the document to prove your name is your birth certificate. However, in some cases, this document may not be available — for example, the courthouse where it was filed may have burned down. Or, perhaps, you changed your name at some point — in which case a court record should document the change. In lieu of a birth certificate, you can use other items to prove your name — a Social Security card, a driver's license, or some other government document.

✔ **Birth date and birthplace:** Again, your birth certificate is the document of choice. If you were born in a hospital, hospital records (containing information about your birth) that were used to create the original birth certificate may exist.

✔ **Death date and place:** Hopefully you don't need to prove this for yourself quite yet, but death certificates and obituaries are good places to find this information for other people. Funeral programs and other mementos can also provide information.

✔ **Marriage date and place:** Naturally, a marriage certificate is the best source of information. You may also have an application for a marriage license and a program from the wedding ceremony (not to mention an invitation to the ceremony or reception). Church records may also show when and where you were married.

✔ **Births of children:** Obviously a child's birth certificate confirms this information. You may have a newspaper announcement of the birth, and if you're a real collector, you may still have the hospital bill!

Of course, you're probably thinking that this information is all common sense. Well, guess what — it is! But it does show you how to relate documents to specific events so that you can enter sources for them in your Family File.

Details, Details, Details

Chances are that you want to store more than just the dates and locations for your vital statistics (and those of your relatives). Yet the main Family Page appears to contain only that information. So what do you do? Take a gander at the three little buttons to the right of the Husband and Wife fields. The first button, labeled More, leads you to some supplemental pages where you can enter facts about you, your current address, medical information, lineage, and notes. (We cover the other two buttons, Scrapbk and Spouses, later in this chapter.)

When you first click the More button, the Facts page appears. It contains five buttons with graphics and labels on the right side of the screen that enable you to navigate among the five supplemental pages. These buttons are called Facts, Address, Medical, Lineage, and Notes. You simply click the button for the page you want to see.

Just the facts

Looking for the perfect place to enter information about your diploma from Betty's Basketweaving School? Or how about the fact that you were included in a special census of the village you lived in during 1998? Look no further than the Facts page, shown in Figure 2-3. This page allows you to store basic information about your life. It automatically reflects some of the events that you entered on your Family Page (such as your birth), and it allows you to add events, characteristics, activities, and places where you've lived.

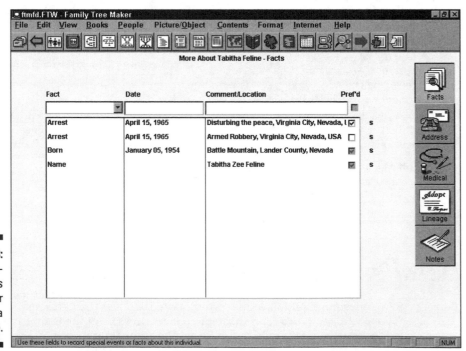

Figure 2-3:
The completed Facts page for Tabitha Feline.

The Facts page has three columns: Fact, Date, and Comment/Location. It also contains the Pref'd check box, where you can indicate a preferred fact if you have more than one date or comment/location for a fact type. The Facts page is simple to complete. Here's what you do:

1. **Open your Family Tree Maker Family Page if it isn't already open.**

   You can use the tabs on the right side of the screen to click through the entries in your database to get to your Family Page. Or you can choose View⇨Index of Individuals.

   To pick Tabitha Feline from our database, we chose View⇨Index of Individuals and then scrolled through the list to find her name. We double-clicked her name, and her Family Page opened up.

2. **Click the More button to the right of your name.**

   The Facts page opens. On the right side of the screen, you see buttons that lead you to the other pages for supplemental and more-detailed information regarding your current address, medical facts, lineage, and notes.

   You need to complete some fields across the top of the Facts page — including the Fact, Date, and Comment/Location fields. You can also click in the Pref'd check box to indicate that this is your preferred fact. We discuss preferred facts in more detail in Step 6.

3. **In the Fact field, choose the type of fact that you're recording from the drop-down list or type in your own selection.**

   Family Tree Maker provides some predetermined Facts that you can select from the drop-down list. These facts are: Adoption, Baptism, Baptism (LDS), Bar Mitzvah, Bat Mitzvah, Blessing, Born, Burial, Caste, Census, Christening, Confirmation, Confirmation (LDS), Cremation, Degree, Died, Education, Elected, Emigration, Endowment (LDS), Excommunication, First Communion, Graduation, Immigration, Military Service, Mission (LDS), Name, Namesake, Nationality, Naturalization, Occupation, Ordination, Probate, Property, Religion, Residence, Retirement, Sealed to Parents (LDS), Social Security Number, Temple, and Will.

   Of course, you're bound to have some types of facts that aren't included in Family Tree Maker's predetermined list, so you can add them yourself. It's easy to do. All you have to do is type in whatever you want to call the fact. Then after you complete the other fields (we get to those steps in just a minute) and press the Enter key, Family Tree Maker opens a dialog box that acknowledges that you've entered a new fact and asks if you want to add it to the list. Click OK, and your new fact name is added to the drop-down list.

For example, say that Tabitha was somewhat of a scoundrel in her younger years, and she had some run-ins with the law. You want to enter an arrest as a fact, but arrest is not one of the choices in the drop-down list. So in the Fact field, type in **Arrest**. (Now you're hooked. You have to complete the rest of the steps and this example before you can find out what Family Tree Maker does with your new fact.)

4. **Tab over to the Date field and enter the date on which the event occurred.**

   You can enter the date as numerals (01/01/1965) or spell it out (January 1, 1965), whichever you prefer. If you enter only two digits for the year, Family Tree Maker prompts you to choose a four-digit year so it knows whether the event was in 1765, 1865, or 1965. Then Family Tree Maker automatically converts the date to the default format with the month spelled out and listed first (January 01, 1965). If you prefer the day-month-year format for dates, then you need to reset the default setting.

   For our example, we entered the date 04/15/1965 (because Tabitha was only eleven at the time, we won't hold it against her). After pressing Enter upon completing the entire fact, Family Tree Maker converts the date to April 15, 1965.

5. **In the Comment/Location field, enter any brief comments about the event or the location where it occurred.**

   When entering a location for this event, we recommend that you provide the town, county or parish, and state. You can also include the country.

   The Comments/Location field is equipped with Family Tree Maker's Fastfields feature. As soon as you start typing, Family Tree Maker starts guessing what you're entering, based on names of locations that you've entered before. The program remembers up to 50 location names for common use. (For more about Fastfields, see Chapter 3.)

   Notice that a little trash bin icon pops up next to the Comments/Location field as soon as you start working with this field. This trash bin works along with the Fastfields feature. If you click the trash bin, Family Tree Maker erases that location from the Fastfields list. If you're entering the name of a new place, you can click the trash bin and erase all the previous entries to the list, or you can just keep typing in the field, and eventually Family Tree Maker recognizes that it's a new location.

   Continuing with our example, we entered the information about Tabitha's arrest: Disturbing the peace, Virginia City, Nevada, USA.

6. **If you want this fact to be the preferred one in your database, click in the Pref'd check box.**

Undoubtedly, a time will come when you have conflicting information about a fact. Although this isn't likely to happen in the data about yourself, it can be a common occurrence when researching your ancestors. This is where the Pref'd option comes in. This option allows you to specify which fact you believe is the true one until you can prove that it is.

In keeping with our example, say for a moment that we have a Fact entry for an arrest of Tabitha on the same date and at the same location but for a different crime (maybe armed robbery). The Pref'd check box enables you to choose which crime was more likely, based on your knowledge of Tabitha and her other past activities. If it is more likely that she was arrested for disturbing the peace, then you can click in the Pref'd check box for that fact. Family Tree Maker then gives it preference over the armed robbery information in the list and in any reports you generate. Of course, she could have been charged with both crimes at the same time — but we sure hope not.

7. **Press the Enter key on your computer.**

   When you press Enter, your new fact appears on the list below the fields.

   If the type of fact you entered does not yet appear in the Fact drop-down list, like our example of Arrest, then Family Tree Maker opens a dialog box, asking if you want to add it to the list. Click OK, and your new fact name is added to the drop-down list.

   After you've entered more than 13 facts, a scroll bar appears on the right side of the page for you to use to navigate the list of facts.

8. **Enter the source of the information.**

   Don't forget to add the source of your information by pressing Ctrl+S (press the Ctrl and S keys simultaneously).

To see the completed Facts page for Tabitha, refer to Figure 2-3.

On a street called. . . .

Unless you're a bit forgetful, the Address page, shown in Figure 2-4, may not seem to serve much of a purpose when recording information about yourself (which is the focus of this chapter). But it's a handy feature if you plan to share your database with others and want to be added to their family reunion or newsletter mailing lists. And eventually we think you'll find that this is a convenient feature when tracking down your relatives to send them things like invitations and announcements.

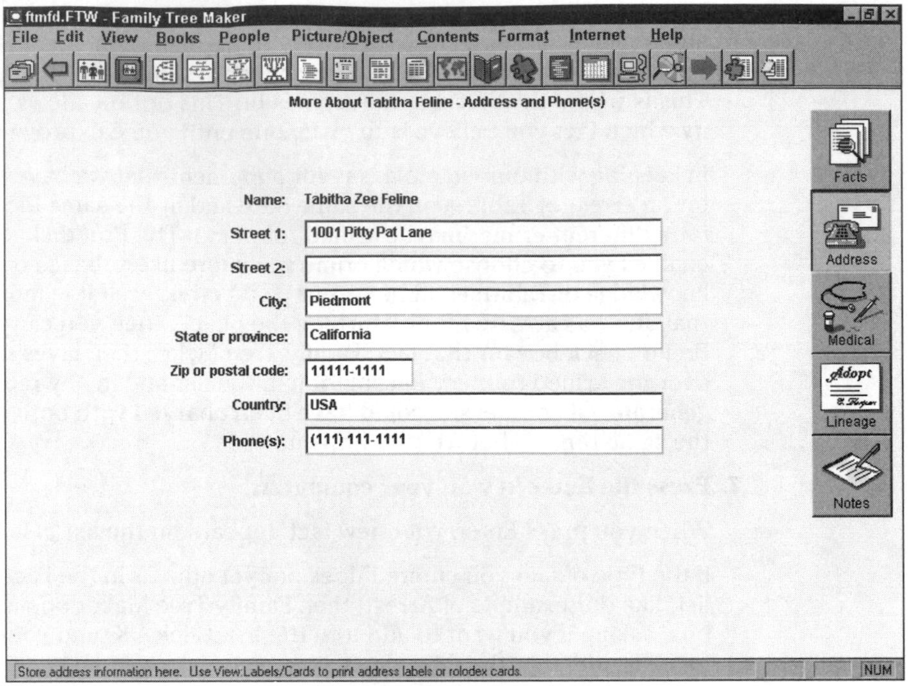

ftmfd.FTW - Family Tree Maker

File   Edit   View   Books   People   Picture/Object   Contents   Format   Internet   Help

More About Tabitha Feline - Address and Phone(s)

Name:	Tabitha Zee Feline
Street 1:	1001 Pitty Pat Lane
Street 2:	
City:	Piedmont
State or province:	California
Zip or postal code:	11111-1111
Country:	USA
Phone(s):	(111) 111-1111

Facts

Address

Medical

Lineage

Notes

Store address information here.   Use View:Labels/Cards to print address labels or rolodex cards.   NUM

Figure 2-4:
The Address
page for
Tabitha
Feline.

Follow these steps to add your own address to the file:

1. **Go to your Family Page (if you're not already on it).**

   Use the tabs on the right side of the screen or choose View⇨
   Index of Individuals to get there. We use Tabitha Feline as our example
   (see some of our preceding examples in this chapter if you're not sure
   who Tabitha is).

2. **Choose View⇨More About⇨Address.**

   This step brings up the Address page. (Of course, if you prefer to click
   buttons rather than use pull-down menus, you can get here by clicking
   the More button to the right of the Name field and then clicking the
   Address button on the right side of the Facts page.)

   Notice that Family Tree Maker has already entered a name in the Name
   field by copying the name off the Family Page.

3. **Enter your street address in the Street 1 and Street 2 fields.**

   Don't feel like you have to stretch out your street address to fill both
   fields if you have a regular old address like we do — one that takes up
   only one line. Family Tree Maker provides the second line in case you
   need it for some reason. Maybe you have some fancy ranch or estate

name that you like to include in your correspondence. Family Tree Maker provides the two lines just for such a purpose, so you can put the ranch name on the first line and the actual street address of your residence on the second line.

We entered Tabitha's make-believe address of 1001 Pitty Pat Lane on the Street 1 line.

4. **Type the name of your town, city, or village in the City field.**

We like to pretend that Tabitha lives in Piedmont so that's what we typed for City.

5. **Type the name of your state or province in the State or Province field.**

We entered California for Tabitha's address.

6. **Type your zip or postal code in the appropriate field.**

Not knowing the exact zip code for Piedmont, California, we just entered 11111-1111 for Tabitha.

7. **Be sure to tab down and enter your country in the Country field.**

Most people know that California is in the United States, but just to be thorough, we went ahead and typed USA.

8. **Tab to the final field and enter your telephone number(s).**

We entered Tabitha's phone number of (111) 111-1111.

Wasn't that easy? You're all done entering your address and phone number(s). Now you're set . . . unless you move, that is.

All things medical

Some genealogists pursue their family histories just to find out medical information. They want to know whether any hereditary diseases run through their veins. And others think that knowing medical information adds color to a family's history. You may be interested to find out personal characteristics (like height and weight) about your ancestors, as well as what ailments afflicted poor Aunt Gertrude and how many limbs Uncle Bo lost in that unfortunate accident of 1901. The Medical page in Family Tree Maker stores just this kind of information for you.

The Medical page, shown in Figure 2-5, has fields where you can enter a height and weight, as well as a cause of death. And in a free-form field, you can provide more detail about illnesses, surgeries, serious ailments, physical or mental disabilities, or just about anything medical.

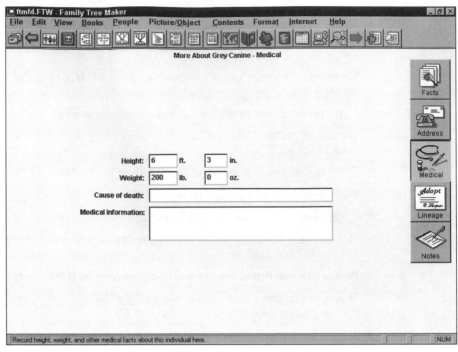

Figure 2-5:
The Medical
page for
Grey
Canine.

Follow these steps to add information about your medical history to the file:

1. **Open your Family Page in Family Tree Maker.**

   Use the tabs on the right side of the screen to click through the entries in your database to get to your Family Page. Or choose View⇨Index of Individuals. (For a refresher on how to use the Index of Individuals, take a look at Chapter 3.)

   To mix things up a bit, we use Grey Canine for our example here. We already had the Family Page for Tabitha Feline open, which happens to be the Family Page for Grey, too, because he's Tabitha's husband.

2. **Click the More button to the right of your name.**

   This action opens the Facts page. Down the right side of the screen, you see buttons that lead you to the other pages for supplemental and more-detailed information regarding current address, medical facts, lineage, and notes.

3. **Click the Medical button.**

   The Medical page appears.

4. **Enter your height in feet (ft.) and inches (in.) in the Height fields.**

   We entered 6 feet and 3 inches for Grey.

5. **Tab down and enter your weight in pounds (lbs.) and ounces (oz.) in the Weight fields.**

   Don't worry if you fib a little bit about your weight — Family Tree Maker won't tell anyone. Well, it won't tell anyone you don't let it tell when you share your database with others.

   We typed 200 in the pounds field and left the ounces field blank (Grey doesn't have a scale that measures that precisely).

6. **Tab down to the Cause of Death field.**

   Of course, if you're reading this book, then you're obviously not deceased. So you don't need to put any information about yourself in this particular field. However, you want to complete this field when entering information about some of your ancestors and others in your database.

7. **Tab to the Medical Information field and type any information you want in this field.**

   Now's your chance to lament every ache and pain you've ever had, if you so choose (provided it all fits in the field). Seriously, you may want to include only chronic conditions that would be of interest to future generations, unless a funny or interesting tale goes along with a particular non-chronic ailment you suffered. Then you want to list the ailment here and include the funny story in the Notes section (which we cover in a later section of this chapter).

   Our example person, Grey, is in pretty good health, so we didn't type any ailments in this field.

   Also keep in mind that you can add sources for both the Cause of Death and Medical Information fields.

Lineage

Do you have a special title that you use? We mean an official one, not just one you made up (such as Queen of the Universe or Master of All Things Electronic, which happen to be our self-designated titles). Maybe you're a Private in the U.S. Army, you have your doctorate in literature, you happen to be the president of a small country, or you're a minister. Whatever the case may be, you'll want to include your special title in your database. The Lineage page in Family Tree Maker allows you to record your special title.

The Lineage page, shown in Figure 2-6, also enables you to do the following:

✔ Add any nicknames or aliases that an individual may have used.

✔ Assign a reference number to that particular individual (in this case, yourself).

✔ Exclude that individual from any calendars you generate with Family Tree Maker.

✔ Select whether to include both maiden and married names for a female individual in trees and reports, and determine the order of the names.

✔ Indicate the nature of the individual's relationship with his or her father and mother.

✔ Exclude this individual's relationship with his or her father or mother from any trees, charts, or reports you generate with Family Tree Maker.

The fields dealing with the person's relationships with his or her father and mother are enabled only if you've completed a Family Page for the parents.

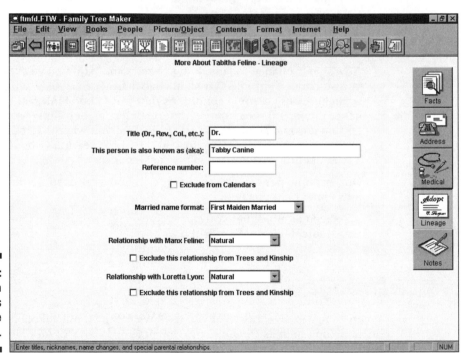

Figure 2-6:
Tabitha
Feline's
Lineage
page.

Follow these steps to complete your Lineage page:

1. Go to your Family Page (if you're not already on it).

Use the tabs on the right side of the screen or choose View⇨Index of Individuals to get there.

For our example, we used Tabitha Feline. We found her Family Page by clicking the tabs on the right side of the screen until we located her.

2. **Choose View⇨More About⇨Lineage.**

   This command opens the Lineage page. (Of course, if you prefer to click buttons rather than use pull-down menus, you can get to this point by clicking the More button to the right of the Name field and then clicking the Lineage button on the right side of the Facts page.)

3. **Type your title in the Title (Dr., Rev., Col., and so on) field.**

   Say you've been knighted by the queen of your country. Then you'd definitely want to enter the title **Sir** in the Title field. As for Tabitha, she's a podiatrist, so we typed Dr. in the Title field.

4. **Tab to the This Person is Also Known As (Aka) field and enter any nicknames or aliases you've used.**

   Be sure to enter your last name, too, when you enter your nickname. When you're ready to generate trees, charts, and reports, you have the option of using nicknames rather than given names. And if you have only the nickname entered here, it may be difficult to tell who the person is on the tree, chart, or report.

   For example, Tabitha Feline usually goes by Tabby. So, we typed Tabby Feline in this field.

5. **(Optional) In the Reference Number field, type in any special number that you want to assign to yourself.**

   You use this field if you prefer a special numbering system to identify your ancestors to more easily tell them apart. Not every genealogist uses this field.

6. **Click in the Exclude from Calendars check box if you want to exclude information about yourself on your Family Tree Maker calendars.**

7. **Select a Married Name Format from the drop-down list. (If the person whose Lineage page you're completing is male, this option doesn't appear.)**

   Your choices are First Maiden Married, First Middle Married, or First Middle Maiden. Your selection here will control how the names of females in your Family File are displayed in trees and reports.

8. **Using the Relationship with [Father] drop-down list, select the most appropriate description for your relationship with the person identified as your father.**

   Your choices are Natural, Adopted, Foster, Unknown, Step, Family Member, and Private.

   If the person listed in the Husband field on your parent's Family Sheet is your biological father, then select Natural. Or, if you were raised by your aunt and uncle, select Family Member.

   We selected Natural for Tabitha.

9. **Click in the Exclude This Relationship from Trees and Kinship check box if you want to exclude any information about the relationship in your trees, charts, and reports.**

   Although the person listed in the Husband field on your parent's Family Page may be your biological father, you may be estranged from him and not want your trees, charts, and reports to reflect the direct line between you and him. Checking this box is the way to mark the relationship for exclusion.

10. **Using the Relationship with [Mother] drop-down list, select the most appropriate description for your relationship with the person identified as your mother.**

    Your choices are Natural, Adopted, Foster, Unknown, Step, Family Member, and Private.

    If the person listed in the Wife field on your parent's Family Page is your biological mother, then select Natural. Or, if you were raised by your aunt and uncle, select Family Member.

    We chose Natural for Tabitha.

11. **Click in the Exclude This relationship from Trees and Kinship check box if you want to exclude any information about the relationship in your trees, charts, and reports.**

    Although the person listed in the Wife field on your parent's Family Page may be your biological mother, you may be estranged from her and not want your trees, charts, and reports to reflect the direct line between you and her. Checking this box is the way to mark the relationship for exclusion.

A note worth remembering

Surely you have some personal stories that you want to include in your family file for future generations to read. Everyone has some. Funny stories, sad stories, even quirky little anecdotes. The Notes page, shown in Figure 2-7, provides room for you to reminisce. It has a free-form field where you can type in any notes you want to include. It works just like a word processor, so type to your heart's content. For more information about formatting and manipulating text in the Notes section, page ahead to Chapter 11.

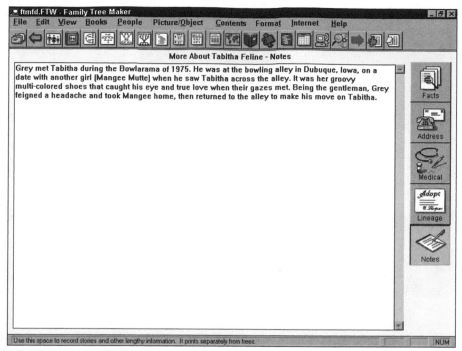

Figure 2-7:
The Notes
page for
Tabitha
Feline.

But for the basics on typing in notes about yourself, follow these steps:

1. **Open your Family Page in Family Tree Maker.**

   Use the tabs on the right side of the screen to click through the entries in your database to get to your Family Page. Or choose View⇨Index of Individuals. (For more on how to use the Index of Individuals, take a look at Chapter 3.)

   We selected Tabitha Feline's Family Page by choosing View⇨Index of Individuals, scrolling to find her name, and double-clicking it.

2. **Click the More button to the right of your name.**

   The Facts page appears. On the right side of the screen, you see buttons that lead you to the other pages for supplemental and more-detailed information regarding current address, medical facts, lineage, and notes.

3. **Click the Notes button.**

   Or you can choose View⇨More About⇨Notes to go directly to the Notes section.

   The Notes page pops up with your cursor on the first line.

4. **Write anything you want about yourself that doesn't fit (either because of topic or space) on one of the other More pages.**

Do you have a funny story about how you met your spouse? How about a touching memory of your grandfather? Here's the place to include these kinds of narratives.

We wrote the following note: Grey met Tabitha during the Bowlarama of 1975. He was at the bowling alley in Dubuque, Iowa, on a date with another girl (Mangee Mutte) when he saw Tabitha across the alley. It was her groovy multi-colored shoes that caught his eye, and true love when their gazes met. Being the gentleman, Grey feigned a headache and took Mangee home, then returned to the alley to make his move on Tabitha.

Proving you exist, Part Deux

We want to mention some more types of documents that can prove events that have occurred in your life. The following are helpful for adding sources to the More About Facts fields:

✔ **Education:** You probably have a diploma or a degree laying around the house, which confirms the dates and places of your education. You may also have tuition bills, financial aid paperwork, or your original application for admission.

✔ **Immigration:** If you immigrated to this country, then you probably have copies of immigration papers, visas, passports, and perhaps naturalization papers that show when you immigrated.

✔ **Military service:** Several documents show military service. You may have a copy of discharge papers, service records (such as orders and leave and earnings statements), retirement letters that show the period of time that you were in the military, and the awards that you received.

✔ **Occupation:** Your occupation may be noted on a variety of documents. You may have copies of offer letters, insurance papers, earnings statements, W-2 and W-4 forms, retirement papers, and other types of personnel paperwork that show your employment at a given company. If you work for yourself, you may have incorporation papers and other government documents reflecting your ownership of a business.

✔ **Property:** If you own property, you may have plat maps, property tax records, mortgages, and perhaps construction or remodeling permits that you can use to prove ownership.

✔ **Residences:** Although you may not have owned property, you probably lived somewhere. In these cases, rental agreements, insurance papers, personal tax returns, and other items can prove residence.

✔ **Religion:** A number of documents may indicate your chosen religion (if any). Baptism certificates, church directories, and other church records can show evidence of membership.

The preceding list covers just a few of the areas in Family Tree Maker. You can certainly find different sources of information for these and other events. Trying to prove all the major events that occurred in your life can be fun — sometimes you even learn a few things about yourself in the process.

Putting Your Mug (er . . . Picture) in the File

Unless you have the talent to spin a good tale out of the facts you've collected and entered, your database may seem a little stale. Pictures and other scanned images can help brighten up your family history. Family Tree Maker has a Scrapbook feature that is wonderful for linking information about people to their photos or to other objects pertaining to them.

Clicking the Scrapbk button to the right of your name on the Family Page takes you to a section where you can link your software to photographs, sound files, and movies (called *objects*) about you. (Or you can use the Scrapbk icon on other people's Family Pages to do the same thing for them.)

Here's how to link these items to Family Tree Maker:

1. **Open your Family Page in Family Tree Maker.**

    Use the tabs on the right side of the screen to click through the entries in your database to get to your Family Page. Or you can choose View⇨Index of Individuals.

    We wanted to use Grey Canine's Family Page, so we clicked the tabs until we found it.

2. **Click the Scrapbk button to the right of your name.**

    Or you can choose View⇨Scrapbook.

    The Individual Scrapbook page appears. Also a Cue Card for Scrapbook pops up, which offers tips and highlights about the Scrapbook feature. If you don't want the Cue Card to pop up every time you open a Scrapbook, click in the check box that says `Click here if you don't want to see this Help Window again`. Then click OK.

3. **Open the Picture/Object pull-down menu and select one of the Insert options.**

    You can choose to Insert Photo CD Picture (if your CD-ROM drive supports the Photo CD format), Insert Picture from File (for supported graphics formats, see Chapter 4), or Insert Object.

4. **Follow the instructions in the dialog boxes that appear.**

   Depending on which Insert option you choose, Family Tree Maker may ask you to place the Photo CD in your CD-ROM drive and then guide you through the process of adding photos from the CD to your Scrapbook. Or it may ask you to provide the filename for the image you want to link and give you the opportunity to browse for the item in your computer's directories. Or you may be guided through the process of creating an object to insert in your Scrapbook.

   We selected a great picture of Grey Canine (see Figure 2-8) — taken not too long ago.

For additional information about using images in the Scrapbook, check out Chapter 4.

Including pictures along with your genealogical data is a nice touch, but they don't do you a lot of good if you don't remember who the people are when you revisit your database years from now. That is why the More About Picture/Object feature is a wonderful thing. You open the More About Picture/Object dialog box, shown in Figure 2-9, by clicking the little down arrow on the lower-right corner of the Scrapbook image/object or by choosing More About⇨Picture/Object. This dialog box allows you to include specific information about the object you've included.

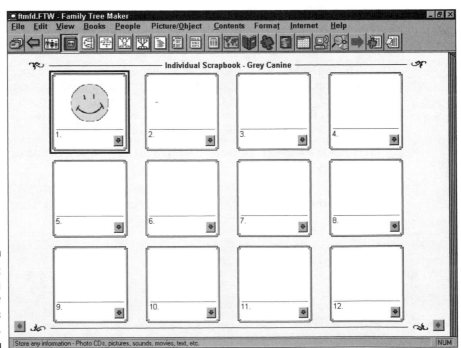

Figure 2-8:
A picture in Grey Canine's Scrapbook.

Figure 2-9:
The More
About
Picture/
Object
dialog box
allows you
to provide
details
about the
objects you
include.

Follow these steps to complete the More About Picture/Object dialog box:

1. **When you're on the Scrapbook page, click the little down-arrow icon in the lower-right corner of the image that you want to provide information about.**

   The More About Picture/Object dialog box appears.

2. **In the Caption field, type the caption that you want to include for your picture/object.**

   This caption can be whatever you like. We recommend that you provide a brief description of what's happening or, if only a few people appear in the photo, include a list of those in the picture.

   For our example, we typed *Grey and Tabitha Canine's Wedding Party* into the field.

3. **Tab down and enter a label in the Category field.**

   You want to be consistent as you make up and use the categories. Doing so helps you more easily print out pictures that have a common theme. You may want to label all the wedding pictures as *Wedding* and birthday pictures as *Birthday*. We recommend that you even take your labeling a step further and identify photos/objects by family. For example, label all of Tabitha Feline's wedding pictures as *Canine/Feline: Wedding*.

4. Go to the next field and enter the object's Date of Origin.

The Date of Origin should be the date on which the original object was created. For example, if you're using a photo that's been scanned, the Date of Origin would be the date on which the original picture was taken — not the date that the picture was scanned.

In our example, we entered the date of origin of June 09, 1975.

5. Choose the type of object from the Type drop-down list.

Your choices are Photo CD Picture, Picture, Sound Clip, Spreadsheet, Video Clip, Word Processor Document, Other OLE Object (OLE stands for Object Linking and Embedding, which allows you to insert a file from one type of program directly into another program), and Unknown.

Choose the type of object that best describes the source of the current picture/object. Ours is a picture, so we chose Picture.

6. Tab to the Description free-form field and enter a description of the object.

This field allows you to provide more information about the picture. You may want to include any special circumstances surrounding the object and perhaps list the location of the original object (if the object is a picture, list who has the original picture).

We typed the following into our description: This is a picture of the wedding party at Grey Canine and Tabitha Feline's wedding. Notice that Grey's suit doesn't fit quite right — that's because he is wearing his brother's suit. His was lost at the cleaners. The original picture is kept in the wedding photo album owned by Grey and Tabitha Canine.

7. Click in the appropriate check boxes to indicate any special Printing instructions.

You can choose from these printing preferences relating to the object:

- **Include in Printed Scrapbook:** This option allows you to specify whether you want the object to appear in printed versions of the Scrapbook. For example, you may not want to include video footage in the Scrapbook.

- **Preferred Picture/Object for Trees:** Here you can designate which objects are the preferred ones for inserting into your family trees. You can designate up to three objects. Then when you print your family trees, you tell Family Tree Maker which set of objects to print.

- **Preferred Picture/Object for Labels/Cards:** Similar to the preferred picture/object, this setting allows you to specify which objects should appear on labels and cards. You can select only one object as the preferred object.

- **Preferred Picture/Object for Fam Grp Sheets:** Again, you can designate the preferred object that shows up when you generate Family Group Sheets. You can specify only one object.

8. **If you want this picture/object included in your Scrapbook slide show, click in the Include in Show check box.**

   Family Tree Maker allows you to put together a slide show of some or all of the images and objects included in your Scrapbook. If you want this particular item included, you need to click in the Include in Show check box. Otherwise, this item will not be included.

9. **If you're using a Photo CD as the source for this image, enter the CD number, photo number, and resolution of the photo in the appropriate fields in the Photo CD section.**

Picking Your Favorite (or Current) Spouse

If you've been married more than once, you're probably wondering whether Family Tree Maker can accommodate you. Well, you and Elizabeth Taylor can rest easy. Family Tree Maker allows you to enter multiple spouses and select which spouse to display on your Family Page and use in your various trees and reports.

Time for a new mate

On the Family Page, the Spouses button to the right of your name takes you to a section where you can add a spouse to your list and select which spouse you prefer to appear on your primary Family Page (that means the spouse who comes up in Family Tree Maker automatically).

Follow these steps to add spouses:

1. **Go to your Family Page (if you're not already on it).**

   Use the tabs on the right side of the screen to click through the entries in your database to get to your Family Page. Or you can choose View⇨Index of Individuals. (For more on how to use the Index of Individuals, take a look at Chapter 3.)

   As it turns out, our favorite example male, Grey Canine, was married once before. Relax, Tabitha knows about it. So we selected Grey's Family Page.

2. **Click the Spouses button to the right of your name.**

   This action brings up the Spouses of [Your Name] dialog box, shown in Figure 2-10, which contains a list of the spouses for whom you've already entered information. If you started by entering information about your current spouse on the Family Page, then only your current spouse's name and your marriage date appear on the list.

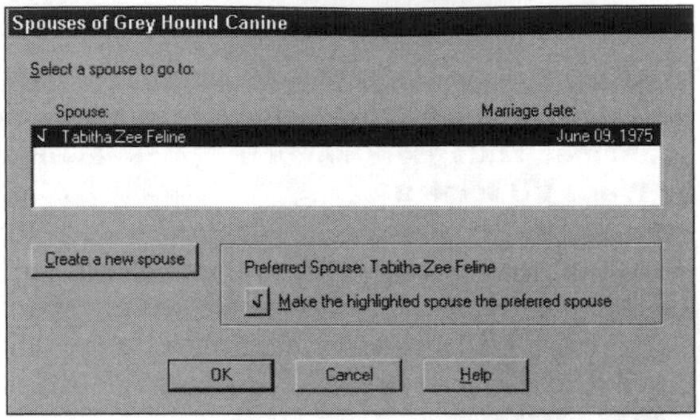

Figure 2-10: The Spouses dialog box.

   In Grey's case, the only spouse currently listed is Tabitha Feline.

3. **Click the Create a New Spouse button.**

   Wow. That could be a dangerous statement, huh? Well, we won't get into how many of you would like to create the perfect spouse. Instead, we focus on the task at hand — creating an entry in Family Tree Maker for another spouse.

   If you've already entered all of your children's names under the current spouse, Family Tree Maker opens a dialog box that asks if you want to attach these children to the new spouse. Your answer depends on whether your children are by your current spouse or a different spouse.

   We typed the name of Grey's first spouse, Ima Lynx, in the Wife field of the new Family Page.

4. **Think back to determine whether your children are by this new spouse and then select Yes or No.**

   If you select No, a new Family Page appears, with your name and birth information already in the appropriate fields. If you select Yes, then all of the children's names and tabs to their Family Pages are displayed on the new Family Page, which contains blank fields for the additional spouse's information.

5. **Complete the blank fields for the new spouse.**

Got a spousal preference?

After you have entered more than one spouse in the database, you need to indicate who is your preferred spouse. Your preferred spouse in Family Tree Maker means the spouse whose name you want to appear on your primary Family Page and on the trees you generate. Of course, you can always change your preferred spouse should your choice fall out of favor for any reason.

Here's how to specify a preferred spouse:

1. **Click the Spouses button to the right of your name on your Family Page.**

   The Spouses of [Your Name] dialog box appears, which contains a list of the spouses for whom you've already entered information.

   In our case, we selected the Spouses of Grey Hound Canine.

2. **Highlight the name of your preferred spouse.**

   Because we like Tabitha so much, we chose her as the preferred spouse.

3. **Click the little check-mark button that says** Make the highlighted spouse the preferred spouse.

   You should see the name of the preferred spouse change as you click the button.

4. **Click OK.**

Entering Extra Marital Details

Aha. We got you with the heading, didn't we? No, this section doesn't deal with infidelities. In it, we discuss extra features for marriage information. Two buttons on your Family Page (right there next to the Marriage Location field) lead you to pages where you can provide detailed information about your marriage to the spouse listed on that Family Page. One is a More button, and the other is a Scrapbk button. We start with the latter.

The Scrapbk button takes you to a Scrapbook page that is essentially like the Scrapbook pages for the Husband and Wife on the Family Page. For information about how to use this feature, take a look at the section "Putting Your Mug (er . . . Picture) in the File," earlier in this chapter.

The More button takes you to a Facts page, where you can enter facts about the marriage, including how it ended (if it did so). And on the right side of the page, you find two buttons — one for the Facts page (that you are currently on) and one for a Notes page. If you click the Notes button, Family Tree Maker takes you to a Notes page that looks identical to the Notes pages for the Husband and Wife (you get to the individual Notes pages by clicking the More buttons next to the names of the Husband and Wife on the Family Page). In the next few sections, we look at the Facts and Notes pages a little closer.

Facts about your marriage

The form on the Marriage Facts page is a lot like the one on the regular Facts page for individuals, with the exception of the Ending Status and Reference Number fields (see Figure 2-11). Also the predetermined facts in the Facts drop-down list are different from those on the individual Facts pages. You can more easily understand some of the differences after you complete the page. Just follow these steps:

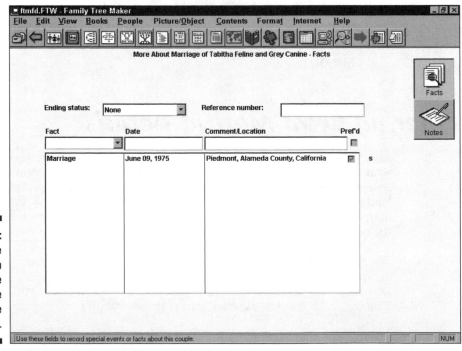

Figure 2-11:
Get the lowdown on the couple on the Marriage Facts page.

1. **Click the More button to the right of the Marriage Location field on your Family Page.**

   This step takes you to the Marriage Facts page on which you need to complete several fields, including Ending Status, Reference Number, Fact, Date, and Comment/Location, and as well as mark the Pref'd check box.

2. **Select an ending status from the Ending Status drop-down list.**

   Your choices in the drop-down list are Annulment, Death of One Spouse, Divorce, None, Ongoing, Other, Private, Separation, and Unknown. Unfortunately, you cannot add to this list by typing in your own term for the Ending Status. If you and your spouse are still married, then choose None.

3. **Tab over to the Reference Number field and assign a special number, if you so choose.**

   You complete this field if you use a special numbering system to identify relationships so that you can more easily tell them apart.

4. **Go to the Fact field and enter the type of fact that you're recording.**

   You can select one of the predetermined facts from the drop-down list, or you can type in your own Fact type. Family Tree Maker offers these choices: Annulment, Death of One Spouse, Divorce, Divorce Filed, Engagement, Friends, Marriage, Marriage Bann, Marriage Contract, Marriage License, Marriage Settlement, Partners, Sealed to Spouse (LDS), Separation, and Single.

   If you want to add to the list of facts, simply type in whatever you want to call the fact. Then after you complete the other fields (we get to those steps in just a minute) and press the Enter key, Family Tree Maker opens a dialog box that asks if you want to add it to the list. Click OK, and your new fact name is added to the drop-down list.

   By the way, you may be wondering how this Fact field is different from the Ending Status field. The Fact field allows you to specify the date and circumstance surrounding the event. It also allows you to include the source of information for the event. The Ending Status field is really a flag in the database that is used when generating reports.

5. **Tab over to the Date field and enter the date on which the event occurred.**

   You can enter the date as numerals (06/09/1975) or spell it out (June 9, 1975), whichever you prefer. If you enter only two digits for the year, Family Tree Maker prompts you to choose a four-digit year. Then Family Tree Maker automatically converts the date to the default format with the month spelled out and appearing first (for example, June 9, 1975). If you prefer the day-month-year format for dates, then you need to reset the default setting by choosing File⇨Preferences⇨Dates & Measures and changing the Date Format.

6. **Tab over to the Comment/Location field and enter any brief comments about the marriage event or the location where it took place.**

   When entering a location for this event, we recommend that you provide the town, county/parish, and state. You can also include the country.

   As with other location fields throughout Family Tree Maker, this one is equipped with the Fastfields feature. So as soon as you start typing, Family Tree Maker starts guessing what you're entering, based on names of locations that you've entered before. The program remembers up to 50 location names for common use.

   When you're entering just a location name, a little trash bin icon pops up next to the Comments/Location field as soon as you start typing. This trash bin works along with the Fastfields feature. Click it to go to Family Tree Maker's next suggestion if you want to save some time typing. If you're entering the name of a totally new place, click it until Family Tree Maker gives you a field with only the letters you typed so far.

7. **If you want this fact to be the preferred one in your database, click in the Pref'd check box.**

   You use this feature when you have two or more facts entered that conflict with each other. It allows you to specify which fact you believe is the true one until you can prove that it is. For example, if your notes contain two different engagement dates for your grandparents and you're not sure which one is correct, you can pick the most likely one for Family Tree Maker to use in reports until you can prove which one is true.

Notes on marriage

How did you propose to your spouse? Or how did your spouse propose to you? Was it romantic or funny? Did you have a traditional wedding or elope to Las Vegas? Was it raining when you got married? These are the kinds of details you want to include in your database in a narrative form for future generations to appreciate. The Notes page (which you get to by clicking the More button next to the Marriage Location field on the Family Page and then clicking the Notes button on the Facts page) is just the place to write it all down. The Notes page is a word processor within Family Tree Maker. For more on how to use Notes, see "A note worth remembering," earlier in this chapter.

Chapter 3

Giving the Lowdown on Others

· ·

· ·

*E*ver heard the phrase that the person who has the most toys when he dies wins? Many genealogists feel that whoever has the most database entries at the family reunion wins. Of course, this gives us the perfect opportunity to preach that having accurate information and source citations is more important than having a great number of entries.

You want to store everything you know about your relatives in Family Tree Maker so that you can easily retrieve information for further research, as well as use the information to create beautiful trees, charts, and reports to share with others. In order to store the information, you must first enter it into the program, which is what you find out how to do in this chapter. We also give you some tips for navigating your way through Family Pages.

Thumbing Through Your Relatives

As you build your database, you need to maneuver through Family Tree Maker to get to new Family Pages to complete. And after you've made quite a few entries in Family Tree Maker, you need to maneuver around to add data and generate trees and reports. So how do you do this, you ask?

You can move around in the Family Pages four ways:

✔ By using the tabs that run down the right side of the Family Page screen.

✔ By using the Index of Individuals.

✔ By using the Find function.

✔ By clicking the box of the person in a family tree you're viewing on your computer.

In the next few sections, we take a look at each of these four methods in more detail.

Tabs

As you enter information about yourself, Family Tree Maker generates links to blank Family Pages for your relatives. It starts by creating a link for your parents, which appears as a tab on the right side of the screen, next to your data. Then if you enter information about a spouse or children, it creates Family Pages for your spouse's parents and your children. The tab for your spouse's parents appears below the one for your parents, and smaller tabs for each of your children appear beneath it.

Family Tree Maker does the same thing for every Family Page you complete. So when you fill in the fields on your parents' Family Page, tabs become available for your father's parents, your mother's parents, and all of their other children (if they have any). And so on, and so on. Figure 3-1 shows Grey Hound Canine's Family Page, where you can see the tabs (links) that run down the right side of the page.

Using the tabs to navigate the Family Tree Maker pages is a breeze. But using them may seem a little monotonous if you need to move through several generations.

Figure 3-1:
The tabs to relatives' Family Pages appear on the right side of the screen.

| Parents of Grey | Parents of Tabitha | Fox Brittany | Gordon |

To open the Family Page for a particular person or set of parents, all you have to do is click a tab. Here is an example:

1. Open Family Tree Maker.

Usually you can just double-click the Family Tree Maker icon on your Windows desktop.

The last Family Page that you were working on as you finished using Family Tree Maker the time before now is the one that appears. Use this Family Page for the purposes of this example.

Say that the last page we were working on was that of Grey Hound Canine and Tabitha Zee Feline. So their page pops up when we open Family Tree Maker this time.

2. On the right side of the Family Page, locate the tabs to other Family Pages.

You see two big tabs and four little, layered tabs. The top big tag is for the Husband's parents. The second one is for the Wife's parents. And the four little ones are for up to four of the couple's children. As you scroll through the list of children (if the couple has more than four), the tabs for the children change to reflect the four whose names are onscreen.

Grey and Tabitha's Family Page has the standard tabs for their parents, and three of the children's tabs are labeled with the names of their three children, as shown in Figure 3-2.

3. Click the tab for the Wife's parents. (If you're an unmarried male, click the tab for your parents.)

For those of you who may need a little refresher on using Windows, you use your computer's mouse to move the cursor to the tab. You knew that, right? Clicking the tab takes you to the Family Page for the Wife's parents.

In our example, the Family Page for Tabitha's parents, Manx Lee Feline and Loretta Lyon, appears.

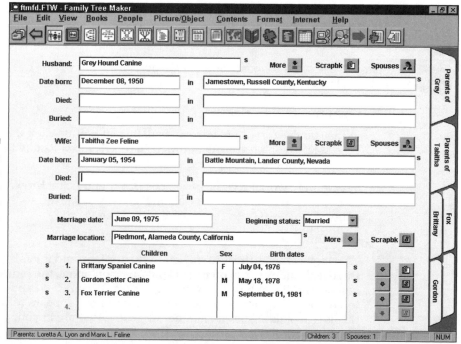

Figure 3-2:
Only three of the children's tabs have names on them because Grey and Tabitha Canine have only three children.

Say you want to access your great-grandparents' Family Page from your Family Page. First you click the tab for your parents. Then you click the tab for either your paternal grandparents (dad's parents) or maternal grandparents (mom's parents), depending on which family line you're following. After your grandparents' page appears, you click the tab for either your grandfather's or grandmother's parents, again depending on which family line you're following. So you click three tabs to access your great-grandparents' Family Page.

Index of Individuals

If you want to access a Family Page that is several generations and family lines from the one where you're starting out, then using the Index of Individuals is the way to go. The Index of Individuals is just what it sounds like — an index of all the names in your database. You can scroll through this list until you find the name of the person you're looking for. Then you just double-click the name, or highlight the name and click OK, or highlight the name and click the Go to Family Page button. Or you can just type the name of the person you're looking for in the Name field at the top of the Index dialog box. Any of these ways take you to the appropriate Family Page.

You can open the Index of Individuals dialog box two ways. First, you can click an icon on the toolbar at the top of Family Tree Maker. It's the one farthest to the left that looks like three index cards stacked on each other. (If you've rearranged your toolbar or changed the icons on it, then the Index of Individuals icon may not be exactly where we've just described it.) The second way to get to the Index of Individuals is to choose View⇨Index of Individuals.

Follow these steps to locate and open a person's Family Page by using the Index of Individuals:

1. **Open Family Tree Maker.**

   In case you've forgotten, you can usually just double-click the Family Tree Maker icon on your Windows desktop. The last Family Page that you were working on appears.

   Say we were working with Grissle Lee Bayer and Leitel Brown Squirrel's Family Page the last time we were in Family Tree Maker, so that page appears when we open the program this time.

2. **Click the Index of Individuals icon on the toolbar.**

   This icon is the farthest to the left of the toolbar, and it has a picture of three little index cards on it. Clicking this icon opens the Index of Individuals dialog box, shown in Figure 3-3. A Name field appears at the top of the dialog box, and most likely a scroll bar appears to the right of the list (depending on the number of people that are in your database). The names in the list are alphabetized by surname.

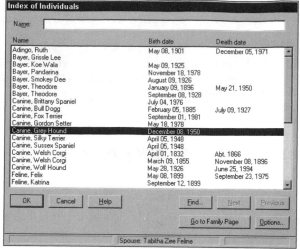

Index of Individuals		
Name:		
Name	Birth date	Death date
Adingo, Ruth	May 08, 1901	December 05, 1971
Bayer, Grissle Lee		
Bayer, Koe Wala	May 09, 1925	
Bayer, Pandarina	November 18, 1978	
Bayer, Smokey Dee	August 09, 1926	
Bayer, Theodore	January 09, 1896	May 21, 1950
Bayer, Theodore	September 08, 1928	
Canine, Brittany Spaniel	July 04, 1976	
Canine, Bull Dogg	February 05, 1885	July 09, 1927
Canine, Fox Terrier	September 01, 1981	
Canine, Gordon Setter	May 18, 1978	
Canine, Grey Hound	December 08, 1950	
Canine, Silky Terrier	April 05, 1948	
Canine, Sussex Spaniel	April 05, 1948	
Canine, Welsh Corgi	April 01, 1832	Abt. 1866
Canine, Welsh Corgi	March 09, 1855	November 08, 1896
Canine, Wolf Hound	May 28, 1926	June 25, 1994
Feline, Felix	May 08, 1899	September 23, 1975
Feline, Katrina	September 12, 1899	

OK   Cancel   Help   Find...   Next   Previous

Go to Family Page   Options...

Spouse: Tabitha Zee Feline

Figure 3-3:
The Index of
Individuals
in our
example
database.

In our example, the Index of Individuals opens with a scroll bar on the right.

3. **Scroll through the list of individuals to find the person you're looking for and then highlight that name.**

We're sure you already know this, but just in case . . . you scroll through the list by clicking the little arrow keys at the top and bottom of the scroll bar, or by clicking the scroll box and dragging it up and down the scroll bar. And you highlight a name by clicking it.

We're looking for Sy Berian Tiegger's Family Page, so we scroll down the list to find his name and then highlight it.

4. **Click the OK button.**

Family Tree Maker takes you to that person's Family Page. For our example, Family Tree Maker takes us to Sy's Family Page.

Find feature

If you don't feel like tabbing through lots of pages or scrolling through the Index of Individuals to find the person you're looking for, you can always use the Find feature. Using the Find feature is a quick and painless process. Just follow these steps:

1. **Open Family Tree Maker.**

Double-click the Family Tree Maker icon on your Windows desktop to open the program. The last Family Page that you were working on appears.

We were just working with Grissle Lee Bayer and Leitel Brown Squirrel's Family Page, so that page appears when we open the program this time.

2. Choose Edit⇨Find Individual.

The Find Individual dialog box appears, as shown in Figure 3-4. In this dialog box, you can search by a variety of things (for example, by name or by date or type of life event).

Figure 3-4:
Locate lost
relatives
with the
Find
Individual
dialog box.

3. Select the item to search by and type in all or part of the person's name or event in the For field.

For our example, we decided to search by name and entered Smokey in the For field.

4. Click the Find Next button.

Family Tree Maker switches the Family Page in the background to the first one it encounters with a name matching the search criteria. If you're not interested in the page that appears, click the Find Next button again, and Family Tree Maker fetches the next Family Page that matches.

Links on trees

It never fails that when you show your pretty pedigree chart (also known as an Ancestor tree) to your dad, he asks about the data you have entered about your great-grandpa and reminisces about when your great-grandpa lived with his family when your dad was a little boy. You get an impulse to flip over to great-grandpa's Family Page so that you can double-check your facts and use the Notes feature to record some of dad's stories. Do you want to scroll through the Index of Individuals to find great-grandpa's page? Nah. Do you want to go through the steps to open the Family Page that you were on so you can click through the tabs? Definitely not. Well, we have good news for you! You can double-click the box that contains information about great-grandpa on your pedigree chart (Ancestor tree) and go directly to his Family Page.

Here's how to get to a Family Page from within a tree:

1. **Open Family Tree Maker.**

   Double-click the Family Tree Maker icon on your Windows desktop. The last Family Page that you were working with comes up.

   We like working with Grey Hound and Tabitha Zee Canine in our examples, so say that their Family Page is the one that comes up.

2. **Create an Ancestor tree for the person whose pedigree you'd like to see.**

   Of course, if the person whose pedigree you'd like to see is not the person whose Family Page you're on, then you need to use the tabs or Index of Individuals to get to the appropriate Family Page (see the two preceding sections for details). For our purposes here, just use the Family Page that you start on to create a tree.

   Creating a family tree can be a multistep process, but for this example, we just need any old Ancestor tree because we're interested in the box links on it. (Check out Chapter 9 to see how to create various trees and charts.) Position your cursor in the field of the person for whom you want to create the family tree and then click the icon on the toolbar that has little blue lines and boxes on it in the form of a pedigree chart. (If you have not customized your toolbar in any way, this icon is the sixth from the left. If you're using Version 7.0, it's the fifth from the left.) Then select whichever format you prefer — fan, standard, or vertical. (For information about these different formats, check out Chapter 9.) Family Tree Maker then creates a family tree on your screen.

   We created an Ancestor tree for Grey Hound Canine by placing the cursor in his Name field and clicking the appropriate icon on the toolbar. We chose the fan format for his pedigree, as shown in Figure 3-5.

3. **Choose an ancestor whose Family Page you want to open and double-click his or her box on the Ancestor tree.**

   In looking at the Ancestor tree for Grey Hound Canine, we noticed that we're missing some location information for Grey's maternal grandparents. We actually just received this information from a cousin who is also researching this family line. So we double-click either Theodore Bayer's box or Ruth Adingo's box to open their Family Page, where we can add this newly found information.

See how simple it is? Of course, this process works the same way if you want to open a Family Page from any of the family trees — Ancestor, Descendant, All-in-One, Hourglass, or Outline Descendant.

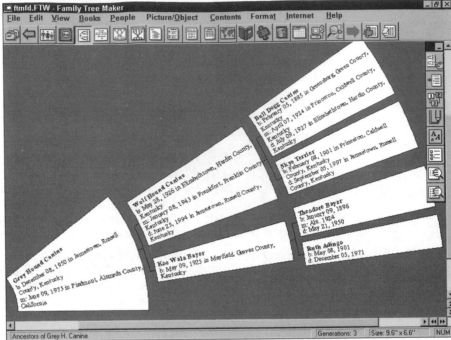

Figure 3-5:
A fan
Ancestor
tree for Grey
Hound
Canine.

Keeping the Goods on Everyone and His Sister

In Chapter 2, we recommend that you start with yourself when entering information into Family Tree Maker and, from there, provide the goods on your spouse, your children, and your grandchildren. Then work your way backward through your parents, grandparents, great-grandparents, and so on. Needless to say, if you've never had a better half or kids, then you can move directly to relatives who preceded you (that is, unless you want to make up a spouse and kids for some odd reason).

The steps to complete a Family Page are the same for all the entries you make — whether you're providing facts about your mom, your granddad, an aunt, or even a great-great-grandmother. So rather than repeat them over and over throughout this chapter — and sound like a broken record — we cover them here, early enough in the chapter that we still have your attention (hopefully).

[You pick the person]'s Family Page

If you're just beginning to populate your database, start on your own Family Page and use the tabs to open the Family Pages of your parents, your in-laws, and your children. If you've already entered information and you're just returning to this section because you can't remember how to complete a Family Page (hey, it happens), then your best bet is to choose View⇨Index of Individuals to select the person whose Family Page you need to work on.

After you reach your destination Family Page in Family Tree Maker, here are the steps to follow to complete a Family Page (Figure 3-6 shows you what a completed Family Page looks like):

1. **Enter the person's full name in the appropriate field.**

   In either the Husband or Wife field, enter your relative's name in this order: first name, middle name, last name. If your relative is a female, be sure to enter her maiden name as the last name. Using her maiden name enables you to see which family line she's really from. Using her married name confuses things — making it difficult to determine whether the Husband or the Wife is really of the married surname line and makes further research on her family line next to impossible because you would be tracking the wrong name.

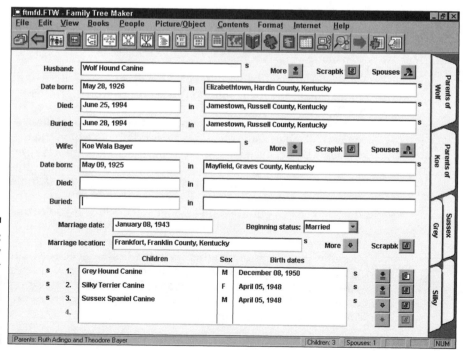

Figure 3-6:
The Family Page for Wolf Hound Canine and Koe Wala Bayer.

If the person doesn't have a last name (surprisingly, this is more common than you may think) or you question whether you have the correct last name for the person, enter \\. For a person with no last name, enter \\ (with no spaces in between). For a person whose last name you don't know yet, use **Unknown**\. And for a person whose last name you question, use *his/her last name*\. For example, if we suspected Bayer wasn't really Koe Wala's last name, we'd enter Koe Wala \Bayer\ in her name field.

Do we have to explain that you choose the appropriate field — Husband or Wife — based on this person's role in the family? Nah . . . you probably already figured that out. You may be questioning, however, what to do with a person who has never been married and, thus, has been deprived of the pleasurable opportunity to fill a husband or wife role. For such a person, use the field that best corresponds with his or her gender. In case you're not sure, that means put a boy's information in the Husband field and a girl's in the Wife's field.

For our example, we entered information about a sample person — Koe Wala Bayer. Canine is Koe Wala's married name, and her maiden name is Bayer. Moving the cursor to the Wife field of the first Family Page, we entered Koe Wala Bayer, because we want her information to reflect her maiden name.

2. **Go to the Date Born field and enter this person's date of birth, including the day, month, and year.**

   Use the Tab key to navigate through the fields or use your mouse to move the cursor. The fields that are initially disabled (such as Date Born, Died, and the Location fields) become active as soon as you type in a name.

   Family Tree Maker automatically converts dates written as all numerals to a format that spells out months. In other words, if you enter 08/05/1962, the system automatically converts the date to the spelled-out format (August 05, 1962) unless you change the default format. Also, be careful when using all numerals for dates in which the day is 1 through 12, because Family Tree Maker also automatically converts the order of the date to whatever the default settings dictate. Initially, the software has a default format of month, day, year. (So if you enter 08/05/1962, Family Tree Maker assumes that 08 is the month, not the day, and writes out the date as August 05, 1962.) If you're using the numerals 13 through 31, the order in which you enter your dates doesn't matter — Family Tree Maker assumes that any number greater than 12 is the day, regardless of whether its in the first or second position. Many genealogists prefer to enter dates in this order — day, month, year. If you prefer this order, you can change Family Tree Maker's default settings to accommodate you. Just choose File➪Preferences➪Dates & Measures and change the Date Format.

Family Tree Maker can't read your mind (even though it seems to sometimes), so you need to enter four digits for years. Otherwise, it doesn't know whether '62 means 1762, 1862, or 1962. If, by chance, you forget and enter only two digits, Family Tree Maker scoffs at you. Actually, it just prompts you to use a four-digit year.

There are an awful lot of catches to entering dates, aren't there? Well, you're almost finished with this field. If you don't know exactly when an event took place, you can approximate a date by using *circa* or *about*. Family Tree Maker automatically converts *circa* or *about* to an abbreviation. Whether it uses Cir or Abt in the field depends on your preference. The initial default is Abt.

In our example, we tabbed over and entered Koe Wala's date of birth in the Date Born field. Her birthday is May 9, 1925. So we entered 05/09/1925 in the field, and Family Tree Maker converted it to May 9, 1925.

3. **Tab over to the In field and enter the person's place of birth.**

   Always include as much information as possible in every field, including the town, county or parish, and state of a person's birth. If you want, you can also include the country. Koe Wala was born in Mayfield, Kentucky so we entered Mayfield, Graves County, Kentucky, USA.

   When you start typing the location, Family Tree Maker usually starts guessing what you're typing. All the location fields in Family Tree Maker have this feature, called Fastfields. Family Tree Maker guesses what you're entering based on names of locations that you've entered before. The program remembers up to 50 location names for common use.

4. **Tab down to the Died field and complete it, if appropriate. Then do the same for the In field for the place of death.**

   Of course, if your relative is still among the living, you don't enter any information in these fields at this time. And no, just because you enter a date and place for your mother-in-law doesn't mean that your wish will come true. Family Tree Maker is a powerful tool, but not that powerful!

   Because our sample gal is alive, we didn't enter any information in these fields at this time.

5. **If you're using Version 7.0, tab down to the Buried field and complete it, if appropriate. Then do the same for the In field for the place of burial. If you're using another version of Family Tree Maker, skip this step.**

   As with Step 4, if your relative is still among the living, you don't enter any information in these fields at this time.

   Because Koe Wala is alive and well, we didn't enter any information in these fields.

6. **Enter information about the person's spouse or significant other. If he or she never had a spouse or significant other, skip to Step 7.**

   Where you enter the spouse's information depends on whether you used the Husband or Wife field for the person you consider the main focus of this Family Page. (If you're entering information about a significant other or life partner and you don't really like the designations Husband and Wife, you can change them by adjusting the Beginning Status field, which we cover in a few minutes.) After the date and place of birth fields are active, tab down and enter the spouse's information in the Date Born and In fields. If the spouse has died, you also want to include information about his or her passing in the Died and In fields.

   Koe Wala is married to Wolf Hound Canine, so we typed his name (in that order) in the Husband field. Then we provided his date of birth in the Date Born field and his place of birth in the In field.

   If the person you're focusing on was married more than once, you can enter information about multiple spouses and select which spouse you want to use in your reports and trees. You just click the Spouses button next to the person's name and follow the instructional boxes. For more information about entering multiple spouses, take a look at Chapter 2.

7. **Enter the person's marriage information in the Marriage Date, Beginning Status, and Marriage Location fields.**

   The Marriage Date and Marriage Location fields are disabled until you enter names in both the Husband and Wife fields. After the fields become active and you finish entering the basic information about the Husband and Wife, tab down to the Marriage Date field and enter the date of their wedding. In the Marriage Location field, enter the town, county or parish, and state where they tied the knot. If you want, you can also include the country.

   Koe Wala and Wolf eloped and were married by a justice of the peace in Kentucky while he was home on leave from World War II. So we entered January 08, 1943 in the Marriage Date field and Frankfort, Franklin County, Kentucky, USA in the Marriage Location field.

   The Beginning Status field reflects the relationship status between the persons whose information appears in the Husband and Wife fields. It's blank until both fields have information, and then it assumes Married for the relationship, unless you specify otherwise. If the Beginning Status field reflects the wrong status for the relationship of the two people, choose a different status from the drop-down list. Your choices are Friends, Married, Other, Partners, Private, Single, and Unknown. Also, the Beginning Status field controls titles for some of the other fields on the Family Page. If you select Friends or Partners for the relationship status of the two people, Family Tree Maker automatically changes the labels on the Husband and Wife fields to Friend or Partner, and the Marriage Date and Marriage Location fields to Meeting Date and Meeting Location.

Because Koe Wala and Wolf were married, we left the Beginning Status field set to its default setting — married.

We also wanted to include some of the details about Koe Wala and Wolf's elopement in our database so that future generations will know the romantic tale. After all, while on a brief respite from serving Uncle Sam overseas, Wolf came home to find that the little pest next door — Koe Wala Bayer — had grown into a beautiful, young lady. He wooed her for all of a week before they snuck off in the middle of the night to get married in the state capital. If you click the More button next to the Marriage Location field, you can record Facts or Notes about the marriage. You can even include pictures or other multimedia by clicking the Scrapbk button next to the More button. For more detailed information about using these functions, check out Chapter 2.

8. **If this person has children, enter information about them in the fields at the bottom of your Family Page. Include their names, sex, and birth dates. If this person doesn't have kids, skip this step.**

We recommend that you include anyone you consider to be this person's child whether they are his or her bloodline or not. This means including all biological children, adopted children, stepchildren, and foster children. You can designate the nature of their relationship with this particular person on the Lineage page, which we cover in "He was also known as . . . ." later in this chapter. And we suggest you enter the children in their birth order — in other words, list the child who was born first on the first line and then list subsequent children in order of the date on which they were born.

Family Tree Maker can be a little deceiving when you're entering facts about children. At first glance, you may think that you can enter information about only one to four children, but this isn't the case. To add a fifth or subsequent child to the list, just press Enter after recording the previous child's date of birth; Family Tree Maker then brings up a fifth or subsequent line for you to use. (You can also use the scroll bar to access additional lines — the scroll bar appears after you enter the fourth child's information.) Enter each child's full name, sex, and date of birth in the appropriate columns.

In our example, Koe Wala and Wolf have three children: Sussex Spaniel, Silky Terrier, and Grey Hound, and their dates of birth are October 30, 1943, April 5, 1946, and December 8, 1950, respectively. We entered Sussex Spaniel Canine in the first line of the first column. Then we tabbed over and selected M to indicate that he's a male, and then tabbed to the final column and entered his birth date. After we pressed Enter, the cursor dropped to the next line, ready for us to enter information about Silky.

We want more. . . .

The Family Page enables you to track the basic information about your relatives — names, dates and locations of births, marriages, and deaths (burials too, if you're using Version 7.0). Although this information is important, it doesn't paint much of a picture of your relative's life. Digging up all sorts of dirt on everyone and storing it in your database makes your genealogy more thorough — and colorful, too. Five supplemental pages to the Family Page allow you to store more insightful details about your relatives' lives.

The five supplemental pages handle facts about a person, addresses, medical information, lineage details, and notes. Clicking the More button next to the person's name on the Family Page takes you to the first supplemental page, the Facts page. From there, you can click the navigation buttons on the right side of the screen to access the other supplemental pages.

A matter of fact

Where did Uncle Angus live and when? When did Aunt Babs travel with the circus as the bearded lady? Did great-grandpa Harry graduate from high school? You can record answers to these kinds of questions on the Facts page.

Some of the events that you enter on the Family Page are automatically copied to the Facts page. For example, when you enter a person's date of birth on the Family Page, Family Tree Maker automatically copies it to the Facts page. In addition, you can add other events, characteristics, activities, and places to the Facts page, as shown in Figure 3-7. This page provides enough room for you to enter the type of fact, the date, and a comment or location. And you can even select preferred facts, if you have conflicting information about an event. For step-by-step instructions on entering facts, check out Chapter 2.

He lives where?

The Address page allows you to record a person's last-known address. It's a handy feature when you need to print labels and lists of relatives for whatever purpose — holiday cards, invitations to reunions, family newsletters, and so forth. The page itself is pretty self-explanatory, but if you want to follow step-by-step instructions, you can find some in Chapter 2.

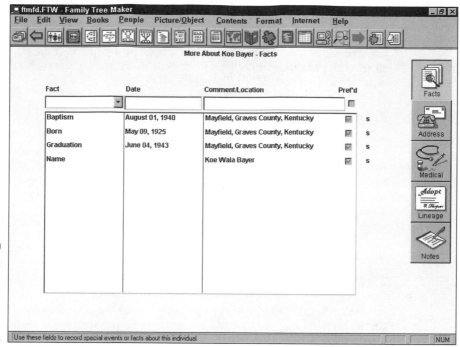

Figure 3-7:
A completed
Facts page
for Koe
Wala Bayer.

She was 6'5" and 200 pounds

How tall was your grandmother, and how much did she weigh? What did she die of? Did she have any chronic medical conditions? The Medical page provides space to record all of these details — fields where you can enter height and weight, as well as a cause of death. And then in a free-form box, you can provide more detail about illnesses, surgeries, serious ailments, physical or mental disabilities, or just about anything medical. For specific information about completing this page, check out Chapter 2.

He was also known as. . . .

Was your uncle Dr. Dudley, Colonel Dudley, or plain old Mr. Dudley? Did he go by Dud instead of Dudley? You can record all of these things and more on the Lineage page. This page handles titles, nicknames and aliases, reference numbers, and information on the relationships between the individual and his or her parents. It also enables you to exclude people from calendars and exclude relationships from your trees and reports. There's also a field that appears for females that enables you to choose the format of their names on trees and reports (whether to include both the maiden and married names and in which order). The fields on the Lineage page are clearly labeled so you can figure out what information goes where, and you can indicate relationships with parents by choosing from drop-down lists. If you want to follow an example walk-through, see Chapter 2.

Keeping notes on everybody

You probably have some stories about various family members that you want to include in your family file for future generations to read. Stories about nutty Aunt Rita, memories of great-grandpa, and a narrative that your mother wrote when she was 12. The Notes page has room for all of these things. It works just like a word processor. For more information about formatting and manipulating text in the Notes section, see Chapter 11. And for step-by-step guidelines for recording notes, take a peek back at Chapter 2.

Picture this

You've probably heard the saying, "A picture is worth a thousand words." We think this is especially true of photographs of ancestors. Seeing what they looked like, how they dressed, and what their homes were like speaks volumes about them. Pictures can help you tell your stories and enhance your genealogy. Family Tree Maker allows you to include your pictures with your database so that you can create trees and reports that enable others to put a face with a name when looking at your presentations. And not only does Family Tree Maker let you store photos (actually, it stores scanned images, not actual photographs), but it also handles all sorts of multimedia objects.

To get to the scrapbook, click the Scrapbk button that appears to the right of the person's name on the Family Page. (Or if you want to link to a scrapbook for a couple's marriage, click the button to the right of the Marriage Location field.) You can add scanned photographs, sound files, and movies (called *objects*) to the scrapbook. Chapter 2 provides step-by-step instructions for attaching items in the scrapbook.

Picking on Your Children First

Aside from you and your spouse, who do you know the most about? You may answer Michael Jordan or Julia Roberts, depending on your interests outside of genealogy. But we'd be willing to bet that the truth of the matter is that you know more about your kids than just about anyone else. In fact, information about your children is so closely tied to you that they first appear on your

Family Page in Family Tree Maker. Funny how that works. Even when they're going through their awkward and sarcastic stages, they're still part of your family, and Family Tree Maker expects you to claim them.

Entering information about your children seems like a natural progression after completing the Family Page fields and supplemental pages about yourself and your better half. Of course, if you don't have any children, you don't need to rush out and get (or create) some. You can just leave the Children fields at the bottom of your Family Page blank.

After you complete your Family Page, including listing any children that you have, Family Tree Maker creates Family Pages for each of the children. To access these Family Pages so that you can provide more detailed information about your children, use the tabs on the Family Page you're on or use the Index of Individuals. (Not sure how to use the tabs or index? Check out "Thumbing Through Your Relatives," earlier in this chapter.) And then follow the steps in "Keeping the Goods on Everyone and His Sister," earlier in this chapter, to complete each of your children's Family Pages.

When you're entering information about your kids, don't forget to cite your sources. In particular, reference primary and secondary source documents that support what you already know about your kids — such as birth, baptism, and marriage certificates. (For more about citing sources, flip over to Chapter 6.) And be sure to include your amusing and touching stories about them on the Notes page, and scanned pictures — if you have some — in the Scrapbook.

Entering and organizing information about children can be a challenging process — which is only fitting because the same can be said of raising children! How do you account for an adopted child, a stepchild, or a foster child in Family Tree Maker? What if you didn't enter your children in their birth order, but you want your Descendant tree to show them that way? Who says the kid has the same last name as his father? What if your child has two sets of parents? Family Tree Maker addresses all of these questions with various features. And these features work when you're dealing with all children in Family Tree Maker, not just your children.

The nature of the relationship

What is the nature of your relationship with your son? No, we don't really want to know that you think he's a know-it-all teenager and he thinks you're a boring old geezer. What we're getting at here is whether he is your natural child, adopted child, stepchild, foster child, or something altogether different.

Family Tree Maker enables you to record the nature of the relationships of children to their parents on the Lineage supplemental page. You choose the appropriate relationships with the father and mother from drop-down lists. Your choices are Natural, Adopted, Foster, Unknown, Step, Family Member, and Private. For more on what the Lineage page is and how to complete it, check out the "He was also known as. . . ." section, earlier in this chapter, and the step-by-step instructions in Chapter 2.

Ordering your kids around

What? You forgot to list your eldest daughter on your Family Page and now she's showing up at the bottom? How could you do such a horrible thing ? Okay, seriously, you're not likely to forget one of your own kids, but you may overlook your ancestors' kids. Or maybe you didn't have a complete list of your ancestors' children when you entered their data, and now you have a census record that lists all of them by name. So you add the children, but the end result is a list that is not in birth order. Rest easy — Family Tree Maker allows you to change the order of children (sort them), as well as move a child or insert a child's name.

Sorting the children

Do you have so many children that you can't keep them straight? Did you end up with a jumbled list in Family Tree Maker in which your last born is first and your first born is somewhere in the middle? Or maybe you're just not very good with dates so you had to hunt down all of the children's birth certificates, and because you found them in random order, you entered them in random order. Whatever the case may be, you can sort your kids' entries by birth order. Just choose People⇨Sort Children. A dialog box then opens, asking if you want to sort the children in their birth order (oldest first). Click OK to rearrange the kids or click Cancel to stop the transaction.

Moving a kid

Maybe you entered one child out of order. Rather than sorting the whole list, you can choose to move just that child's name to its appropriate location in the hierarchy of children. Just follow these steps to move a kid:

1. **Position your cursor on the line where that child's name appears (or highlight the name) and then choose People⇨Move Child From.**

   A dialog box opens, asking whether you want to move this child to a new position in the list.

2. **Click OK and then move the cursor to the appropriate position in the list.**

3. **Choose People⇨Move Child To.**

   Family Tree Maker then moves the kid's name to the new position.

Inserting a child's name

Did you forget to list a child? So now you want to add him, eh? And knowing you, you don't want to put him at the bottom of the list and then have to sort the list to get all those kids in birth order. Lucky for you, Family Tree Maker has a feature in which you can simply insert the kid's name and information on the line where this kid belongs. Just follow these steps to insert a child's name:

1. **Position your cursor in the list of children on the Family Page in which you need to add a kid.**

2. **Choose People⇨Insert Child.**

   Family Tree Maker inserts a blank line above the line where your cursor is sitting. So if your cursor is on the first child's name, Family Tree Maker inserts the line for a new child on the first line and drops the first child's name down to line two.

3. **Enter the child's basic information (name, sex, and date of birth) on that line.**

   Family Tree Maker creates his or her Family Page.

He wanted a name change, so we gave him one

Family Tree Maker automatically uses a father's last name for all the children listed on the father's Family Page. By father's name, we mean the last name of the person listed in the Husband field. If a child has a different last name, you need to fix it manually, which is easy to do. Just change the name on the list of children on the Family Page and press Enter. Family Tree Maker asks you if the person with the new name is the same person as the one with the old name. Click Yes, and Family Tree Maker changes the name.

Attaching children to their parents without a Snugli or rope

Can you imagine what kind of backache you'd have if your children were attached to you at all times? Heck, the thought of carrying a 145-pound, 15-year-old son is flat-out scary. But we're not really talking about physically attaching children to parents. We're talking about attaching their Family Pages to multiple parents' Family Pages.

In several situations, a child can have more than one set of parents. With adoptions, some children have biological and adoptive parents that they need to accommodate in their Family Tree Maker database. In divorces and deaths, some children gain stepparents. And foster care enables some children to claim multiple parents. Family Tree Maker allows you to give a child more than one set of parents so that your database reflects these situations. Chapter 5 covers this feature in detail — giving you more information and step-by-step instructions.

Telling Stories about Your Parents

After you've provided data about yourself, your spouse or significant other, and your kids (if you have any), we recommend you start to work on your parents. You open their Family Page by using the tab on your own page or by using the Index of Individuals (see "Thumbing Through Your Relatives" for instructions). For hints on completing a Family Page, refer to "Keeping the Goods on Everyone and His Sister," earlier in this chapter.

Be sure to cite sources for your parent's information as you complete their Family Page. You may have copies (or the originals) of birth, baptism, marriage, or death certificates; newspaper articles about them; permits and licenses for their business; land records; tax records; and old church or city directories. For details about entering source information, check out Chapter 6.

Also, you want to include — on the Notes page — stories about your parents that you heard from them or events that you witnessed. Things like how they met, their favorite activities, offices they've held (elected or appointed to government, church committees, or social organizations), and their dreams. In the Facts page, you may want to identify their occupations and educational levels. And don't forget to attach scanned photographs or maybe videotaped interviews to their file by using the Scrapbook feature.

Don't Leave Out Gramps

As you fill out your parents' Family Page, Family Tree Maker creates blank Family Pages for their parents and your siblings. And the process works the same way as you go back through the generations: Each time you fill out a Family Page, Family Tree Maker creates pages for parents and children. We recommend that you work going backward through the generations, recording information on your direct ancestors first.

Of course, the number of Family Pages you have to complete multiplies and branches out. Sometimes you may be confused about whose page you should complete next — do you pick your grandfather's parents over your grandmother's parents? Our suggestion is to go with the line that you know the most about and then come back and pick up other family lines. After you've completed the pages for your direct ancestors, come back to your parents' Family Page to begin working on other relatives — your siblings and their families, then your aunts and uncles, and so forth.

Ain't No Relation of Mine

Oh sure, everyone has a person or two in the family tree that they would rather not claim. You know, Uncle Zeb who has a few too many cobwebs in his attic (and we don't mean the attic in his house). But those aren't the non-relations we're talking about here. We're referring to people who aren't related to us, but we wish were — individuals who have a special place in our families but technically aren't related by marriage, birth, or adoption. How do you account for these people in Family Tree Maker?

We touch on how to handle significant others or life partners in "[You pick the person]'s Family Page," near the beginning of this chapter, so we won't rehash that here. The main thing you need to know about entering information about a relative's significant other or life partner is that you enter it in the spouse's field on the relative's Family Page. And by changing the Beginning Status of their relationship on the Family Page, Family Tree Maker changes some of the terms on the Family Page. For example, the Husband and Wife fields become Friends or Partners fields, and the Marriage Date and Marriage Location fields become the Meeting Date and Meeting Location fields.

If you're dealing with an unrelated person who doesn't really fit into the family structure, then you create a Family Page in your database that isn't linked to the rest of your family. This way, the people you identify on this unlinked Family Page won't appear in your trees, charts, and reports.

Follow these steps to create an unrelated Family Page:

1. **Open Family Tree Maker.**

   Typically all you have to do is double-click the Family Tree Maker icon on your Windows desktop. The last Family Page you were working on appears.

2. **Choose People⇨Add Unrelated Individual.**

   Add Unrelated Individual is the first option on the People drop-down menu. A blank Family Page appears.

3. **Complete the Family Page by entering the person's information.**

   For guidance on completing the Family Page, take a look at "[You pick the person]'s Family Page," earlier in this chapter.

4. **To return to a family member's Family Page, choose View⇨Index of Individuals.**

Of course, if you later discover that this person was indeed related to your family somehow, you can always link his or her Family Page to the family by using the Attach features. You can attach a person as a spouse or child. See Chapter 5 for guidance on fixing your database.

Importing Your Ancestors

One last thing that we need to talk about is importing individuals. No, we don't mean loading all of your relatives up and bringing them to live with you. What we're talking about is importing a GEDCOM file that you received from another researcher.

As you may recall, GEDCOM is a standard file format that genealogical databases use so that researchers can share their information. After you receive a GEDCOM file from another researcher, you can import it into Family Tree Maker

You should always review the new Family File (after you've imported it) to ensure that all of the elements that you're expecting are contained in the new Family File. Some programs are better than others at exporting and importing GEDCOM files, so many things could potentially go wrong with the import. Things to look for are accurate dates and whether all of the notes and sources imported correctly.

Here are the steps to import a GEDCOM file:

1. **Choose File⇨Open Family File.**

   This step opens the Open Family File dialog box.

2. **Select GEDCOM in the Files of Type drop-down list.**

   You can see only GEDCOM files (and directories) when GEDCOM is selected.

3. **Select the GEDCOM file to import and click Open.**

   This generates the New Family File dialog box.

4. **Type a new file name into the File Name field and click the Save button.**

   You should see the Import from GEDCOM dialog box.

5. **Select your preferences for importing the GEDCOM file.**

   The Import from GEDCOM dialog box (see Figure 3-8) contains a few options. The first asks if the location field is too long, do you want to keep the first or last part of the location? It also gives you the option of deleting the underscore from names, and adding spacing in the location fields. You can also choose which Facts you want to import, although Name, Birth, Marriage, and Sex are always imported. Normally, you are safe using the defaults here, which we recommend unless you have experience with working with GEDCOM files. Click OK after you are satisfied with the selected options.

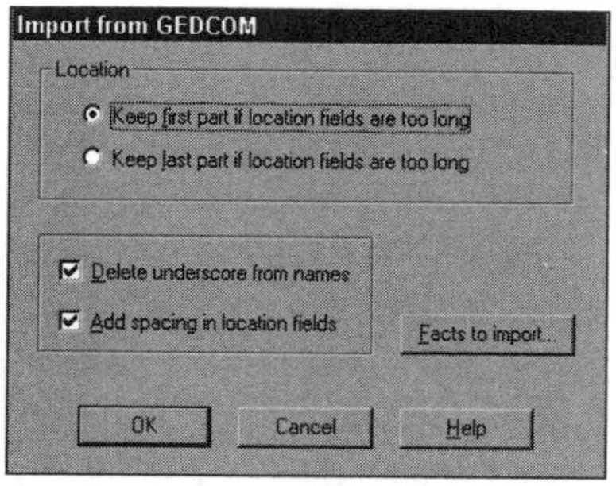

Figure 3-8:
The Import
from
GEDCOM
dialog box.

6. **Click OK after the import is finished.**

   When Family Tree Maker is finished importing the file, it provides a message and notes any warnings or errors that were generated during import. Even if no errors were reported, it's still a good idea to check all of the information. After the import is complete, you may see a message asking if you want to run a new FamilyFinder report. If you do, just click OK. If not, click Cancel and then OK.

If you eventually decide that you want some or all of the contents of your new Family File merged with the Family File you've been working on, simply select File⇨Append/Merge Family File and follow the prompts.

Chapter 4

Say Cheese! (Using the Scrapbook Feature)

• •

In This Chapter

▶ Finding out some benefits to using multimedia in Scrapbooks

▶ Creating multimedia objects — pictures, sound, and video

▶ Adding objects to Scrapbooks

▶ Working with OLE objects

▶ Adding captions to your images

▶ Building a slideshow

• •

*W*e all have scrapbooks full of embarrassing photos from when we were young. Often we like to look through them to reminisce about the way things were, and our kids like to page through them and make fun of the clothing styles at the time.

The problem with these traditional scrapbooks (other than your mother pulling them out to show off your adorable baby pictures) is that they are not really all that exciting — at least not in the way that our interactive society views excitement. The pictures and their handwritten captions sort of just lie there, lifeless. That is, until now. With Family Tree Maker, you can create a multimedia scrapbook complete with pictures, sound, and video. And, with a little creativity, you can even entertain the kids of the interactive generation.

This chapter focuses on Family Tree Maker's Scrapbook feature. We take a quick look at how to create multimedia objects, include these objects in your Scrapbook, and use the Scrapbook to organize your research.

Multimedia, It's Not Just for Kids

We know that some of you probably shiver when you see the word multimedia. It sounds so complex, so difficult to deal with. After all, multimedia involves state-of-the-art technology and requires really expensive computers and gadgets. Well, not really. If you can work a VCR, you probably can handle the types of equipment necessary to scan pictures or capture video. In fact, some companies have created products that make working with multimedia easier than working the VCR.

Do some of you still need convincing? Here are some of the benefits of using multimedia in Scrapbooks:

✔ **Document preservation.** Electronic scrapbooks are an excellent way to preserve documents that may otherwise deteriorate over time. For example, how many of you have old, yellowing newspaper articles that continue to fade over time? Why not scan them so that if the paper becomes unreadable, you still have the digitized version of the document?

✔ **People preservation.** No, we're not talking embalming here. But we are talking about a way to preserve the voices and images of people who have passed on. For example, Matthew had the opportunity to interview his grandmother and record it on audio tape. Now that she has passed on, her descendants can still hear her telling family stories and answering questions about her life. You can also do the same thing with video. Descendants can view their ancestors in action and see firsthand some of the famous family traits that they inherited.

✔ **Entertainment for the kids.** Seeing great-grandma act silly may be a thrill for children. Not only is it entertaining, but it may get the kids interested in finding out more about their family, allowing you to pass on all that you know about family traditions. Who knows, they may be budding genealogists.

If these aren't enough reasons, we're sure that you can come up with some on your own if you put your mind to it. Either way, we suggest adding a little spice to your Family File with multimedia.

You Gotta Have Input Before You Can Output

We know this may come as a shock to you, but multimedia objects don't create themselves. Something must digitize the pictures, sound, and video and allow these objects to be saved to a storage device (like a hard drive, floppy disk, Zip disk, or CD-ROM). To give you a little insight, in the next few sections we take a quick look at a few ways that multimedia objects are created.

Attachments from your buddy

One of the easiest ways to get multimedia objects is to have friends and family members send them to you already digitized. They may e-mail you pictures, send you collections of objects on disk or CD-ROM, or allow you to download objects from the Internet.

Typically, these objects are already in a format that Family Tree Maker can accept. If they aren't, then you need to get a graphics program that can convert the files into something that you can use. These graphics programs come in a lot of different shapes and sizes (and price ranges, for that matter). If converting a file is not something that you'll be doing often, then you may want to look for *freeware* (a program that is available on the Internet or on disk at no cost) or *shareware* (a program that is made available by the author for a small fee). A good place to start your search is at Shareware.com (www.shareware.com). Or you can just ask your buddies and relatives to save the objects in a format that is compatible with Family Tree Maker. For more on compatible file formats, see "A bit about file formats" later in this chapter.

Scanned images

One of the greatest technological advancements for genealogists like yourself is the scanner. A scanner works much like a photocopier. When you photocopy a document, you lay the document on the bed of the copier, and the copier creates a copy of the object and prints it to paper. A scanner also creates a copy of the object, but it saves the object as an electronic file instead of printing it to paper.

Many types of scanners are available. Here are a few of them:

- **Flatbed:** This scanner is what many people think of when they hear the word scanner. The flatbed scanner looks like a photocopier. You lay a document on the bed of the scanner, start the scanning program, and the scanner does the rest. These scanners come in different sizes. Some can only hold letter-size documents, whereas others can handle legal and odd paper sizes. Also some come with document feeders that allow you to place several documents in the scanner at a time. Flatbed scanners usually require you to insert the necessary expansion card into one of the empty expansion slots inside your computer. This can be tricky to do with a laptop, so you may want to use a flatbed scanner only with a desktop computer (although there are exceptions to this).

- **Handheld:** Handheld scanners were originally a low-cost alternative to the more expensive flatbed scanners. However, as the prices of flatbeds have dropped, handhelds have become less plentiful. Handhelds serve a couple of purposes. First, they can scan objects that you can't easily place on a flatbed scanner. They are ideal for scanning oversized photographs and documents. In fact, we used a handheld scanner to scan a picture that was still in a picture frame (the relative did not want us to take the picture out of the frame — it's a long story). Second, handheld scanners are especially useful for taking on the road. They tend to be very compact and easy to pack with a notebook computer. Many handhelds plug into the parallel or serial ports on your computer, so they don't require you to install a card. Unfortunately, the quality of scans of a lot of handhelds are not on the same level as their flatbed counterparts. Also, it sometimes takes multiple scans (which then need to be stitched together), just to scan an ordinary sheet of paper.

- **Snapshot:** Snapshot scanners are useful for creating electronic images of photographs that measure 5 x 7 inches or smaller, because they're designed to work primarily with that size of photograph. Snapshot scanners are compact and come in external (no computer card required) and internal (card installation required) varieties. You feed the photograph into the scanner, and the scanner captures an image before sending the photo back out. Some snapshot scanners have removable tops that you can use as handheld scanners in order to capture images larger than 5 x 7 inches. One caution with snapshot scanners: You may not want to use them with old, fragile photographs. Feeding the photographs through the scanners can damage them.

- **Sheetfed:** No, sheet scanners won't scan your linens (at least not very easily). Sheetfed scanners are typically a little wider than a regular sheet of paper (8½ inches across). They're still rather compact, as far as scanners go, but all are external. You feed the photograph or document into the feeder on the scanner, and the scanner captures an image as the document goes through. Like some snapshot scanners, some sheetfed scanners have removable tops that you can use as handheld scanners in order to capture images larger than 8½ inches across. Use caution when using these scanners with fragile photographs because they can be damaged as you feed them through. In fact, we suggest using only a flatbed scanner for old photographs.

✔ **Slide:** Slide scanners have become more popular lately. They allow you to digitize those old family reunion and vacation slides that you have laying around the attic. You can purchase slide scanners by themselves, or buy one of the new flatbed scanners that comes with slide attachments.

Lots of specialty scanners are available, as well. For example, you can purchase transparency scanners, Advanced Photo System (APS) scanners (the film that is used in newer Kodak cameras), negative film scanners, microfilm scanners, and (in case you feel the need to scan the business cards that your cousin, the insurance salesman, always gives you) business card scanners. There are also multi-purpose machines that can not only scan documents but can also print, photocopy and fax. These machines are made by manufacturers such as HP, Canon, and Brother and you can find them at your local electronics or office supply store.

If you don't want to purchase a scanner, another option is to have someone do the scanning for you. Most copy and print shops have the capability to scan photographs and documents, and some even allow you to do it yourself.

Photo CDs

A relatively new option in photo development is the Kodak Photo CD. The Photo CD is a collection of digital photographs stored on a CD-ROM that is produced at the same time that your film is developed. Many film developers now offer the Photo CD as an option, much like double prints are an option. The Photo CD is a good choice when you don't have a scanner but still want to preserve your photographs in a digital format.

Sound cards

Most new computers come with sound cards — especially if the machines have CD-ROMs. Sound cards allow you to hear music, games, and sound effects from the programs that run on your computer (sound beyond just beeps, that is). Many of these cards have jacks on the back of them that allow you to hook up input devices (such as tape recorders or stereo systems) so that you can record. In order to do this, you have to use special software that is capable of translating the signal coming from your tape recorder into a digital format that the computer can store. This software usually comes with a sound card, although you can find more sophisticated programs at your local software store.

Video capture boards

Similar to a sound card, a video capture board is a card inside of your computer that enables you to grab images from your camcorder, VCR, DVD player, or other video playback device. You can use moving images or still pictures, depending on your video capture board and the accompanying software. Some computers are shipped with video capture as standard, but generally that's not the rule. Video capture boards can have some high-end computer requirements, so be sure that your computer system can handle a particular video capture board and software program before making your purchase.

We should also note that some companies produce external video capture products. You can hook up these products to your Universal Serial Bus (USB) port (if your computer supports this type of device). Also, there are new products on the market that act as TV tuners that allow images to be captured to disk. Check the documentation that came with your computer to figure out whether any of these are a good option for you.

Digital cameras

Digital cameras are one of the newer technologies to capture genealogists' interest. Being able to take all your photographs with a camera that downloads the images directly to your computer is exciting! Depending on the model, you store the digital pictures within the camera's memory, or on compact flash cards, or on 3½-inch disks. With the models that store the images internally, you must take the extra step to download the images to your computer through a serial cable. Some models save the images to a floppy disk. When using these models, you simply insert the disk into your computer and copy the files to your database.

As with every other computer peripheral, if you're considering purchasing a digital camera, carefully read the package and hardware/software requirements to make sure that your computer system can support the equipment.

Digital camcorders

Digital camcorders are also doing their part to shape the way that genealogists store information. The most common digital camcorders come in the 8mm format and are either digital-only or hybrid camcorders. Digital-only camcorders can only record and play digital tapes. Hybrid camcorders (such as the Digital 8 products by Sony) can play and record standard 8mm tapes as well as digital tapes.

Many digital camcorders have extra features that make them fun to use (such as fancy transitions, titling, and so forth), and some even have so many features that you can't think of any occasion when you would use them. And some camcorders allow you to take still digital pictures. You can download the video and still pictures to your computer without purchasing extra hardware.

Start Scrapbooking!

Enough of the small talk. You're ready to start putting that Scrapbook together. No need to go in search of that dried-up pot of glue or the two-sided adhesive tape; you can cut and paste the electronic way by using the Scrapbook feature of Family Tree Maker.

Inserting pictures from a file

If you don't have a scanner, your first question may be, "Where would I get a scanned picture?" Maybe another researcher sent you a picture that he scanned or possibly you downloaded an image from a Web page. The key is that you have a scanned picture and you want to include it in your Family File. So if you have a scanned picture that's already been saved to a file and you want to place the picture into the Scrapbook, follow these steps:

1. **Select the Family Page of the individual who is the subject of the scanned photograph.**

   You can use the tabs on the right side of the screen to navigate to your Family Page. Or you can choose View➪Index of Individuals. (For more on using the Index of Individuals, take a look at Chapter 3.)

   We decided to add a picture of our old friend, Grey Canine.

2. **Click the Scrapbk button to the right of the individual's name or choose View➪Scrapbook.**

   This step creates the Individual Scrapbook page. You may encounter a Cue Card, giving you some information about Scrapbook options. If you don't want the Cue Card to pop up every time you open a Scrapbook, click in the check box that reads Click here if you don't want to see this Help Window again. Then click OK.

3. **Choose Picture/Object➪Insert Picture.**

   You can choose Insert Photo CD Picture, Insert Picture from File, or Insert Object. Because you have a picture from a file, choose Insert Picture from File.

4. **Select the picture that you want to add in the Insert Picture dialog box.**

   Once you select the image, Family Tree Maker guides you through the process of creating an object to insert in your Scrapbook.

   We selected a great picture of Grey Canine — taken not too long ago. We selected the Insert Picture from File option.

   The Insert Picture dialog box appears and shows you the contents of your computer on the left side and has a preview pane for your picture on the right side, as shown in Figure 4-1.

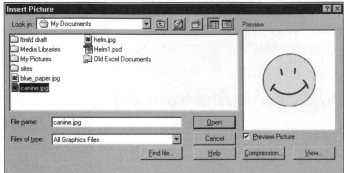

Figure 4-1:
Find your picture with the Insert Picture dialog box.

5. **In the Insert Picture dialog box, select a picture.**

   You select a picture in this dialog box in the same way that you select files when using Windows Explorer or File Manager. You can also search for files by clicking the Find File button. After you locate the picture, either double-click it or highlight it and then click the Open button.

   If you want to preview the picture to make sure that it's really the one you want to use, just click in the Preview Picture check box, located below the Preview screen. If you select the Preview Picture option, two more buttons become available. The Compression button allows you to set the size of the picture when imported into Family Tree Maker (we talk more about compression later), and the View button allows you to see the picture in a larger size.

   After you select a picture, the Edit Picture dialog box appears, as shown in Figure 4-2.

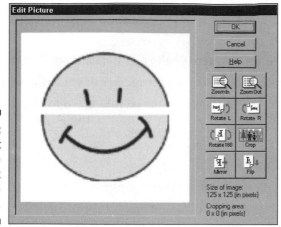

Figure 4-2:
The Edit
Picture
dialog box
with the
white bar.

In some versions of Family Tree Maker, you may encounter a white bar running through your image. This is a known bug with the Family Tree Maker graphics viewer. It can be annoying, but should not adversely affect the import of your picture.

6. **Adjust the picture to find the right look.**

This dialog box allows you to make simple edits to the picture including rotating, cropping (or cutting the picture to focus on a specific part), mirroring (essentially turning the picture around, as if you were viewing it in a mirror), and flipping (vertically) the picture.

You can rotate the picture by clicking the Rotate L (left), Rotate R (right), or Rotate 180 buttons until the picture appears the way you want it. If the picture is facing the wrong direction, use the Mirror and Flip buttons to position it correctly.

Cropping a picture (or cutting it down to size) is a really simple in Family Tree Maker. When you move your cursor over the picture in the Edit Picture dialog box, the cursor turns from an arrow to a cross — more specifically, a crosshair. This crosshair allows you to designate a specific area of the picture for cropping. Follow these steps to crop a picture:

1. **Move the crosshair to the upper-left corner of the area where you want the selection to begin.**

If you need a closer look at the image you are editing, use the Zoom In button. If you need to return to normal size, use the Zoom Out button.

2. **Click and hold down the mouse button while you drag the cursor to the lower-right part of the selection, and then release the button.**

   You should see a square on the picture, marking the selection area.

3. **Click the Crop button to cut the picture down to the selected area.**

   If you don't like the way that the picture is cropped, just click the Cancel button, and the picture returns to the way it was when you started. Keep in mind that if you click the Cancel button, all the other changes that you made to the picture (during this session) are cancelled as well.

7. **Click the OK button when the picture looks the way that you want.**

   A thumbnail (small version of the picture) of the picture is inserted into the first box in the Scrapbook (assuming that you don't have any other pictures in the Scrapbook).

   You can view the full picture at any time by double-clicking the thumbnail of the picture in the Scrapbook.

   If you need to adjust the contrast of pictures that you entered into the Scrapbook, simply select the picture and choose Picture/Object⇨Contrast. Then use the sliding scale to darken or lighten the contrast and click OK.

Family Tree Maker allows you to store up to 2,000 objects in the Scrapbook for each person and marriage. So, you have plenty of room to add all those multimedia nuggets — provided you have enough space on your computer to store all these graphical images.

Inserting Photo CDs

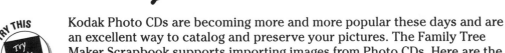

Kodak Photo CDs are becoming more and more popular these days and are an excellent way to catalog and preserve your pictures. The Family Tree Maker Scrapbook supports importing images from Photo CDs. Here are the steps to import a picture from a Photo CD into a Scrapbook:

1. **Open the family member's Scrapbook in which you want to insert the image.**

2. **Click the box where you want to insert the picture.**

3. **Choose Picture/Object⇨Insert Photo CD Picture.**

   Another option is to right-click on a Scrapbook box and choose Insert Photo CD Picture from the menu that appears.

   After you choose the option from the menu, the Insert from Photo CD dialog box appears. This dialog box contains three buttons labeled Find, View, and Resolution.

4. **Select a picture to add to the Scrapbook.**

   To find a picture on the Photo CD, click the Find button. You are presented with a field labeled Find Photo Number. Just type in the photo number that you would like to add to the Scrapbook and click OK.

   After you've selected a picture, you can use the View button to see it at its full size.

   The last button that you can select is the Resolution button. Using this button, you can change the size and compression ratios for the picture. The default settings for these ratios are usually good, but you can change them if you want. For more on compression ratios, see the section "Compressing Uncle Zeke," later in this chapter

5. **Click the OK button to insert the picture into the Scrapbook.**

6. **After you're back at the Insert Photo CD dialog box, you can click the OK button.**

   When you do this, the Edit Picture dialog box appears, where you can edit the image.

7. **When you're happy with the way the picture looks, click the OK button.**

   This action returns you to the Scrapbook page, and your picture should now appear as a thumbnail in one of the Scrapbook boxes.

Some versions of Family Tree Maker appear not to support the newer versions of Kodak's Picture CD. For example, we tried to import pictures from a CD that we just had made in October 1999 in to Family Tree Maker Version 7.0. When we attempted to import a picture, we were given an error message that the program could not read the CD. We had no problems reading the CD with the Kodak software on the same machine. We found that the way around this is to import the picture as a picture from a file and then find the appropriate picture on the CD. In our case, the Picture CD had the pictures in JPEG format which made it easy to import.

A bit about file formats

Family Tree Maker supports several standard graphics file formats. Knowing these formats ahead of time helps you avoid trying to add images that Family Tree Maker doesn't support. The eight file formats that the Scrapbook supports are

- ✔ Windows Bitmap (*.bmp)
- ✔ FlashPix Format (*.fpx)
- ✔ JPEG Interchange Format (*.jpg, *.jff)
- ✔ PhotoCD Format (*.pcd)

✔ Zsoft Image (*.pcx)

✔ Photoshop 3.0 Format (*.psd) — the program says 3.0, however, we were successful in adding a Photoshop 5.0 file to the Scrapbook

✔ Tagged Image Format (*.tif)

✔ Windows Metafile Format (*.wmf)

The notable file formats that Family Tree Maker does not support is the Graphic Interchange Format (*.gif), a popular format on the World Wide Web, and Encapsulated PostScript (*.eps). (Presumably, this was due to licensing issues.) So make sure that anything you get from the World Wide Web is not in GIF or EPS format.

Compressing Uncle Zeke

Another thing you want to keep in mind when placing pictures in the Scrapbook is the *file compression ratio*. File formats such as the JPEG Interchange Format allow you to specify the compression ratio of the picture. In other words, you can control the size of the file. The tradeoff is that the quality of the picture decreases with the file size. So decide on an acceptable level of quality for the pictures that you intend to store in the Scrapbook. If you intend to use the Scrapbook as a preservation archive, then you probably want to decrease the compression. If you are merely keeping pictures in the Scrapbook for family trees, then you can set the compression rate higher.

You can adjust the compression ratio by clicking on the Compression button found underneath Preview in the Insert Picture dialog box. After clicking the button you are presented with ten radio buttons with compression levels from 1:1 to 28:1. Select the desired ratio and click the OK button.

When using the Family Tree Maker compression feature, keep an eye on the Disk Space Needed area of the Change Compression dialog box, shown in Figure 4-3. It gives you a good indication of what the final size of the object will be after it's compressed.

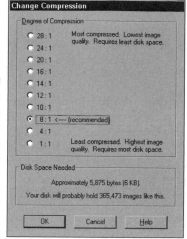

Figure 4-3: The Disk Space Needed area is the key to keeping your hard drive happy.

Getting Those Ol' OLE Objects in There

In addition to photographic images, you can insert a number of other objects into the Scrapbook. These objects include sound and video files or files from other programs such as word processors or spreadsheets. The only prerequisite is that you create these other objects by using a software program that supports *Object Linking and Embedding* (OLE). Object Linking and Embedding allows users to create an object (a graphic of some sort) in one piece of software and then place that same object in another piece of software.

For example, say that you have an old, worn picture of your great-grandfather. You decide to scan it into a graphics program, such as Photoshop, so that you can touch up the picture. After you have the picture looking the way that you want it, you save it in Photoshop's file format. Normally, you can't use that file in another software program, unless it specifically accepts Photoshop files. That's where OLE comes in. OLE allows you to import that object into Family Tree Maker, without Family Tree Maker needing to be specifically configured to handle Photoshop files (although Family Tree Maker does accept Photoshop files without OLE, pretend for the moment that it doesn't). It works the same way with word processing files, video captures, sound bites, and spreadsheets (and a whole lot more).

You can import an OLE object into Family Tree Maker's Scrapbook three ways, which are as follows (drum roll, please):

 ✔ Import an OLE object that is an existing file.

 ✔ Import a new OLE object from its original program.

 ✔ Paste an OLE object from the Clipboard.

Existing OLE objects

Importing an OLE object that is in an existing file is easy, just follow these steps:

1. **Select the box on the Scrapbook page where you want to insert the object.**

2. **Choose Picture/Object⇨Insert Object.**

    The Insert Object dialog box appears, as shown in Figure 4-4.

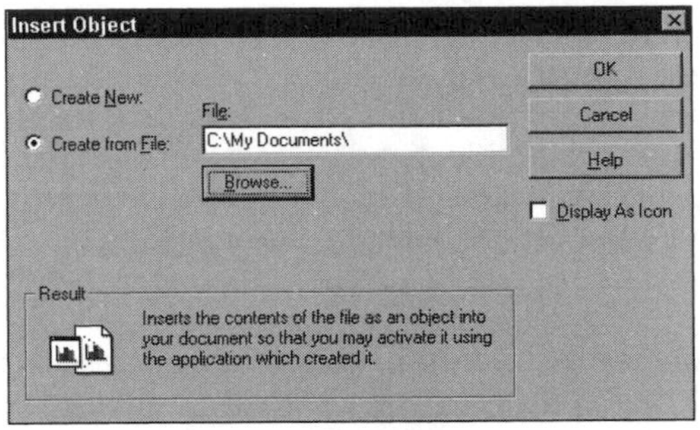

Figure 4-4:
The Insert
Object
dialog box,
with the
Create from
File twist.

> **Insert Object**
>
> ◯ Create New:
> ◉ Create from File: File: `C:\My Documents\`   [Browse...]
>
> [OK] [Cancel] [Help]
>
> ☐ Display As Icon
>
> Result
> Inserts the contents of the file as an object into your document so that you may activate it using the application which created it.

3. **Select the Create from File option on the left side of the dialog box.**

    The dialog box then displays a field where you can type in the filename of the OLE object. If you don't know its exact location, click the Browse button and locate the file.

4. **After you locate the file, click OK.**

    The object should appear as a thumbnail in the Scrapbook.

Some documents don't show up well as thumbnails. So consider displaying the file as an icon in the Scrapbook box. To do this, open the Insert Object dialog box and select the Display As Icon option. When the Display As Icon checkbox is marked, two things are added to the Insert Object dialog box — a picture of the icon and a button marked Change Icon. Then click the Change Icon button and either accept the default icon or choose another. Finally, change the Label field to something that is more descriptive than simply *Document*. When finished, click the OK button twice, and the object is inserted in the Scrapbook.

New OLE objects

Importing a new OLE object from its original program is a little more involved than importing it from an existing file, but it's not too complicated. Just follow these steps:

1. **Choose Picture/Object➪Insert Object.**

   The Insert Object dialog box appears, as shown in Figure 4-5.

Figure 4-5: Create New OLE object portion of the Insert Object dialog box.

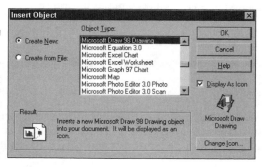

2. **Select the Create New option on the left side of the dialog box.**

3. **Scroll through the list of the OLE object types and select the object type that you want to create.**

4. **Click the OK button to launch the application in which you build the OLE object to import.**

5. **After you finish creating the object in the application, close the application.**

   The object should appear as a thumbnail in the Scrapbook.

Pasty OLE objects

The final way to insert an OLE object is to paste it into the Scrapbook from the Clipboard. Maybe you created a note in the Windows WordPad program that you want to add to the Scrapbook. All you have to do is choose Edit⇨Copy, which places the object on the Windows Clipboard. Then, open the Scrapbook page for the individual, select a box, and then choose Edit⇨Paste Special. Select how you want the object to be placed into the Scrapbook and then click the OK button. And you're done!

Scanning Your Ancestors

One of the new features in Version 7.0 is the ability to download pictures from your digital camera or scan images or documents directly into Family Tree Maker. This can save you some time and some system resources since you can avoid having several programs open at the same time. To scan a picture or document into the Scrapbook just follow these steps:

1. **Go to the scrapbook where you want to place the picture or document.**

   Once you are in the scrapbook, click in the block where you want the picture or document placed.

2. **From the menu bar, select Picture/Object⇨Insert Picture from Scanner/Camera.**

   This generates the Select Source dialog box. Listed in the box are the scanners and digital cameras for which your computer has drivers. If your scanner is not listed, you may need to reinstall your scanner or camera device driver. See your scanner or camera documentation for more details.

3. **Highlight the scanner that you wish to use and then click the Select button.**

   A dialog box labeled Getting Image appears and your scanner software launches. Make whatever adjustments you need to the image and then click whatever button or command your scanner software uses to finish the scanning process (consult your scanner manual for more information). Once your scanner program finishes, the scanned picture will pop up in the Edit Picture dialog box in Family Tree Maker.

4. **Make any adjustments to the picture or document in the Edit Picture dialog box and then click OK.**

   This will place your scanned picture or document into the scrapbook.

Just like adding a picture from a file, keep in mind the size of the image when you scan it. You may want to crop the picture in order to reduce its size. Also, most scanner programs allow you to change the resolution of the scan to a smaller resolution, as well as reduce the overall amount of colors in the picture. Both of these reduce the space that the scanned picture consumes.

Knowing Who's Who (Using Captions and Other Detail Recorders)

We love to get a hold of old pictures of our family. We scan them and insert them into our Family Tree Maker Scrapbook. But, after a few years (okay, maybe even weeks), our memories start to fade, and we have trouble remembering who is in the pictures. Is it Uncle Ed or Aunt Edna that's sitting on that horse? (Yes, unfortunately, telling them apart is sometimes difficult now that Aunt Edna quit going to the salon for her weekly facial waxing.) Well, that's where the More About Picture/Object dialog box comes in handy. This dialog box allows you to record information about the object — things such as its date of origin and a description, and you can even categorize the object and specify under what conditions to print the it.

Here's how to add information to the More About Picture/Object dialog box:

1. **Click the little down arrow icon in the lower-right corner of the Scrapbook image you want to provide information about.**

   This action opens the More About Picture/Object window, shown Figure 4-6.

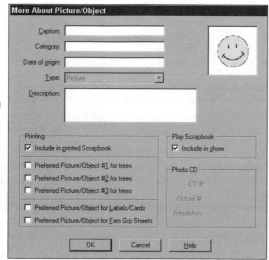

Figure 4-6: Keep your objects straight with the More About Picture/ Object dialog box.

2. **Type a caption for your picture/object in the Caption field.**

   This caption can be whatever you'd like. We recommend that you provide a brief description of what's happening and list the people in the photo, if there aren't too many.

3. **Tab down and enter a label in the Category field.**

   Be consistent as you make up and use the categories. That way, you can easily print all the pictures that have a common theme. You may want to label all the wedding pictures as *Wedding* and birthday pictures as *Birthday*. We recommend that you even take your labeling a step further and identify photos/objects by family. For example, label all of Tabitha Feline's wedding pictures as *Canine/Feline: Wedding* or *Feline: Wedding*.

4. **In the Date of Origin field, enter the date that the original object was created.**

   The date of origin is the date on which the *original* object was created. For example, if you're using a photo that's been scanned, the date of origin is the date on which the original picture was taken — not the date the picture was scanned.

5. **In the Type drop-down list, select the type of object.**

   Your choices are Photo CD Picture, Picture, Sound Clip, Spreadsheet, Video Clip, Word Processor Document, Other OLE Object, and Unknown.

   Select the type of object that best describes the source of the current picture/object.

6. **Tab to the Description free-form field and enter a description of the object.**

   For example, you could put in a description such as the following: "This picture of Gray Canine was taken at his 31st birthday party. The copy of the picture used for this scanned image is in the possession of Tabitha Canine."

7. **Select any special printing options in the Printing area.**

   You can choose from several printing options relating to the object. They include

   • **Include in Printed Scrapbook:** This option allows you to specify whether you wish the object to appear in printed versions of the scrapbook. For example, you may not want to include video footage in the scrapbook.

   • **Preferred Picture/Object for Trees:** Here you can designate which objects are the preferred ones for inserting into your family trees. You can designate up to three objects. When it comes time to print your family trees, you then tell Family Tree Maker which set of objects to print.

- **Preferred Picture/Object for Labels/Cards:** Similar to the preferred picture/object, this setting allows you to specify which objects will appear on labels and cards. You can only select one object as the preferred object.

- **Preferred Picture/Object for Fam Grp Sheets:** Again, you can designate the preferred object that shows up when you generate family group sheets. Only one object can be specified.

8. **Select the Include in Show option if you want this picture/object included in your Scrapbook slide show.**

   Family Tree Maker allows you to put together a slide show of some or all of the images and objects included in your Scrapbook. If you want this item included, select the Include in Show option. Otherwise, this item isn't included.

Keep in mind that the more details you put into the More About Picture/Object dialog box, the better you'll be able to keep track of the hundreds or thousands of pictures. Taking the time to annotate details now saves you a lot of time later.

Sailing Through the Scrapbook

Now you have hundreds of objects in an individual's Scrapbook. Aunt Betty wants you to print a copy of that picture of Aunt Edna on the horse, and now you need to find it amongst all the darling pictures of her. Now we detail some ways to easily navigate through the Scrapbook.

First you need to go to Aunt Edna's Family Page and click the Scrapbook button. You can navigate through the Scrapbook three ways. One way is by using your mouse, another is by using keyboard shortcuts, and the final way is by searching the Scrapbook.

Using the mouse is probably best for those who just want to page through the Scrapbook. To do this, locate the two arrows in the lower corners of the Scrapbook, as shown in Figure 4-7. One arrow points left, and the other points to the right. If you have pages either in front of or behind the current Scrapbook page, then the arrows appear black, and you can click them. If the arrows are gray, then they are disabled, and no Scrapbook pages are in that direction. To go forward in the Scrapbook, just click the arrow in the lower-right corner of the Scrapbook. You can page backward by using the arrow in the lower-left corner of the Scrapbook. Makes sense, doesn't it?

The keyboard way takes a little more effort. So we created handy-dandy Table 4-1 to help you out.

Figure 4-7:
The arrow
navigation
buttons
allow you to
turn the
Scrapbook
page.

Table 4-1	The Keys to Navigation
Direction	*Keys*
To navigate one object at a time	Use the left-, right-, up-, and down-arrow keys. Or use the Tab key to go to the next object and Shift+Tab to go to the previous object
To go to the first object on the current Scrapbook page	Press the Home key
To jump to the last object on the current Scrapbook page	Press the End key
To move to the first object on the first Scrapbook page	Press Ctrl+Home
To move to the last object on the last Scrapbook page	Press Ctrl+End
To go to the next Scrapbook page	Press the Page Down key
To go to the previous Scrapbook page	Press the Page Up key

And now we come to the topic of searching for objects. Sometimes you just can't bear the thought of wading through all those pictures. Why not let Family Tree Maker do some of the work for you? After all, you earned it.

Follow these easy steps to search for an object:

1. Go to the individual's Family Page and click the Scrapbook icon.

This step takes you to the individual's Scrapbook page.

2. Choose Edit⇨Find Picture/Object.

Magically, the Find Picture/Object appears.

3. **In the Search drop-down list, select the field that you want to search.**

   The Search field, shown in Figure 4-8, gives you several options, including:

   - **Include Object for Play Scrapbook:** You can either search for items that are marked to be included or not included when playing the Scrapbook.

   - **Include Object in Printed Scrapbook:** Search for items that are designated to be printed in the Scrapbook (or those that are not designated to be printed).

   - **Picture/Object Caption:** Search the Picture/Object Caption (defined in the More About Picture/Object dialog box) for a particular set of words.

   - **Picture/Object Category:** Remember the categories that you can set up in the More About Picture/Object dialog box? This is where they come in handy. Here you can search for objects that match the stated category.

   - **Picture/Object Date:** This search examines the Date of Origin field in the More About Picture/Object dialog box for a match.

   - **Picture/Object Description:** Searches the Description field found on the More About Picture/Object dialog box.

   - **Picture/Object Type:** The More About Picture/Object dialog box provides the option of designating eight types of objects. These include Photo CD Picture, Picture, Sound Clip, Spreadsheet, Video Clip, Word Processor Document, Other OLE Object, and Unknown. You can choose to include or exclude the object types in the search field.

   - **Preferred Picture/Object:** You can also search for pictures/objects that were designated in the More About Picture/Object dialog box as the Preferred Picture/Object for Family Group Sheets, Preferred Picture/Object for Labels/Cards, and Preferred Picture/Object for Trees.

Figure 4-8:
The Find
Picture/
Object
dialog box
with the
Search
drop-down
list.

4. **After entering your search criteria, click the Find Next button.**

    Family Tree Maker highlights the first object in the Scrapbook that meets your criteria. To go to the next object, click the Find Next button. To go to the previous object, click the Find Previous button.

5. **After you find the object that you're searching for, click the Cancel button.**

This search technique works well when locating objects in one relative's Scrapbook. If you need to search for objects across several individuals' Scrapbooks, choose Edit⇨Find Individual. For more on this option, see Chapter 3.

Arranging Your Scrapbook

As with any kind of Scrapbook, you want to organize your information the best that you can. Sometimes, you need to change the order of the objects, add or remove objects, and even move or copy an object from one Scrapbook to another. Fortunately, Family Tree Maker allows you to change your mind and rearrange your Scrapbook as often as you like.

Sorting the Scrapbook

To change the order of your Scrapbook items, you use the Sort Scrapbook command. Here's how to do it:

1. **Open the Scrapbook that you want to sort.**

2. **Choose Format⇨Sort Scrapbook.**

    The Sort Scrapbook dialog box appears, as shown in Figure 4-9. It gives you the option of sorting the Scrapbook by caption, category, or date.

3. **Select a sort option and then click OK.**

    The Scrapbook is sorted, and you return to the Scrapbook page.

Figure 4-9:
Sort to your
heart's con-
tent with the
Sort
Scrapbook
dialog box.

Moving and copying objects

To move or copy an object between two Scrapbooks, you use the old cut and paste maneuver. Here's how:

1. **Open the Scrapbook where the object resides and select the object (by clicking it).**

2. **Choose Edit⇨Cut Picture/Object to move the object or choose Edit⇨Copy Picture/Object to copy the object.**

3. **Locate the Family Page where you want to paste the object and click the Scrapbk icon.**

   The Scrapbk icon resides between the More and Spouses icons on the Family Page.

4. **Select the box in the Scrapbook where you want to paste the object and choose Edit⇨Paste Picture/Object.**

   Family Tree Maker inserts the object into the Scrapbook.

You can continue to paste the same object into different Scrapbooks as long as the object remains on the Windows Clipboard.

Removing an object

To remove an object from the Scrapbook, simply select the object and press the Delete or Backspace key. Family Tree Maker opens a dialog box asking you to confirm that you want to delete the object. Click Yes, and the object disappears. If you make a mistake and want the object back, just choose Edit⇨Undo.

Playing the Old Scrapbook Game

One of the neat features of the Family Tree Maker Scrapbook is the ability to *play* the Scrapbook. Playing the Scrapbook consists of building a slideshow. You build the slideshow by selecting the Include in Show option in the More About Picture/Object dialog box for each desired object. You may not want to have every object in your slide show, especially OLE objects that contain multiple pages, or audio or video clips.

After you designate what will be in the slideshow, check the lineup of the objects to make sure they're in the order that you want them. If you need to change the order of the objects, you need to sort the Scrapbook (see "Sorting the Scrapbook," earlier in this chapter).

If you're all set to play the Scrapbook, simply choose Picture/Object⇨Play Scrapbook. The Play Scrapbook dialog box appears and asks you to indicate the duration that you want to view each object in the slideshow (in seconds). Set the number by typing it into the field or by using the up and down arrows to increase and decrease the time. Click OK, and the first object appears on your screen. After the slideshow ends, you return to the Scrapbook page.

 If you're impatient with the amount of time it takes to move to the next object, you can always click the left mouse button and move things along. We certainly like to move things along from time to time.

A Few Points to Ponder

You need to keep a few things in mind when adding images, sound, and video to your Scrapbook. The first consideration is the amount of free hard drive space on your computer. Every time that you add something to the Scrapbook, the size of your Family File increases. If you have a computer that does not have a lot of free space, then you're limited in the number and quality of items that you can place in your Scrapbook.

If you find that you're pressed for space, you can do a few things to give yourself (and your computer) a little more breathing room:

> ✔ **Be selective in what you put into a Scrapbook.** Just because you have the capability of placing 2,000 objects per person in a Scrapbook doesn't mean that you should. If you're pressed for space, put only the most significant things into the Scrapbook. For example, rather than including four pictures of the same individual at the same age, reduce the number to just one and reference the location of the other three pictures in the Notes section of your Family File or in the Description section of the included picture's More About Picture/Object dialog box.

- ✔ **Reduce the number of duplicate copies of pictures in your Scrapbook.** If you have a picture, video, or other object that pertains to more than one person, you can save space by placing the object in one individual's Scrapbook and then referencing the object in the Notes section of the remaining individuals' Family Files.

- ✔ **Use compression to reduce the size of pictures in your Scrapbook.** The quality of a picture has a direct impact on the amount of space the picture occupies on your computer. A way to reduce the size of a picture is to increase the compression of the picture file. The tradeoff is that the picture is reduced in quality with a higher compression. The best thing to do is to experiment with different compression ratios and see which has the best balance of size and quality for your picture.

- ✔ **Crop out unnecessary space from your images.** One of the best ways to reduce the size of your picture file is simply to reduce the size of the picture. If you have a picture of an ancestor where the ancestor is in the middle of a picture and the rest of the picture is dead space, then crop the picture to show just the ancestor.

- ✔ **Snip the video.** Videos take up a lot of space on a computer. To keep the space to a minimum, use a graphics program to cut unnecessary footage from the video.

Another factor to consider is the amount of memory that your computer has (that is, the amount of RAM). The more objects that you place in your Scrapbook, the more memory that is consumed when you display the Scrapbook. So, if you have a computer that does not have a lot of memory, you may run into problems displaying items, or they may take a lot of time to appear. A lack of memory can also cause programs to crash and other odd things to happen on your computer screen. Again the best thing to do is to limit the amount of objects that you keep in a Scrapbook. Or, of course, you can add more RAM to your computer (that is, if your computer can accept more RAM). For more specifics about the amount of RAM in your computer, consult the manuals that came with your computer.

Chapter 5

Deleting Undesirables (And Other Ways to Fix Data)

*F*ace it: Everyone makes mistakes. And when you're entering tens, hundreds, or even thousands of names and other kinds of information into Family Tree Maker, you're likely to err from time to time. So there's no use crying over spilt milk. (We thought we'd get in as many clichés as possible.) What you need to know is how to find and fix the errors in your database. That's where this chapter comes in. It covers everything from watching and searching for errors, to getting rid of people who are just taking up space in your database, to correcting links you created by mistake.

To Err Is Human. . . .

Are you prone to typos? Sometimes when you're moving along, typing at the speed of light (well you do, don't you?), you don't realize you've made a boo-boo. Family Tree Maker tries to help you make as few mistakes as possible. Nice, isn't it? It tries to help you avoid making mistakes through a function called error checking. And, should it let an error slip by, it then goes searching for mistakes, at your command, two different ways. In the next few sections, we explore how Family Tree Maker watches for mistakes and what kinds of errors it looks for, and we examine the error messages that you may encounter.

On the lookout for errors

Having a second set of eyes is always helpful. Of course, we don't literally mean having a second set attached to your person. In fact, that may not be helpful at all — considering all the taunting and staring you'd have to endure. Not to mention how difficult it would be to get glasses that fit. Seriously, what we mean is that having someone else looking over your shoulder helps you avoid mistakes. Family Tree Maker can be that someone when you're working on your genealogy.

In addition to having a spell-checking feature, Family Tree Maker has error-detecting features. Family Tree Maker watches for errors in your Family File three ways:

- ✔ **Error Checking:** Keeps an eye out for possible mistakes as you're typing.
- ✔ **Find Error:** Reviews your Family File at your request and stops at each potential mistake, giving you the opportunity to fix it.
- ✔ **Data Errors report:** Generates a report that shows any errors.

In the next few sections, we examine spell checking and each of the error checking methods closely.

An old standby: Spell checking

If you're like us, you probably rely on your word processor (and other computer programs) to identify spelling errors. And you've come to expect that all programs have this capability. So why should your expectations of Family Tree Maker be any different? They needn't be because Family Tree Maker has spell checking, too. The only catch is that Family Tree Maker's spell checking works only on the Notes sections of your Family Pages and on the Books that you create with the software.

You can set up spell checking to review all the notes and text items in your Family File, or just specific parts. (The specific parts are one or all of the text items in a Book or a particular Notes section for an individual or a marriage.) Here's how you use spell checking:

1. **Depending on which sections you want to spell check, start from the particular Notes page, the particular Book, or any of the Family Pages (if you want to run spell check on all Notes pages and Books in the Family File).**

   If you're spell checking all the Notes and text items in your Family File, you can start from any Family Page, tree, or report. If you're checking one text item in a Book, go to that text item to start. If you're checking all the text items in a Book, you need to start from the Book Outline. And, lastly, if you're spell checking a particular Notes section (for an individual or marriage), you need to go to that specific page.

2. **Choose Edit➪Spell Check.**

   Spell checking searches through your Family File, Notes section, or text items looking for misspelled words. If it finds something it thinks may be spelled incorrectly, a Spell Check dialog box opens.

3. **Review the spelling in the Spell Check dialog box. If necessary, fix it by selecting one of the suggestions or by typing in your own word. Then click Change or Ignore, depending on what you want Family Tree Maker to do.**

   The Not in Dictionary part of the dialog box identifies the misspelled word. And Family Tree Maker suggests possible spellings for you to select from, or you can type in the proper word yourself. You can also click the following buttons:

   - **Ignore:** Skip the misspelling.
   - **Change:** Fix the misspelling.
   - **Add:** Add this spelling to the list of approved words.
   - **Close:** Quit spell checking.

   Spell checking changes the spelling of that word or ignores it and then continues looking for errors. Each time it finds a possibly misspelled word, a dialog box appears.

4. **Repeat Step 3 for each misspelled word.**

   After the process is complete, a box appears, telling you that the spell check is finished.

5. **Click OK.**

And that is spell checking in a nutshell. It works a lot like spell checking in other computer programs, don't you think?

Caution as you go

Whereas Family Tree Maker's spell checking works only on certain parts of the program, Error Checking looks over the Family Pages. Error Checking helps you watch for name and date errors as you're typing — things like strange characters in a name, nicknames being used as a first name, and dates that are not logical. You determine things that you want the program to watch for and prompt you about so that you can fix them as you go. Unless you change the default settings, Family Tree Maker uses Error Checking automatically. But you need to know how to turn the function on and off anyway, so here are the steps:

1. **Choose File➪Preferences➪Error Checking.**

   The Error Checking dialog box appears, as shown in Figure 5-1, where you can select which errors you want Family Tree Maker to watch for.

2. **Select either or both of the options and then click OK.**

Your two choices are Name Errors and Unlikely Birth, Death, and Marriage Dates. If you don't want the program to watch for these errors, you can deselect the options.

Figure 5-1:
Family Tree
Maker can
watch for
name and
date errors
as you enter
information.

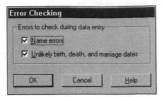

Now, if Family Tree Maker questions one of the names or dates you've entered, a dialog box opens, prompting you to review the information for accuracy. And, if you made a mistake, you can fix it right then and there.

Hunting for errors

Have you ever known someone who thrives on finding mistakes in other peoples' work? Sure, you have. We've all known someone like that. Family Tree Maker's Find Error function is just like that someone. Well, maybe not just like him or her — Find Error may not be quite as nitpicky or thorough, but it's not for lack of trying. It's just that Find Error is restricted to looking for name and date errors.

Find Error differs from Error Checking (see the preceding section) in that it's a search function you run on your entire Family File at one time instead of a feature that double-checks your work as you go. However, the two do look for the same kinds of mistakes. Here's how you run Find Error:

1. **Choose Edit⇨Find Error.**

   A Find Error dialog box appears, where you determine which errors you want Family Tree Maker to search for. Your two choices are Name Errors and Unlikely Birth, Death, and Marriage Dates.

2. **Select either or both of these search options and then click OK.**

   Find Error starts searching through your Family File. Each time it finds something suspect, a Find Error dialog box opens, describing the error and giving you the opportunity to fix it. (You may have noticed that the dialog box to set your error-searching options and this dialog box have the same name.) You have several choices in this Find Error dialog box: Find Next (which takes you to the next possible error), Close (which ends the search), Help (which gives you on-screen guidance), or AutoFix (which suggests a fix that you can accept or reject). You can also select an option to have Family Tree Maker ignore this particular error from now on.

3. **Fix the error as appropriate.**

4. **Click Find Next to continue looking for errors.**

5. **For each possible name or date error that Find Error discovers, repeat Steps 3 and 4.**

   When Family Tree Maker is done looking for errors, a dialog box opens, telling you that it's finished.

6. **Click OK.**

You're done running the Find Error search. Easy, wasn't it?

Reporting on errors

Are you the type of person who likes to see a whole list of possible errors instead of being told one error at a time? If so, then you'll probably prefer to use the Data Errors report instead of the Find Error search function in Family Tree Maker.

The Data Errors report identifies name, date, and other errors in just a few short seconds. It has three columns: the name of the person whose Family Page has the error, that person's birth date (for identification purposes in case you have two or more people with the same name), and a description of the potential error. After looking through the list, you have to manually go to each Family Page and make any corrections. You create the Data Errors report in the same way that you create any of the other Family Tree Maker reports. Here's how:

1. **Click the Report button or choose View➪Report.**

   The Report button is the thirteenth from the right or sixth from the left on the default toolbar (if you're using Version 7.0, it's the twelfth from the left and eighth from the right). It's the one with little blue lines in columns on it.

   This step opens up the report that you were working on most recently. So if you were last using a Data Errors report, then that's what comes up, and you can skip Steps 2 through 4. If you were using some other type of report, then you need to change formats.

   Also a Cue Card for Report pops up, which offers tips and highlights about the reporting feature. If you don't want the Cue Card to pop up every time you open a Report, click in the check box that says `Click here if you don't want to see this Help Window again`. Then click OK.

2. **Click the Format button on the side toolbar or choose Format⇨ Report Format.**

   The Format button is the top one on the vertical toolbar that's on the right side of the screen (unless you've moved it). It has a picture on it of a finger pointing to two pieces of paper.

   The Report Format box appears, where you select the type of report you want.

3. **Scroll through the list and highlight Data Errors.**

4. **Click OK.**

   Family Tree Maker generates the Data Errors report.

Go through the Data Errors report to determine which Family Pages you need to visit to add or correct information. Then go to those pages and make any necessary changes.

What did that say?

You can receive three types of error messages in Family Tree Maker: name, date, and other errors. If Error Checking and Find Error uncover any potential mistakes, they generate name and date error messages, and the Data Errors report reflects all three types of messages. Let's take a look at all three types.

Notification of name errors

Family Tree Maker reviews the various name fields in your Family File and identifies potential problems. Here's a list of the name error messages and what they mean:

- ✔ `Are [person's name] and [person's name] the same person? Answer YES if you are changing the spelling.` You see this message when you're changing the spelling of a name.

- ✔ `There may be a title in the name field.` Family Tree Maker compares the names in your database to a predetermined list of possible titles (such as Dr., Col., or Rev. and their spelled-out counterparts) and lets you know if it finds a possible title in a name field. (You should record titles on the Lineage page; see Chapter 2 for details.) You also receive this message if an individual's name can be considered a title — such as King or Princess, as shown in Figure 5-2.

- ✔ `The name may contain a nickname.` You get this message if you set a name in quotes in a name field. Family Tree Maker assumes you're trying to enter a nickname. (You record nicknames on the Lineage page; for details, see Chapter 2.)

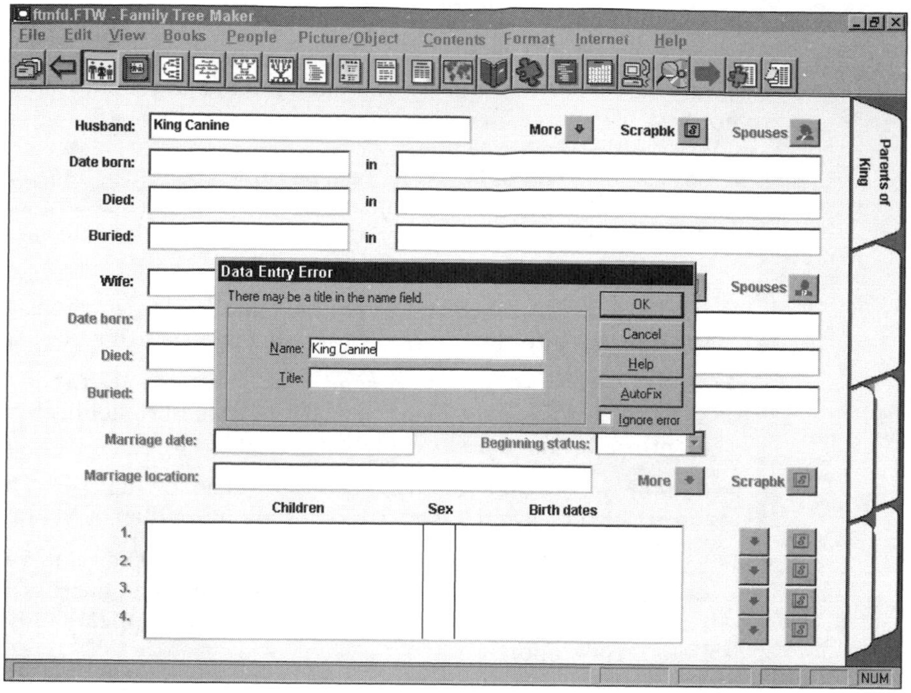

Figure 5-2:
Names that
can be
considered
titles (such
as King or
Princess)
generate
error
messages.

✔ [Wife's name] has the same last name as her spouse [Husband's name]. Generally this indicates that you entered someone's married name instead of their birth name. You should enter birth names only on the family page. (You get a variation of this message on the Data Errors report. It says, Possibly used married instead of maiden name in the marriage to [Husband's name].) The program picks up on the fact that the individuals listed as *Husband* and *Wife* on a Family Page have the same surname. To avoid confusion and make researching easier, use maiden names for all females.

✔ The name may have too many or too few capital letters. Typically, you see this message if you entered a surname in all upper-case letters (capital letters) or failed to use capital letters at all.

✔ The name may contain an illegal character. Somehow *one* of these characters has made it into a name field: ~ ! @ # $ % ^ & * _ + = | : ; " < / ( ) [ ] { } 1 2 3 4 5 6 7 8 9 0.

✔ Possible misplaced dash in the name. A dash is in the name where it shouldn't be (at the beginning), or you've entered two dashes somewhere in it (usually when hyphenating a compound surname).

Dating problems

Just as Family Tree Maker searches the name fields for name errors, it looks over any date fields for date errors. And if it finds any, it uses these messages to notify you:

- ✔ `Child's birth date occurred before [parent] was 13 years old.` Family Tree Maker compares the Date Born fields for parents and their children, and then generates this message if the dates are not compatible.

- ✔ `Child's birth date is after mother's death date.` If a child's Date Born is after the mother's Died date, you get this message.

- ✔ `Child's birth date occurred too long after father's death date.` This message appears if a child's Date Born field is ten or more months after the date in the father's Died field.

- ✔ `Mother was older than 50 at the time of child's birth.` Surprise! Mom's and kid's birth dates are more than 50 years apart.

- ✔ `Birth date is more than 20 years after the marriage date of [parents' names].` The child's Date Born and parents' Marriage Date are 20 or more years apart. (This message appears only on the Data Errors report.)

- ✔ `Birth date before the marriage date of [parents' names].` You guessed it: Family Tree Maker thinks the child was conceived out of wedlock or arrived earlier than expected. (This message appears only on the Data Errors report.)

- ✔ `Individual's marriage date occurred before age 10.` You get this message if the month and year in the Date Born field are less than ten years earlier than the Marriage Date.

- ✔ `Death date is before birth date.` This message is pretty clear — the year of death is earlier than the year of birth.

- ✔ `Death date is more than 120 years after birth date.` Gee, can you guess what might generate this message? You're absolutely right. The Date Born and Died dates are 120 years or more apart.

- ✔ `Not in birth order in the children list.` The kids are out of order on the parents' Family Page. (This message appears only on the Data Errors report.)

- ✔ `[Event date] is empty.` A particular date field is empty. (This message appears only on the Data Errors report.)

- ✔ `This date contains a word or character I don't understand.` Something strange is in a date field.

And that's not all, folks

Family Tree Maker identifies a couple of errors that don't fit into the name or date categories. So, appropriately enough, they are categorized as other errors. Here are the messages you receive when other errors are detected or suspected:

- ✔ No parents, no children, and no spouses. This sounds like a strange message, doesn't it? You're probably wondering how a person can have no relations — after all, everyone has parents. Well, typically this error appears if you've detached a person from his or her family. You probably intended to fix a relationship mistake but forgot to reattach this person to the correct family members. (See "All You Need to Know About Relationships," later in this chapter.)

- ✔ [Name of field] may have incorrect capitalization. Family Tree Maker notices if you entered information in a field in all uppercase (capital) letters and, if so, gives you this message in the Data Errors report.

Without a Trace (Erasing People)

Have you ever researched a person or family with a familiar surname only to discover (after hours of work, of course) that you are not related to them? If you already entered information about them into your database, you'll want to remove them or otherwise correct your mistakes so that their information doesn't distract or mislead you (or others who copy your database). Deleting individuals or even groups of people is a relatively easy process in Family Tree Maker. Allow us to explain how to rub out — oops, we mean delete — people.

G'bye not-your-uncle Angus

Once upon a time, you got a bad lead. A guy with the same name as your great-grandfather's brother appeared in some records near where Gramps lived. You assumed that he was related, so you gathered copies of everything you could find on him. Now, after spending countless hours researching and entering facts about this guy into your database, you find out that he isn't even remotely related to your family. What do you do? In just a few steps, you can delete all that you know about him from your database.

Here's how to delete a person from Family Tree Maker:

1. **Go to the Family Page of the person you want to delete.**

   You can get to the Family Page by using the tabs on the right side of the screen or by choosing View⇨Index of Individuals and then scrolling through the list until you find the person you're looking for. (For more information about navigating through Family Pages, see Chapter 3.)

Say we just discovered that Fluffy Canine (about whom we've been collecting information) wasn't a member of our ancestor's family. We open Fluffy's Family Page by using the Index of Individuals.

2. **Click in the person's name field — whether it's the Husband or Wife field depends on the person's family role and/or gender.**

   Where you click in the name field doesn't matter. In our example, we clicked Fluffy's name.

3. **Choose People⇨Delete Individual.**

   Family Tree Maker asks whether you're sure that you want to delete this person. The message that we see asks specifically about deleting Fluffy's information.

4. **If you're sure you want to delete this person, click Yes. If you're not sure, click No.**

   We are absolutely positive that we want to delete Fluffy's information, so we click Yes. All the information about Fluffy is deleted, including her name and birth, marriage, and death data. She is also removed from the Family Page where she was listed as a child.

Be careful when you're deleting individuals from your database. If you happen to delete a person you didn't really intend to get rid of, you can always use the undelete feature (Edit⇨Undo Delete Individual) to restore that person. But you have to do so immediately after you make the deletion. If you perform any other function(s) after deleting the person, you lose the opportunity to use the undo feature.

Also remember that when Family Tree Maker deletes people, it deletes everything about them — all basic information (names, dates, and birth, marriage, and death information), supplemental information (on the More About pages), and links to all family members. If you delete a person who was the link between two generations in one of your family lines, you have to manually reconnect those generations (see "All You Need to Know About Relationships," later in this chapter).

There goes the whole family

Just as you may need to delete an individual for whatever reason, at some point you may need to delete a whole group of people. Maybe a branch of the family turns out not to be blood-related, so you don't want them in your database. Or maybe you're preparing a copy of your database to share with another researcher who is interested only in your paternal lines. You don't want to provide everything you have on your maternal lines, so you want to delete the maternal group.

Follow these steps to delete a group:

1. **Make a copy of your Family File by selecting File⇨Copy/Export Family File, providing a filename and directory for the copy, and clicking Save.**

2. **Using the copy of your Family File, generate one of three family trees (Ancestor, Descendant, or Outline Descendant) containing information about the group of individuals you want to delete.**

   To create any of the three trees, choose View⇨[Ancestor Tree, Descendant Tree, or Outline Descendant Tree] or use the appropriate button on the toolbar. You need to be on the Family Page for either the furthest-back ancestor or furthest-forward descendant in order for every person in the family group to show up on the tree. For more about generating trees, check out Chapter 9.

   Because we're going to share our database with another researcher who's working on the Canine family lines, we want to delete the Feline side of the family from a copy of the database. We go to Tabitha Feline's Family Page, and from there, we create an Ancestor tree.

3. **Choose People⇨Delete Individuals in [Ancestor, Descendant, or Outline Descendant] Tree.**

   The dialog box shown in Figure 5-3 appears, asking whether you really want to delete these people. We see the dialog box asking if we really want to delete all the Feline ancestors.

4. **If you're sure you want to delete these people, click Yes. If you're not sure, click No.**

   You can get to the Family Page by using the tabs on the right side of the screen or by choosing View⇨Index of Individuals and then scrolling through the list to find the person you're looking for. (For more information about navigating through Family Pages, see Chapter 3.)

   Because we're sure we don't want to share information about the Felines, we click Yes.

In addition to using the Ancestor, Descendant, and Descendant Outline trees to delete groups of people, you can also create a report to do so. This process requires a few more steps than using one of the trees, however. After clicking the Report button or choosing View⇨Report, you have to designate which individuals to include in the report. Do this by clicking the Individuals to Include button on the right side of the report. The Include dialog box opens and allows you to choose Selected Individuals, then click the Individuals to Include button on the box to identify those to include. After you've identified the people to include in your report, delete them by choosing People⇨Delete Individuals.

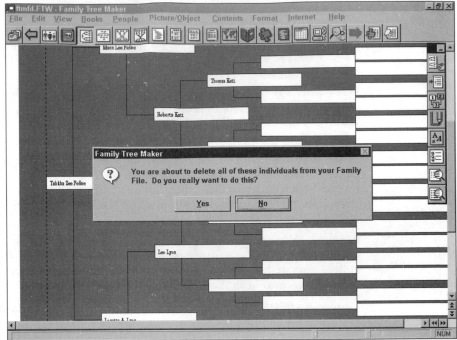

Figure 5-3:
Delete a
group of
individuals
by using an
Ancestor
tree and
the Delete
Individuals
command.

As with deleting individuals, you need to be careful when you're deleting groups of people from your database. If you delete a group that you didn't really intend to get rid of, you can always use the undelete feature (Edit⇨Undo Delete Individuals) to get them back. But you have to do so immediately after you've completed the deletion. If you perform any other function(s) after deleting the people, you lose the opportunity to get them back with the undo feature.

Also remember that all the connections these people had with others in your database are severed. So you may need to reconnect other family members manually (see "All You Need to Know About Relationships," later in this chapter).

All You Need to Know about Relationships

While we can't give you all of the answers about every relationship, we can explain how to handle relationship issues in Family Tree Maker. We have relationship advice about attaching spouses and children, and about merging entries for duplicate individuals that we share with you here.

Forming attachments

Are you attached to your spouse and children (if you have any)? Like having them around, huh? Well, your ancestors were probably attached to their families and liked having them around, too, which is a good thing for you when researching. To continue making your researching (and record-keeping) easier, make sure that you've identified *attachments* (or relationships, if you prefer) correctly and that spouses and children are attached to the proper relatives in your database.

In several circumstances, you may need to repair attachments (or relationships) in Family Tree Maker. Maybe you entered information wrong — heck, we all get in a hurry sometimes. Or possibly you identified a relationship incorrectly — putting a spouse on a person's brother's page accidentally. And in some circumstances, you need to form another relationship — such as for an adopted, step, or foster child who has multiple sets of parents.

Now we take a look at how to attach and detach spouses and children in order to fix relationships in Family Tree Maker. If you have a spouse who, for whatever reason, is showing up married to the wrong person in your database, you need to manually instruct Family Tree Maker to detach that person from the wrong mate and attach him or her to the correct one. This also holds true for a child whose name is showing up in the list of children on the wrong Family Page. Of course, you need to work in sequence here — detach the person from the wrong relationship first and then attach him or her to the right relationship. Knowing this, follow these steps to detach a person:

1. **Go to the Family Page on which the person is mistakenly placed.**

   To get to the appropriate Family Page, choose View⇨Index of Individuals and then select the person's name from the list. Or you can click the tabs on the right side of the Family Pages to find the person you're looking for.

   Say that we mistakenly identified Smokey Dee Bayer as Katrina Feline's spouse. Really, Katrina is married to Smokey's brother, Ted Bayer. So we go to the Family Page that has Smokey Dee Bayer as the Husband and Katrina Feline as the Wife.

2. **Move the cursor to the name of the spouse that you want to detach.**

   Because we want to detach Katrina, we move the cursor to her name field.

3. **Choose People⇨Fix Relationship Mistakes⇨Detach Spouse.**

   If this spouse is attached to children on this Family Page, Family Tree Maker notifies you and asks if you really mean to detach him or her, as shown in Figure 5-4. Because we're sure that Katrina's spousal relationship needs fixing, we clicked Yes.

Figure 5-4:
Family
Tree Maker
double-
checks to
make sure
that you
really want
to detach a
spouse who
is attached
to children.

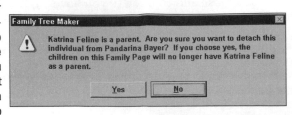

Family Tree Maker then displays a message, telling you that the individual has been detached.

4. Click OK.

You're done detaching the spouse. Now you need to reattach him or her on the appropriate Family Page. So follow these steps:

1. Go to the Family Page where the spouse belongs.

Choose View⇨Index of Individuals to get to the right Family Page. Or you can use the tabs on the right side of the Family Pages to find the person you're looking for.

We know from the preceding steps that Katrina's husband is really Ted Bayer. So we go to Ted's Family Page.

2. Choose People⇨Fix Relationship Mistakes⇨Attach Spouse.

A list of people in your database appears, from which you choose the person to attach as a spouse.

We scroll through the list until we find Katrina Feline's name.

3. Highlight the person's name and click OK.

A dialog box opens, asking if you're sure you want this person to be the spouse of the other person. In our case, it asks if we want to make Katrina Feline the spouse of Ted Bayer.

4. Click Yes.

A box appears, telling you that the attachment is complete, a fact that you can see for yourself in the Family Page.

You also follow the preceding steps to detach and attach children who have been placed with the wrong parents. But say that you have an adopted child who has two sets of parents. You entered the information about one set of parents when you created the child's Family Page. Now to acknowledge the second set of parents in Family Tree Maker, follow these steps:

1. Go to the Family Page on which the person who has multiple sets of parents appears on the list of children.

Use the tabs on the right side of the Family Pages to find the Family Page or choose View➪Index of Individuals. Then select the person's name from the list.

Say that Grey Hound and Tabitha Zee Canine's youngest son, Fox Terrier Canine, is adopted. We use the Index of Individuals to go to the Family Page for Grey and Tabitha, where Fox is listed as a child.

2. Click the person's name on the list of children.

We click in Fox's name field.

3. Choose People➪Other Parents.

The Parents of [Person's Name] dialog box appears. It shows a list of parents, a button for creating new parents, and a check box for selecting which set of parents are the *preferred parents*. (Preferred parents are the ones you want Family Tree Maker to default to.) The parents you already entered should appear at the top of the list of parents. (See Figure 5-5 for an example.)

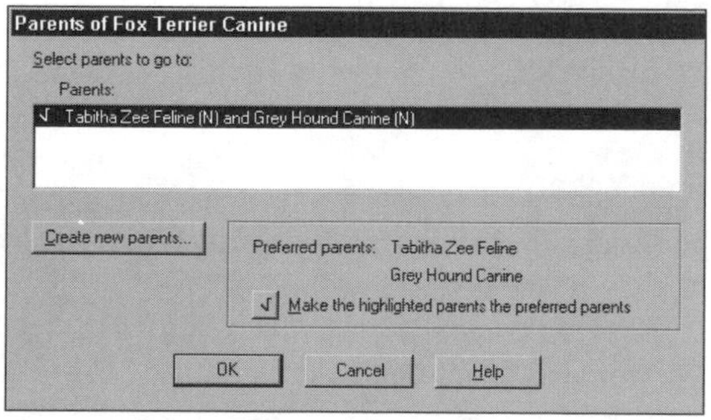

Figure 5-5:
Use this dialog box to create additional parents for a person.

Parents of Fox Terrier Canine

Select parents to go to:

Parents:

√ Tabitha Zee Feline (N) and Grey Hound Canine (N)

Create new parents...

Preferred parents: Tabitha Zee Feline
Grey Hound Canine

√ Make the highlighted parents the preferred parents

OK   Cancel   Help

In our example, the Parents of Fox Terrier Canine dialog box appears. Grey Hound Canine and Tabitha Zee Feline are listed as parents.

4. Click the Create New Parents button.

The Create New Parents dialog box opens. In the Create section, you select whether to create two new parents, another father, or another mother. You can also indicate the person's relationship with his or her father and mother.

5. **Select whether you want to create two new parents or one (father or mother). Indicate the person's relationship with the parent(s) and then click OK.**

   Most of your choices for relationship status with parents — adopted, foster, unknown, step, family member, and private — are the same as on the Lineage page (see Chapter 2).

   For Fox, we chose to add two new parents and listed his relationship with both as Adopted. After clicking OK, Family Tree Maker asks us if we also want to attach Fox's siblings to these parents. Because we do not, we click No. A new, blank Family Page appears.

6. **Complete the new Family Page with the new parents' information.**

   See Chapter 3 for guidance on completing the Family Page.

Of course, now that you have more than one set of parents for this person, you need to indicate which are the preferred parents. You do this by choosing People⇨Other Parents, highlighting the preferred parents, and clicking the little arrow icon that marks the preferred parents. Then click OK.

Dealing with those darned duplicates

In some cultures, family gatherings represent the dating pool from which the single relatives can choose. So, what do you do when those kissin' cousins get hitched? Intermarriages present a bit of a challenge when organizing and storing genealogical data. After all, the two individuals who are married share ancestors somewhere along the way. Luckily, Family Tree Maker accommodates them quite well by allowing you to merge Family Pages for duplicate individuals. Here's what you do:

1. **Open Family Tree Maker.**

   Double-click the Family Tree Maker icon on your Windows desktop. The last Family Page that you were working with appears.

   Grissle Lee Bayer and Leitel Brown Squirrel's Family Page opens because that's the one we were working with most recently.

2. **Visit the appropriate Family Pages where the cousins are listed as children and ensure that you've completed the basic information about them (name, sex, and date of birth). If not, do so now.**

   Use the tabs or the Index of Individuals to get to the Family Pages you need. Make sure that you're using the Family Pages in which the cousins' parents are identified in the Husband and Wife fields, and the cousins themselves are listed as children.

   Say that Sy Berian Tiegger and Pandarina Bayer got married. We take a look at Ben Goal Tiegger and Silky Terrier Canine's Family Page to make sure we have Sy listed as a child, and we look at Smokey Dee Bayer and

Katrina Feline's Family Page to make sure that Pandarina's information is listed under children.

3. Go to the Family Page of one of the cousins.

Click the cousin's tab on the Family Page where you currently are. (After all, you're following these steps closely, and you just finished double-checking the information on the Family Pages, right?) We call this person Cousin #1 for the sake of this demonstration.

We picked Sy Berian Tiegger's Family Page because his was easiest to get to from Ben Goal Tiegger and Silky Terrier Canine's Family Page. Thus, Sy becomes Cousin #1. So it stands to reason that Pandarina is Cousin #2.

4. Complete any fields for which you have information about Cousin #1.

Sy's date of birth already appears in a field, so we add the location. Because he is still among the living, we don't worry about the death information (or burial information either if your using Version 7.0).

5. Enter Cousin #2's name in the spouse's Name field exactly as it appears on the children list of his or her parents' Family Page. And enter Cousin #2's date of birth in the Date Born field exactly as it appears on his or her parents' Family Page. Then press Enter.

The name and date of birth must be exactly like the entries on the parents' Family Page, or the merge won't work. When you press Enter, a message box appears, asking whether this person is the same as the other person who shares that name and date of birth.

We typed Pandarina Bayer in the Wife field and November 18, 1978 in the Date Born field. When we pressed Enter, a box appeared with this message: Is this Pandarina Bayer spouse of Sy Berian Tiegger the same as Pandarina Bayer child of Smokey Dee Bayer?

6. Click the Yes or No button depending on whether this person is the same.

Because it is the same person in our example, we clicked the Yes button. The Merge Individuals window opened for us to compare the two entries and see whether they are the same person (see Figure 5-6).

7. If you want to merge the two entries, click the Merge button; otherwise, click the Don't Merge button or Cancel button.

Because we want to merge the two Pandarinas (because they are the same person), we clicked Merge.

Now the blank Family Page for Cousin #2 is merged with the Family Page for Cousin #1. So when you click the tab for Cousin #2's parents, you go directly to the appropriate, already completed Family Page.

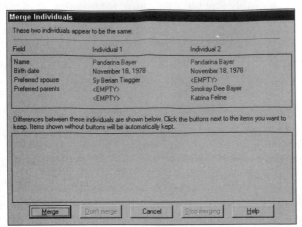

Figure 5-6:
The Merge
Individuals
window
allows you
to review
duplicate
entries to
see if they
are for
the same
person and,
if so, to
merge them.

Part II
Your Handy-Dandy
Research Partner

The 5th Wave   By Rich Tennant

"Perhaps you're right. Maybe he is taking this pedigree
business a bit too far."

In this part . . .

This part takes a look at how Family Tree Maker can help you in your research efforts. First, you find out why citing sources is so important, and then you explore the tools that can make your life a little easier. Rounding out this part, you take a trip online to see the research aids available from Family Tree Maker Web sites.

Chapter 6

Mandatory Chapter on Citing Sources

● ●

In This Chapter

▶ Finding out the importance of citing sources

▶ Using the Master Sources feature

▶ Citing sources

▶ Deciding what source information to include

▶ Creating a Bibliography report

● ●

*I*f you're a fan of TV shows about lawyers, you know it takes a certain amount of evidence to convict a person. Remember how many times Perry Mason got his clients off the hook because he proved the evidence didn't point to them? Whether these shows reflect reality is debatable, but it's not debatable that genealogists need to have evidence to support conclusions they make about their ancestors. Just having an old family legend as your source simply isn't good enough.

We would be remiss if we didn't address the importance of citing sources. As a genealogist, your mission is to collect information about your family's history as well as evidence to support your findings. But you can't expect others to trust your findings on faith. And you can't accept others' findings on faith either. You need to record exactly where you find your facts so that you or others can return to the sources, should you need to do so. This chapter discusses the importance of citing sources, as well as explains how you can track evidence supporting your work with Family Tree Maker.

Compelling Reasons for Citing Sources

Imagine that you received a package from Aunt Lola yesterday. In it is a booklet that she put together about your maternal family lines — a booklet that contains many pieces of information you've been missing in your genealogy. It includes birth and death dates for ancestors that you haven't been able to trace. It also contains interesting and funny stories about your great-great-grandpa's first trip into the city and a pedigree chart showing that you're a descendant of Daniel Boone. Of course, some of the information in Aunt Lola's book conflicts with data you've found yourself — data for which you have your own sources. You want to know where Aunt Lola got her information so that you can determine which facts are correct. But nothing in the booklet is footnoted, so you can't determine exactly where the information came from.

So you flip to the back of the book to see the bibliography — at least if you have a general idea of where the information came from, you can get copies of the sources and dig through them yourself. No bibliography. Problem? Yes. Frustrated with Aunt Lola? An even bigger yes. How do you know that Aunt Lola's account of your family lines is accurate? How do you know where to go to double-check Aunt Lola's information and compare it to your own? This scenario illustrates why you need to cite sources.

Citing sources validates your research and enables you or others to take a another look at the information sources should you need to. Now that you know the *why* of citing sources, you're ready to move on to the *how*.

Master Sources to the Rescue

Chances are pretty good that you'll use some sources over and over again in your research. Wouldn't it be nice if you had to enter most of the bibliographic information about those sources only once? Then you could click a button or something to access that source to attribute facts to it. Master Sources to the rescue!

Family Tree Maker's Master Sources feature allows you to provide basic information about a source (book, article, interview, or just about anything) that you can use again and again, which saves you some time and typing. When you have a specific citation to make (where you point directly to the page or part of the source that proves a particular fact), you can use the Master Source with the source citation. (We discuss source citations in just a minute.) We think of Master Sources as similar to a bibliography.

Follow these steps to set up a Master Source:

1. Choose Edit⇨Edit Master Sources.

The Master Source dialog box opens, as shown in Figure 6-1. Six buttons appear across the top of the window — New, Delete, Next, Previous, First, and Final. The Source Information section is where you enter the Master Source information.

The Source Information section has fields for you to provide the Title of Source, Author/Originator, Publication Facts, Source Media, Call Number, Source Location, Comments, and Source Quality. It also includes the Find Master Source button.

And across the bottom of the window are three buttons — OK, Cancel, and Help.

Figure 6-1:
A completed
Master
Source
dialog box.

2. **Click the New button to add a new master source.**

   If you're simply looking through your master sources, use the Next, Previous, First, or Final buttons and skip the remaining steps in this example. If you're deleting a master source, click the Delete button and then confirm the deletion when Family Tree Maker asks if this is really what you want to do.

   In our example, we click the New button because we're providing information about a document that we haven't referenced before.

3. **In the Title of Source field, enter the name of the source.**

   If the source is a book, simply type in its name. If it's an article, be sure to include the name of the article and the title of the publication (newspaper, magazine, or whatever). If your source is a World Wide Web site, provide the name and URL for the site. If you're using an audio or video tape, list the name of the tape. And if you're interviewing someone, enter his or her name here.

   Say that our sample source is a book about the descendants of Welsh Corgi Canine, written by his great-grandson Wolf Hound Canine. In the Title Source field, we type the name of the book, *Those Wild Dogs of Kentucky: The Canine Family.*

4. **Tab down and type the name of the person who wrote or prepared the source in the Author/Originator field.**

In the Author/Originator field, we enter Wolf Hound Canine because he's the author of *Those Wild Dogs of Kentucky: The Canine Family.*

5. **In the Publication Facts field, enter the copyright date, the name of the publisher or manufacturer, and the place of publication/manufacture.**

   Check the source to find the publication information. You may have to look a little harder for publication information on a CD-ROM, Web site, or other electronic media than you have to look in a book or magazine. But most electronic media do have a publisher or manufacturer and copyright information that you can enter here.

   For our example, we look at the front of the book and gather the necessary data. Then we enter it in the Publication Facts field. We type this: *Copyright 1983. Dog Days Press, Inc. Lexington, Kentucky.*

6. **Using the Source Media drop-down list, select the type of media that the source is.**

   Your choices are Book, Card, Census, Church Record, Civil Registry, Electronic, Family Archive CD, Interview, Letter, Magazine, Manuscript, Map, Microfiche, Microfilm, Newspaper, Official Document, Other, Photograph, Tombstone, Unknown, and Video.

   Our source is a book written by Wolf Hound Canine, so we select Book as the Source Media.

7. **Tab over and enter the Call Number (if one exists) for the source.**

   Typically, call numbers apply to books and periodicals at the library. If you're using a Web site, person, or audio/video tape as the source, you may not have a call number to provide. If you want, you can use this field to provide some other identification number for the source.

   If we had checked out the book at the library, it would have a call number that we could enter here. Because we used Grey Hound Canine's copy, we don't know what the call number is. So we leave this field blank.

8. **In the Source Location field, enter information about the place where you found this source, whether it was a library, a courthouse, an archive, in a person's possession, or whatever.**

   Be sure to include the name of the town, county or parish, state or province, and country.

   We looked at the book while visiting Grey at his home. In the Source Location Field, we enter this: Grey Hound Canine's personal library. Jamestown, Russell County, Kentucky.

9. **In the Comments field, provide any comments or clarifications that you feel are necessary.**

   This field is a good place to provide a description of the source and the date on which you reviewed it.

   In the Comments field, we type, Read this book while visiting Grey at his home in June 1990. Grey told us that Wolf Hound Canine had to pay for the books himself so he had only five printed. Grey does not know the location of the other four books.

10. Tab down to the Source Quality field and complete it.

This is a very subjective field. You determine what values to enter here, so you have the choice of using numbers (1 being excellent, 5 being good, and 10 being poor), words (excellent, good, poor), or some other scale.

Compared to the other sources we've used to gather information about the Canines, this book is fair. We noticed that Wolf Hound Canine didn't always cite his own sources, which makes us question some of the information contained within the book. For this reason, we rate the quality of this source as *Fair,* or a number 8 on a scale of 1 to 10 (with 1 being excellent and 10 being poor).

11. After you've completed the entire dialog box, click OK.

You're done entering this source. If you want to create other Master Sources at this time, click New instead of OK. Family Tree Maker automatically saves the source that you just entered and takes you to a blank Master Sources dialog box to complete.

After you enter a Master Source (or maybe even several), return to the Family Page. You'll notice that this page shows no indication that you created a Master Source entry. That's because, as we said before, the Master Source feature is like a bibliography. Remember when you wrote research papers for school? Did you put a little mark on every page to indicate that you used the books listed in your bibliography? No — it was assumed that you used the sources in your bibliography when preparing the paper. The same assumption holds true here.

When you quoted or paraphrased a particular source in your research paper, however, you included a footnote or endnote (or at least you should have). Likewise, when you create an actual source citation, Family Tree Maker leaves a little mark on the Family Page. What is the mark, you ask? Now that we have you in suspense, you'll have to keep reading to find out — the very next section answers your questions.

Creating Sources (And We Don't Mean Fabricating Them)

Just as you can think of Master Sources as a bibliography, you can think of *source citations* as footnotes or endnotes. Source citations are exactly what they sound like — windows in which you cite a specific source for a fact. Typically, source citations point readers directly to the place where they can find the same information that you found.

Follow these steps to create a source citation in Family Tree Maker:

1. **Go to the field for which you need to cite a source.**

   Make sure that your cursor is positioned somewhere in the field that needs a source citation. You can provide source citations for any of the following fields: Name, Date, and Location (Family Page); Fact, Date, and Comment/Location (Facts Page); and Cause of Death and Medical Information (Medical Page).

   Suppose that we want to cite a source for Grey Hound Canine's birth. We want to document that we obtained information from his birth certificate, so we click in the Husband field of Grey's Family Page.

2. **Choose View⇨Source.**

   Or you can press Ctrl+S. The Source-Citation dialog box appears, as shown in Figure 6-2. Across the top, you find the New, Delete, Next, Previous, First, and Final buttons.

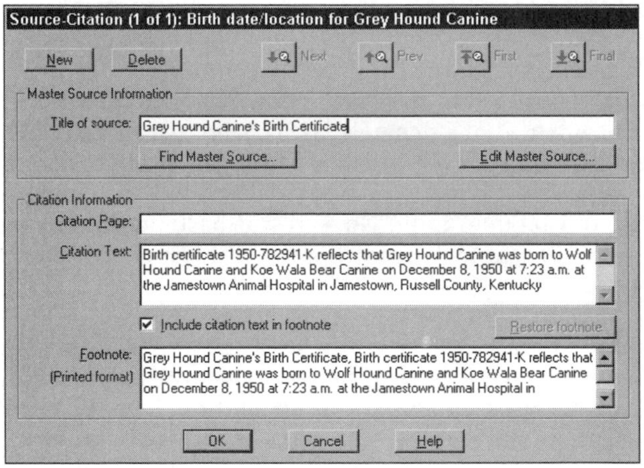

Figure 6-2:
The Source-
Citation
(1 of 1): Birth
Date/
Location for
Grey Hound
Canine
dialog box.

Source-Citation (1 of 1): Birth date/location for Grey Hound Canine

New | Delete | Next | Prev | First | Final

Master Source Information

Title of source: Grey Hound Canine's Birth Certificate

Find Master Source... | Edit Master Source...

Citation Information

Citation Page:

Citation Text: Birth certificate 1950-782941-K reflects that Grey Hound Canine was born to Wolf Hound Canine and Koe Wala Bear Canine on December 8, 1950 at 7:23 a.m. at the Jamestown Animal Hospital in Jamestown, Russell County, Kentucky

☑ Include citation text in footnote | Restore footnote

Footnote: Grey Hound Canine's Birth Certificate, Birth certificate 1950-782941-K reflects that
(Printed format) Grey Hound Canine was born to Wolf Hound Canine and Koe Wala Bear Canine on December 8, 1950 at 7:23 a.m. at the Jamestown Animal Hospital in

OK | Cancel | Help

The dialog box is divided into two parts. In the Master Source Information area, you find the Title of Source field and the Find Master Source and Edit Master Source buttons. The second section is called Citation Information, and it has fields for Citation Page, Citation Text, and Footnote. If you click in the Include Citation Text in Footnote check box, Family Tree Maker includes the citation word for word in the footnote.

The OK, Cancel, and Help buttons appear at the bottom of the screen.

3. **Enter the name of the source in the Title of Source field or click the Find Master Source button and search for the title among the Master Sources you've already created.**

If you've already created a Master Source for this source, then you don't need to type the name in the Title of Source field. Instead, you can select the title from your Master Sources list. (For more information about Master Sources and how to create them, see the preceding section, "Master Sources to the Rescue.") If you're not likely to use the source for more than one or two facts, then just enter the necessary information here in the Source-Citation dialog box.

Because we're using Grey's birth certificate as a source for only two fields, creating a Master Source isn't necessary. Instead, we simply type Grey Hound Canine's birth certificate in the Title of Source field.

4. In the Citation Page field, identify the page on which the information appears.

Of course, if your source is something other than a book or article, you may not have a page number to cite. You can always enter other information about the source in this field, such as the date you interviewed a source or gleaned information from a Web page.

The birth certificate is a single page, so we don't have any page numbers to cite. However, it does have a reference number that the county clerk used when filing the document, so we enter that number here.

5. In the Citation Text field, provide the section of text that contains the fact you're citing.

Here is where you can type the information verbatim from the source.

We paraphrase the birth certificate like this: Birth certificate 1950-782941-K reflects that Grey Hound Canine was born to Wolf Hound Canine and Koe Wala Bear Canine on December 8, 1950 at 7:23 a.m. at the Jamestown Animal Hospital in Jamestown, Russell County, Kentucky. . . . (Of course, we could list everything from the certificate, but we know you're getting eager to move on.)

6. Select the Include Citation Text in Footnote option, if you so choose.

If you select this option, the citation text in the footnote will match what appears in the Citation Text field. If you deselect the option, the citation text does not appear in the footnote.

We don't want the entire text to appear in the footnote, so we deselect the option.

7. Review the footnote and make any changes that you want.

If you want to change the footnote in any way, here's your chance to do so — just type over what's already there. The footnote contains bibliographic information from this source citation's Master Source and the page number that you entered in the Citation Page field. It can also include the actual citation, if you select that option.

Our footnote simply states the title of the document (Grey Hound Canine's birth certificate) and the reference number that we listed under Citation Page. This information looks fine to us, so we make no changes to it.

8. **Click OK.**

   Family Tree Maker takes you back to the Family Page. You should see an *s* next to the field for which you just entered a source citation.

   We click OK and go back to the Family Page for Grey Hound Canine.

We can hear you now, "What do I do if I have several documents proving a particular fact?" Relax. Family Tree Maker has thought of everything. You can enter multiple source citations for a fact. Just follow the preceding steps, and between Steps 2 and 3, click the New button at the top of the window. A blank Source-Citation dialog box appears, in which you enter the additional source information. If you ever need to delete a source (for example, you find a primary source that disproves a source you've already cited), follow Steps 1 through 2 and then click the Delete button. If you're just looking through your citations, you can use the Next, Previous, First, and Final buttons to navigate.

Deciding Which Information to Include

You may be wondering whether to use a particular format when recording bibliographic sources and citations. If you were preparing your genealogy strictly the old-fashioned way — writing it by hand or typing it on your old typewriter — you would need to follow style guidelines to ensure that you recorded the sources correctly. (We are partial to *The Chicago Manual of Style,* 14th Edition.) But because you're recording the information in your Family Tree Maker database, you don't need to worry about remembering certain formats for the various types of sources. Family Tree Maker has dialog boxes specifically for entering Master Sources and citing sources, and takes care of the formatting for you. (See the preceding two sections for more about Master Sources and citing source information.)

Although Family Tree Maker takes care of the formatting, you still may find it helpful to know the types of information to include in your source citations. Here are some guidelines on what to include, depending on the type of source you're using:

✔ **Person:** Include the person's full name, relationship to you (if any), the specific information you learned from this person, the contact data (address, phone number, e-mail address), and the date and time you communicated with the person.

✔ **Record:** Include the name or type of record, record number, number of the book in which the record is kept permanently (such as Deed Book 1), the name and location of the record-keeping agency, and any other pertinent information.

- ✔ **Book, magazine, or newspaper:** Include all bibliographic information — the name of the article and publication, the author's name, the copyright date, the publisher's name, the place of publication, and the page number(s).

- ✔ **Microfilm or microfiche:** Include all bibliographic information (see the guideline in the preceding bullet) and note the document media (microfilm roll, microfiche), document number, and repository name.

- ✔ **Web site:** Include the name of the copyright holder for the site (or the name of the site's creator and maintainer if no copyright appears on it), the name of the site, the site's address or Uniform Resource Locator (URL), the date the information was posted or copyrighted, and any contact information for the site's copyright holder or creator. You can also include a description of the site and why it is pertinent to your research.

- ✔ **E-mail messages:** Include the name and contact information for the sender, the title/subject of the e-mail message, the name of person(s) to whom the note was sent, the date that the message was sent, and a brief description of the note's contents.

- ✔ **Newsgroups:** Include the name and address of the newsgroup, the name and contact information of the person who posted the relevant message, the title/subject of the message, the date that the message was posted, and a brief description of the message.

Of course, the fields in Family Tree Maker's Master Sources and Source-Citation dialog boxes can't match all the types of information we just described. Can you imagine how long the labels on the fields would be? Or how many fields it would take if each type of information had its own field? The fields in these dialog boxes work best for citing books, so you may need to be creative in deciding which field to use when recording information about sources other than books. For example, if you're citing an e-mail message, you may want to record the date of the message in the Citation Page field. If you printed a copy of the e-mail message, you may have a page number to use as well. Why not put both of them in the Citation Page field?

Reporting on Your Sources

When you put together a book in Family Tree Maker (see Chapter 11), you'll want to include a Bibliography report on the sources you've used in your research. Or maybe, you'll have another need for the report — for example, another researcher asks you about the evidence you've used, or you're making a research trip and want a quick reference to see which sources you've already reviewed.

Follow these steps to generate a Bibliography report:

1. **Choose View⇨Report.**

   Or click the Report button on the toolbar. If you're looking at the default toolbar, the Report button is the thirteenth button from the left with the picture of a gray piece of paper with blue lines printed on it (if you're using Version 7.0, it's the twelfth button from the left and the eighth from the right). After you click this button, the last type of report that you created appears.

   A Cue Card for Report may pop up, offering help with the various customizing features. If you don't want the Cue Card to pop up every time you customize a report, select the option labeled `Click here if you don't want to see this Help Window again`. Click OK to continue.

2. **Choose Report⇨Report Format.**

   Or click the Format button at the top of the toolbar on the right side of the screen. A Report Format dialog box appears, and you can select a report by clicking it and then clicking the OK button (or you can just double-click the report).

3. **Select the Bibliography option and then click OK.**

   The Bibliography of Sources report appears.

4. **Customize the report, if you so desire.**

   You can customize your bibliography by using the series of buttons that appear on the toolbar on the right side of your screen. You can customize the type and size of the font, the title and footnotes, the individuals to include, the report format (standard or annotated), and the source references. For more about customizing your bibliography, check out Chapter 10.

5. **Use your bibliography in a book or just as a reference.**

   You can print your bibliography by choosing File⇨Print Bibliography of Sources. Or you can add it to the list of items to include in the book you're making in Family Tree Maker. For specific information about creating a book, flip ahead to Chapter 11.

Don't Delay — Enter Your Sources Right Away

Here is our most important piece of advice about recording sources (drumroll, please): Enter your information and sources as soon as possible into your Family File. The longer that you wait to enter the information, the more likely that you'll forget about the sources you used (things like quality and accuracy). Having your source information is important when you discover that two sources conflict with each other. When this happens, it's nice if you can remember if a source was reliable and provided other information (for which you used this source in a citation) that seems accurate. If so, then perhaps the reliability of that source is better than the conflicting one.

Entering your sources as soon as possible also helps lessen the risk of forgetting where a particular set of photocopies came from and what they are copies of. You can easily get in a hurry at the library or archive — especially if it's about to close. If you're rushing to make those last few copies, you may not take the time to list the source on each page. Then when the pages get separated, you may have problems figuring out what the source of the information was. We suggest entering the information and sources in your Family File as soon as you get home. Think of this task as doing a little homework right after you get home from school.

Many people enter information that they gathered on a research trip but, for the sake of time, decide to enter the source data later. You know who you are. (And here's a little confession so that you know we're human — one of us has a tendency to do this, too.) Unfortunately, devoting a day to entering sources into Family Tree Maker rarely happens, and soon you start filing things away and forget to enter the sources. A few months later, when someone asks you for a source, you have to scramble to find where you filed it. So we encourage you not to put off entering your source information. A little up-front work saves you a lot of time later on.

Chapter 7

Tools to Make Your (Research) Life Easier

*I*n this fast-paced world, finding the time to research your genealogy is difficult enough, but trying to stay organized at the same time is even more challenging. Often people are in such a hurry to collect as much information as possible that they overlook aids that can help them. (Heck, one of Family Tree Maker's aids even does some of the work for you!) This chapter examines four features of Family Tree Maker that can make research in your genealogical life a little easier.

Keeping a Journal of Your Progress

You've probably had those dreams where you're in school and your teacher calls on you to answer a simple question, but you can't remember the answer. Your heart starts beating faster, and you freeze. You can't even muster up something plausible to buy some time. Total panic sets in, and then you wake up.

You may get this same feeling sometimes when you're researching. You walk into an intimidating library, or you discover a genealogical gold mine of a Web site, and then you freeze. Where do I start first? Don't I already have that record? What is the name of that book I've been looking for?

Researching doesn't need to be so stressful. Family Tree Maker wants to help you. It's here for you. Here to store all of your findings. Here to produce beautiful trees for you. Here to assist you in your research. Yes, you heard — well, read — us right. Family Tree Maker can help you in your research by keeping you organized and letting you check your progress with the Research Journal feature.

The Research Journal consists of two parts: a To Do checklist and a list of possible research leads called a FamilyFinder Report. We discuss the Research Journal in more detail in the following sections.

The scoop on your Research Journal

Are you the kind of person who needs to be reminded to do things? Maybe you have an assistant at work and a spouse or roommate at home who serve this function. Maybe your better half provides you with a honey-do list once a week, and you get some fantastic reward upon completing all the items. (You know what a honey-do list is, right? It's that list from which the center of your universe reminds you, "Honey, do this. Honey, do that.") Well, Family Tree Maker doesn't want to miss out on any of the action. It wants to vie for your time with genealogical tasks, so it has a list for you, too.

Even if you're the best-organized person on the planet (okay, second-best organized because April's mother is the best organized), having a checklist of the things you need to do is helpful. The list serves as a reminder of what you still need to accomplish and is an assessment tool to see how far you've come. The To Do list that Family Tree Maker creates for you is part of the Research Journal feature.

Just follow these steps to generate the Research Journal:

1. **Choose View⇨Research Journal.**

   In Version 7.0, choose View⇨FamilyFinder⇨Research Journal, which takes you directly to the Research Journal, so you can skip Step 2.

   A dialog box opens in which you can click Yes to create a FamilyFinder Report or click No to go directly to the Research Journal. (See the following section for more on the FamilyFinder Report.)

2. **Click No to go to the Research Journal.**

   The My Research Journal page appears, as shown in Figure 7-1.

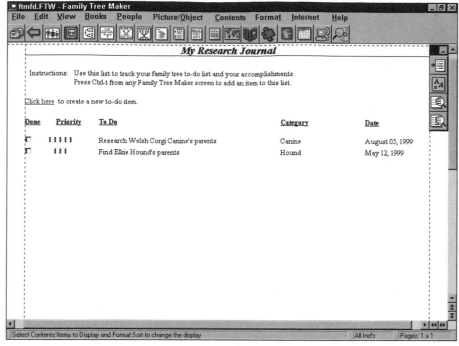

Figure 7-1:
My
Research
Journal
(without the
FamilyFinder
report).

My Research Journal contains five columns: Done, Priority, To Do, Category, and Date. So what do these labels mean, you ask? Allow us to explain in the following list:

✔ **Done:** After you complete the To Do item, click in this check box. Marking completed items enables you to generate a report listing only incomplete items so that you can quickly assess what you need to work on.

✔ **Priority:** You determine the priority of each item in your To Do list by using a scale of one (lowest priority) to five (highest priority).

✔ **To Do:** This is an item on your list of things to do. To add a new To Do item, click the Click here link at the top of the list. (We discuss creating, editing, and deleting To Do items, later in this chapter.)

✔ **Category:** You can assign your own categories to items as you create or edit them. You may choose to categorize your items by type, such as *Primary Record* or *Family Legend*.

✔ **Date:** This column is where you can record whatever date you want to associate with this To Do item. You may want to use it for a due date, or a completion date, or some other date that marks a milestone in your research of this item.

FamilyFinder Report

Wouldn't it be handy to have a research assistant that you could send out to collect genealogical information for you? Even having someone to identify possible leads for you could save you valuable time and energy. Did you know that you already have someone (well, a something anyway) that can do this for you? It's called the FamilyFinder Report, and it's part of your Research Journal.

Family Tree Maker generates the FamilyFinder Report — at your request — by comparing the data in your Family File to various resources on the Internet and the Family Archive CDs from Broderbund. (For more about the Family Archive CDs, check out Chapters 8 and 14.) The report lists potential matches between your information and the resources for you to follow up on.

Creating the FamilyFinder Report is simple. Just follow these steps:

1. **Choose View⇨Research Journal.**

   In Version 7.0, choose View⇨FamilyFinder⇨FamilyFinder Search/Report. A dialog box appears, telling you that a FamilyFinder Report looks for information about the people in your Family File on the Internet and in the Family Archive CDs. Click OK to continue and skip Step 2.

   A dialog box appears, in which you can click Yes to create a FamilyFinder Report or click No to go directly to the Research Journal.

2. **Click Yes to create a FamilyFinder Report.**

   The Create New FamilyFinder Report dialog box appears, as shown in Figure 7-2. In the Search section, you can select options to search the Internet and the CD FamilyFinder Index. In the Include section, you indicate whether to search for All Individuals or Selected Individuals. If you choose Selected Individuals, click the Individuals to Include button to mark those that you want to include.

   Below these two sections, you find the number of people that FamilyFinder will search for and the amount of time that the search will take.

3. **Decide whether you want FamilyFinder to search the Internet or the CD FamilyFinder Index, and then select that option.**

Figure 7-2:
You use the
Create New
FamilyFinder
Report
dialog box
to set the
parameters
for your
search.

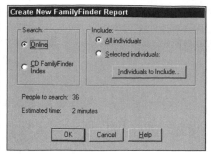

4. **Select the All Individuals or Selected Individuals option.**

   If you choose Selected Individuals, you need to click the Individuals to
   Include button. In the dialog box that appears, you can type a person's
   name in the Name field or use the list on the left to select people.
   Highlight a person's name on the left side and then click the single-arrow
   button to copy the name to the list of people that you want to include in
   the search, which appears on the right side. If you want to include all of
   a person's *ancestors* (direct relatives from whom the person descends)
   and/or *descendants* (direct relatives who descend from the person),
   highlight the person's name and then click the Ancestors or
   Descendants button to add all of that person's ancestors or descendants
   to the Individuals to Include list.

5. **Click OK.**

   A browser window opens, telling you that Family Tree Maker is creating
   your online FamilyFinder Report. It also informs you that Family Tree
   Maker will ding when your report is ready, and that in the meantime, you
   can search through various parts of the Family Tree Maker Web site.

   Of course, if you're not logged on or you don't have Internet access, and
   you indicated that you want to search the Internet, your computer may
   become disoriented trying to create the FamilyFinder Report by using
   the Internet. Something similar happens if you try to search the CDs
   without a CD-ROM drive or without a CD in your CD-ROM drive.

6. **After your computer dings (letting you know that the report is complete), minimize or close your Web browser.**

   Use the little buttons in the upper-right corner of the screen: The underline button minimizes the screen, and the X button closes the program.
   We recommend that you minimize the browser rather than close it. This
   makes it easier to visit any of the Internet matches your FamilyFinder
   search produces.

Closing or minimizing the browser enables you to see Family Tree Maker again. A Cue Card for Research Journal may have popped up. It offers tips and highlights about the Research Journal. If you don't want the Cue Card to pop up every time you open the Journal, click in the check box that says `Click here if you don't want to see this Help Window again`. Then click OK.

You see the FamilyFinder Report shown in Figure 7-3. Near the top of the report is today's date (because you ran the report today). Below that, you find a listing of individuals that may have new matches on the World Family Tree. Information about these matches appears in four columns: Done, Quality, Match, and Source.

The remainder of your FamilyFinder report consists of possible Family Archive CD matches. This information is presented in the same four columns as the World Family Tree matches.

7. **Click a name or folder icon next to a name. Or click the possible match to go directly to its location (or the location that has more information in the case of the CDs) through your Web browser.**

   Clicking the folder expands the information below the entry to show you the possible matches in the source. After you click the possible match in the Source column, your Web browser opens (if you closed it under Step 6) and goes to the URL for the match. If you've already logged off from your Internet service provider, you'll have to reconnect in order to see the match.

   If the possible match is on one of the Family Archive CDs, you have to own or otherwise have access to these CDs in order to follow up on the lead. Clicking the match in your Research Journal takes you to a Family Tree Maker site that provides information about obtaining the CDs (for purchase) but doesn't give you any details about the person who may be your relative. If you have a deluxe version of Family Tree Maker, then you most likely received some Family Archive CDs as a bonus. You can take a look at them to see what the CDs are like. Or, whether you have any of the CDs or not, you can flip to Chapter 14 to read about the bonus CDs that accompany the deluxe version of Family Tree Maker 7.0.

8. **If you visit any of the possible match sites, be sure to click in the Done check box when you return to your Research Journal.**

   Marking the Done check box helps you see, at a glance, which FamilyFinder Report leads you've already followed up on.

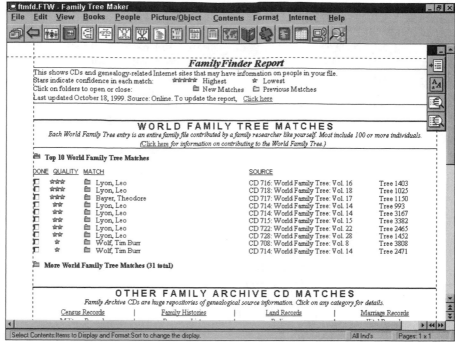

Figure 7-3:
My
Research
Journal
with the
FamilyFinder
Report.

9. Use the Research Journal, with the FamilyFinder Report matches, as your To Do list and research assistant.

Refer to "The scoop on your Research Journal" section if you need to.

If your Research Journal is already open and you failed to request a FamilyFinder Report when you generated your Research Journal, you don't need to worry. You can create one from the Research Journal view. Simply click the little folder icon next to the line that says Create a FamilyFinder Report or choose Edit⇨Create New FamilyFinder Report. Likewise, to update your FamilyFinder Report, choose Edit⇨Update FamilyFinder Report.

When you create your first FamilyFinder Report, Family Tree Maker automatically generates a FamilyFinder Agent for you. (For more about Agents, check out Chapter 8.) This Agent is a computer program that continues to look for information about the individuals listed in your Family File after you've logged off of the Internet or even turned off your computer. If the Agent finds something that may match someone in your Family File, it sends you an e-mail. So the next time you log on, you're greeted with a possible lead. You can then update your FamilyFinder Report to see the new information.

Working with To Do items

Say you're working in your Research Journal — reviewing your To Do items and checking off tasks you've completed. All of a sudden, you realize that you haven't included an entry for a particularly daunting task: collecting a land record for great-grandpa Archibald's property in California. You definitely don't want to forget about this! So you need to add a To Do item to your Research Journal. That's easy enough — just follow these steps:

1. **Open your Research Journal by choosing View⇨Research Journal.**

   If you're using Version 7.0, choose View⇨FamilyFinder⇨Research Journal.

   Your Research Journal opens. (If it doesn't pop up right away, you may need to follow some of the steps provided in "FamilyFinder Report," earlier in this chapter.)

2. **Click the <u>Click here</u> link.**

   The New To Do Item dialog box appears, as shown in Figure 7-4. It consists of a free-form field where you enter information about the To Do item, a field where you indicate the item's priority (from one to five), and Category and Date fields, which are optional.

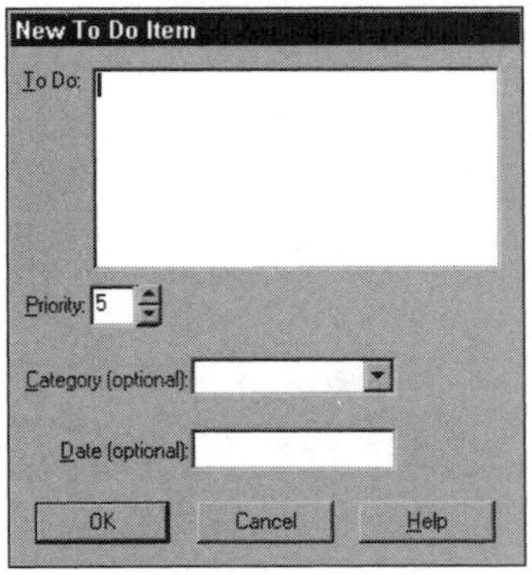

Figure 7-4:
Creating a
new To Do
item.

3. **In the To Do field, enter the task that you need to complete.**

4. **Tab to the Priority field, and select a rating from 1 to 5.**

   Family Tree Maker lists this number of exclamation points beside the To Do item on your Research Journal, which lets you know the item's priority among the tasks you have to do.

5. **(Optional) Tab to the Category field and enter a category.**

   Categories are optional but quite helpful when you're sorting out everything you have to do. Say, for example, you use types of records as your categories (for example, birth certificates, census records, and so forth).

Then you can sort your To Do list by the types of records that you need to get. Or you can use locations as your categories so you can sort and plan your tasks by proximity.

6. **(Optional) Enter a date in the Date field.**

   Like the Category field, the Date field is optional but can also be useful. You can use it to record a due date, a completion date, or the date of some other milestone for that particular To Do item.

7. **Click OK.**

   Family Tree Maker adds your new To Do item to the list in your Research Journal.

In addition to adding To Do items, you can also delete and edit them. To delete an item, simply highlight it and press the Delete key. To edit an item, just click the To Do item that you want to edit. The Edit To Do Item dialog box appears, where you can make any necessary changes.

Sorting your tasks and leads

Do you prefer to organize your research by the locations in which your ancestors lived? Or by the type of records you need to collect? Or by difficulty? If you answer yes to any of these questions, you may not like the way the items in your Research Journal are presented and may want to sort the items into an order that you find easier to work with. No problem. Here's how to sort the items:

1. **Choose Format⇨Sort Research Journal.**

   The Sort Research Journal dialog box appears, as shown in Figure 7-5. In Version 7.0, it allows you to sort only your To Do list. In other versions, it enables you to sort your To Do list and FamilyFinder Report.

Figure 7-5:
You can do
two-level
sorting of
your To Do
list.

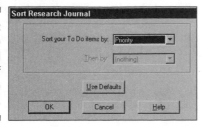

2. **Using the Sort Your To Do Items By drop-down list and the Then By drop-down list, select how you want to sort your To Do list.**

   You have the option of sorting on two levels. In the Sort Your To Do Items By field, select how to sort the list at level one, and in the Then By field, select how to sort the list at level two. Your choices include Category, Date, or Priority for both levels, and you have an additional choice of Nothing for the level-two sort.

   For example, say you want Family Tree Maker to sort your To Do list by category and then place it in due date order. To do so, select the Category option and then the Date option.

3. **Click OK.**

   Family Tree Maker sorts your Research Journal to your specifications.

A Journal made-to-order

If you're not crazy about the standard look of your Research Journal, you can change it. To open the dialog boxes that enable you to customize the format, use the toolbar on the right side of your Research Journal or the pull-down menus. Here are the things that you can customize:

✔ **Items to display in Research Journal:** To open this dialog box, choose Contents⇨Items to Display. You can choose whether to display To Do items that are Done (completed), Not Done (self-explanatory, right?), or Both Done and Not Done. You can also choose whether to show items for All Categories or Selected Categories. Of course, if you choose the latter, you have to designate which categories to include. And, you can choose to show FamilyFinder Report matches — your choices are to show All Matches, Selected Individuals (you then have to select the individuals), or Selected Family Archive CDs (again, you have to choose). Lastly, you can select the Show Only 4 and 5-Star Matches option.

✔ **Text font and size:** Choose Format⇨Text Font, Size, & Style to open this dialog box. You can change the font (its typeface and size) depending on the fonts you have loaded on your computer.

A Place in Time

Are you curious about what historical events occurred during your ancestors' lives? Placing your ancestors in a historical context with the Timeline feature (shown in Figure 7-6) is a great way to enhance your genealogy. And doing so is easier than you may think.

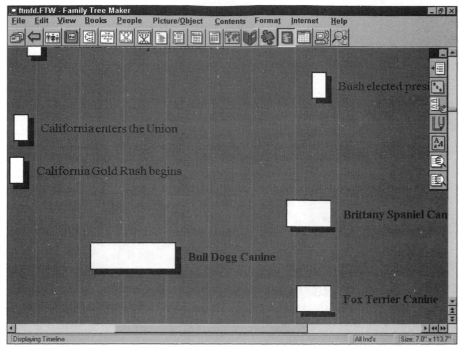

Figure 7-6:
A Timeline
generated
with Family
Tree Maker.

To create a Timeline in Family Tree Maker, choose View⇨Timeline or click the Timeline button on the toolbar (it's the fourth button from the left — the little blue-green piece of paper with white text — unless you're using Version 7.0, which doesn't have an icon for the Timeline). A Cue Card for Timeline may pop up, offering tips and highlights about the Timeline feature. If you don't want the Cue Card to pop up every time you open a Timeline, click in the check box labeled `Click here if you don't want to see this Help Window again`. Then click OK.

You may see a dialog box just before the Timeline appears, informing you that Family Tree Maker cannot estimate birth and death dates for some individuals in your Family File. Anyone for whom it cannot approximate dates are excluded from the Timeline. To proceed in creating a Timeline, just click OK.

The Timeline has horizontal bars indicating the lives of individuals in your database. Behind the horizontal bars are tick marks representing a certain number of years (you can adjust this number if you customize the Timeline). Depending on how many people you include in the Timeline (again, something that you can customize), you may need to scroll down to see the entire chart.

You can customize your Timeline by using the toolbar on the right side of the screen or the pull-down menus. Here are the things that you can customize:

- **Timeline format:** Choose Format⇨Timeline Format to open this dialog box. In it, you can designate the following:

  - How many years, per square inch, the report covers (20, 50, or 100)
  - How often to include a tick mark (in decades)
  - Whether the years flow from left to right or right to left
  - How to display historical events (if at all)
  - Whether to graphically display estimated dates
  - What kinds of historical events to show (for example: Military, Politics, Technology, or United States)

- **Sort:** Choose Format⇨Sort Timeline to open this dialog box. You can sort the Timeline by last name or birth date.

- **Individuals to include:** Choose Contents⇨Individuals to Include to open this dialog box. You can select to include All Individuals or Selected Individuals. If you choose the latter, you need to click the Individuals to Include button and scroll through a list and identify those people to include.

- **Items to include in each box:** Choose Contents⇨Items to Include in Each Box. You can identify the items that you want to appear in each person's box. A list of the available items appears on the left side of the dialog box, and your selected items list appears on the right side. You use the arrow buttons between the two lists to copy items.

- **Text font and size:** Choose Format⇨Text Font, Size, & Style to open this dialog box. You can change the font (its typeface and size) depending on the fonts you have loaded on your computer.

- **Box, line, and border styles:** Choose Format⇨Box, Line, & Border Styles to open this dialog box. You can also change the manner in which the boxes, lines, and borders appear.

- **Title and footnotes:** To open this dialog box, choose Contents⇨ Title & Footnote. Here you can use the standard title or write a custom title. You can also write a small footnote that is added to the Timeline.

Soundexing Your Way to Success

Do you suspect that some of your ancestors changed the spelling of their surnames? It wasn't an unusual thing to do, especially for people who immigrated to the United States. So how do you find documents about these ancestors? Sometimes you just have to guess and check for information under several spellings to be sure that you don't miss something. But other times, you can use a Soundex code.

The *Soundex system* is a method of indexing that finds names that are pronounced in a similar way but spelled differently and places them in groups. Several of the federal censuses are indexed with Soundex. This indexing procedure allows you to find ancestors who may have changed the spelling of their names over the years. For example, you find names like Helm, Helms, Holm, and Holme grouped together in Soundex.

The Soundex code for a name consists of a letter and then three numbers. You can convert names to Soundex the old-fashioned way (a relatively easy and painless process), but why not use Family Tree Maker's built-in calculator? Here's how to use the Soundex calculator to find a Soundex code for a surname:

1. **Choose People⇨Soundex Calculator.**

   The Soundex Calculator dialog box appears. In it, you find the Name field, the Choose button, and a Soundex value.

2. **In the Name field, enter the name for which you want the Soundex code. Or click the Choose button to see a list from which you can select a name.**

   We click the Choose button and scroll through the list until we find Le Tiegger, Anthony. We highlight his name and click OK. Family Tree Maker takes us back to the Soundex Calculator window and enters the surname Le Tiegger in the Name filed. The Soundex value automatically updates to reflect the code of L326, as shown in Figure 7-7.

Figure 7-7:
The code for
Le Tiegger is
L326.

3. **After you finish using the calculator, click Close.**

After you have a list of surnames and their Soundex equivalents, you can use the information to find things. For example, some Web sites enable you to search by using Soundex. They generate a list of sites for you, including sites that have names similar to the one you're researching.

Labeling Your Ancestors

Do you have a family reunion coming up soon? Want to send holiday cards to all of your known relatives? Sending out a questionnaire to collect genealogical information from all your cousins? Organizing your paper files by name? If you answered yes to any of these questions, then you definitely want to familiarize yourself with Family Tree Maker's Labels/Cards feature. It saves you lots of time and energy!

Using the addresses that you provide on the Address page for an individual, you can create labels or cards in a few short steps. Just choose View➪ Labels/Cards, and Family Tree Maker creates a sheet of labels or cards, depending on how you configure your print setup. (We cover your print setup in a minute.)

A Cue Card for Labels/Cards may pop up when you create the sheet. It offers tips and highlights about this feature. If you don't want the Cue Card to pop up every time you open Labels/Cards, click in the check box that says `Click here if you don't want to see this Help Window again.` Then click OK.

You can customize the labels by using the toolbar on the right side of the screen or the pull-down menus. Here are the things you can customize:

- **Items to include in labels/cards:** To open this dialog box, choose Contents➪Items to Include in Each Label/Card. You identify the items that you want to appear on every label or card. A list of the available items appears in a box on the left side of the dialog box, and a box where you copy the names of items to include appears on the right. You use the arrow buttons between the two boxes/lists to copy items. Some of the things you can include are the name, street address, city/state/ZIP, country, age, birth date, anniversary, and so forth of the individuals you choose.

- **Individuals to include:** To open this dialog box, choose Contents➪ Individuals to Include in Labels/Cards. You can select the All Individuals or Selected Individuals option. If you choose the latter, click the Individuals to Include button and scroll through a list to identify the people to include.

- **Options:** Choose Contents➪Options to open this dialog box. You can choose whether to produce one label per household or one per individual. You can also select the option labeled `Print blank rows when fields are empty.`

- **Text font and size:** Choose Format➪Text Font, Size, & Style to open this dialog box.

- **Box, line, and border styles:** To open this dialog box, choose Format➪ Box, Line, & Border Styles.

Family Tree Maker generates the labels or cards to the specifications of various Avery products. The size and shape of the labels or cards depend on the settings in your print setup. To change the size and shape of the labels, follow these steps:

1. **Choose File⇨Print Setup.**

   The Print Setup for Labels/Cards dialog box appears. At the top, it tells you that the setup information affects only the Labels/Card view.

   This dialog box has four sections in which you can: select the printer you want to use, determine the orientation of the paper/sheet of labels or cards, select the paper size and how it is fed into the printer, and work with Avery Labels/Cards. This fourth section is what you want to use here.

   For example, you may need to change the orientation of the paper from portrait to landscape, depending upon how the labels are fed into your printer. You many also need to change the Source under Paper to manual feed if your printer requires it to print labels. The best thing to do is to consult your printer manual for any specific settings that you need to make in the Print Setup dialog box to print labels.

2. **Scroll through the list of labels/cards and select the one you're using.**

   You can make quite a few choices in the list of labels. Use the scroll bar on the right to go through the labels. The first column should match the Avery label number on your box of labels. The second column tells you the size of the label, and the third column tells you how many labels are on a single sheet. This should give you enough information to make the right label choice.

3. **Click OK.**

Now that you know how to change the print setup and create labels, all you have to do is run out to the nearest office supply store and purchase some labels.

Chapter 8

Hit the Web at the Click of a Button

· ·

· ·

*A*dmit it, you're an Internet junky. You like to spend hours on end looking for morsels of information to add to your family history. Even if you don't find anything that applies to your family, you still can't wait to get online again. Are we right? Okay, even if you're not an Internet junky, you'll want to explore the Family Tree Maker Web site because you're likely to find resources that may help you in your research. In this chapter, we look at the Internet research resources that are available through the Family Tree Maker program.

Leave the Driving to Family Tree Maker

Once or twice a year, we travel to New York City. Being from farm country in the Midwest, we probably wouldn't fare too well driving in New York City traffic. Fortunately, when we visit there, we have a driver who takes us around town and makes sure that we get to the right places on time. Wouldn't it be helpful to have a driver take you to valuable research information on the Information Superhighway (that is, the Internet)? You're in luck — the Internet features of Family Tree Maker can help you.

Broderbund Software, the creators of Family Tree Maker, offers three companion sites that can help you further your research goals. These sites are accessible through the Internet option on the Family Tree Maker menu bar. To get to the main page of the Family Tree Maker Web site (which has links to the other two companion sites), choose Internet⇨Go Online. This command opens your Web browser, and you're on your way. However, you can also go directly to the type of information you're looking for, which is what we examine in the remainder of this chapter.

Before we get too far, here is a general idea of what each of the three sites offers:

- ✔ **FamilyTreeMaker.com** (www.familytreemaker.com) is the flagship site of Broderbund's online genealogical resources. It contains links to all the various resources offered by all three sites. Its focus has shifted a little over the past year, concentrating more on the Family Tree Maker product line than on research. However, many valuable research resources are still available from this site.

- ✔ **Genealogy.com** (www.genealogy.com) is a free research site. Many of the resources that formerly were on the FamilyTreeMaker.com site have been relocated to the Genealogy.com site. Plus, many new research tools have been added recently.

- ✔ **GenealogyLibrary.com** (www.genealogylibrary.com) is a subscription-based site that contains a variety of research resources for genealogists. You can find things such as the full text of out-of-copyright books and a collection of digitized records.

Getting Ready to Browse

You need to do some things before you go online. If you did not set up your browser configuration during the Family Tree Maker installation (for more information on installation, see Appendix A), then you need to set it up now. You do this by using the Browser Setup option from the Internet menu, as explained in these steps:

1. **Choose Internet⇨Browser Setup.**

   This command brings up the Browser Setup dialog box, which informs you that you're setting up your browser to access Family Tree Maker's services.

2. **Click the Continue button.**

   A second dialog box (also called Browser Setup) should appear, listing the browsers that Family Tree Maker detects on your computer. If you have more than one browser installed, you can see the other browsers by using the drop-down list, as shown in Figure 8-1. Family Tree Maker suggests which browser to use, but we recommend that you use whichever one you're most comfortable with.

3. **Select your browser type and then click Continue.**

   After you click continue, Family Tree Maker updates the files that it needs to complete the browser setup. You then see a dialog box telling you that the browser has been successfully set up.

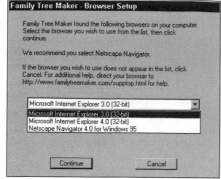

Figure 8-1:
Select your
preference
for a
browser if
you have
more than
one
installed.

After you complete your browser setup, Family Tree Maker should launch
that browser when you select an option from the Internet menu. If you
change your mind and want to use another browser sometime in the future,
just repeat the preceding steps to set up a different browser.

Finding Your Family with the FamilyFinder

By typing an ancestor's name in the Internet FamilyFinder search engine, it
generates a list of Web sites for you. No longer do you need to wander aim-
lessly from one site to another. The Internet FamilyFinder is available on the
FamilyTreeMaker.com Web site. It is a genealogy-specific search engine that
visits and indexes other sites, and then presents them to you upon your
request.

What's in the FamilyFinder Index?

The Internet FamilyFinder searches several different resources at one time.
These resources include

- ✔ Genealogy World Wide Web pages indexed from the Internet
- ✔ The Family Archive CD-ROM collection (produced by Broderbund)
- ✔ Information found on the subscription site GenealogyLibrary.com
- ✔ FamilyTreeMaker.com User Home Pages (individuals who have placed
  the information contained in their Family Tree Maker Family File online)
- ✔ GenForum message boards on the Genealogy.com site (queries about
  surnames and particular locations)

> ✔ Genealogy Classifieds on the FamilyTreeMaker.com site (where Family Tree Maker users can post genealogical–classified ads online)
>
> ✔ The World Family Tree Collection (a collection of genealogical data submitted by genealogists around the world and printed on CD-ROM)

Searching through all of these resources may take a while, especially if you're looking for a common name (such as John Smith). Fortunately, the Internet FamilyFinder allows you to select which of the resources you want it to search. That way, if you're looking only for World Wide Web sites, you don't have to wade through the results from all the Family Archive CD-ROMs.

Using the Internet FamilyFinder

We can sense your anticipation. You've been waiting patiently for us to tell you how to use the Internet FamilyFinder. So without further ado, follow these steps to use the Internet FamilyFinder:

1. **Choose Internet⇨Find Individual on the Internet.**

   Your Web browser opens to the Internet FamilyFinder page on the FamilyTreeMaker.com site (www.familytreemaker.com/iffintro. html). You first see the introduction page for the Internet FamilyFinder. On this page, you can read a brief description of the contents of the FamilyFinder and access some Frequently Asked Questions (FAQs) about it and its Agents (you can find more about Agents in "Secret Agents on the prowl," later in this chapter).

2. **In the Using the Internet FamilyFinder column on the right, click the** <u>**Try Internet FamilyFinder Now!**</u> **link.**

   A new page appears on your screen with a box containing the First Name, Middle, and Last Name fields. Near the bottom of the box is a series of options that you can use to select which areas the FamilyFinder will search. These options include the FamilyArchive CDs, the Internet, GenealogyLibrary.com, the World Family Tree, and certain parts of the Family Tree Maker site itself (User Home Pages, Classified Ads, GenForum message boards, and some online databases).

   If you scroll farther down the page, you'll see some hints for using the Internet FamilyFinder's search capability. If your search doesn't produce the results you were hoping for, take a look at these hints.

3. **Type the name of the individual you're researching in the First Name, Middle, and Last Name fields.**

   If you're looking for only general resources on a surname, just type the surname in the Last Name text box. For example, we decided to do a general search for the surname Canine. We typed *Canine* in the Last Name field and left the rest blank.

4. **Deselect the Search On check boxes for those resources that you don't want Internet FamilyFinder to search.**

   You can choose whether to search the FamilyArchive CDs, the Internet, GenealogyLibrary.com, the World Family Tree, and certain parts of the Family Tree Maker site itself (User Home Pages, Classified Ads, GenForum message boards, and some online databases).

   We want the Internet FamilyFinder to search all the available resources, so we leave check marks in all the Search On boxes.

5. **Click Search.**

   The search engine processes your request and opens the List of Matching Pages, which includes a table with five columns: Name, Date, Location, Found On, and Link. (Figure 8-2 shows an example of a list containing the results for our search on Canine.)

   If you look closely at the Link column, you can see a link to the site where the information was found, along with a summary of the context in which your search term appeared. This way you can see if the search term is used in the correct manner. In our example search, we can see whether the word Canine is used for someone's surname or for a reference to the animal of the four-legged variety.

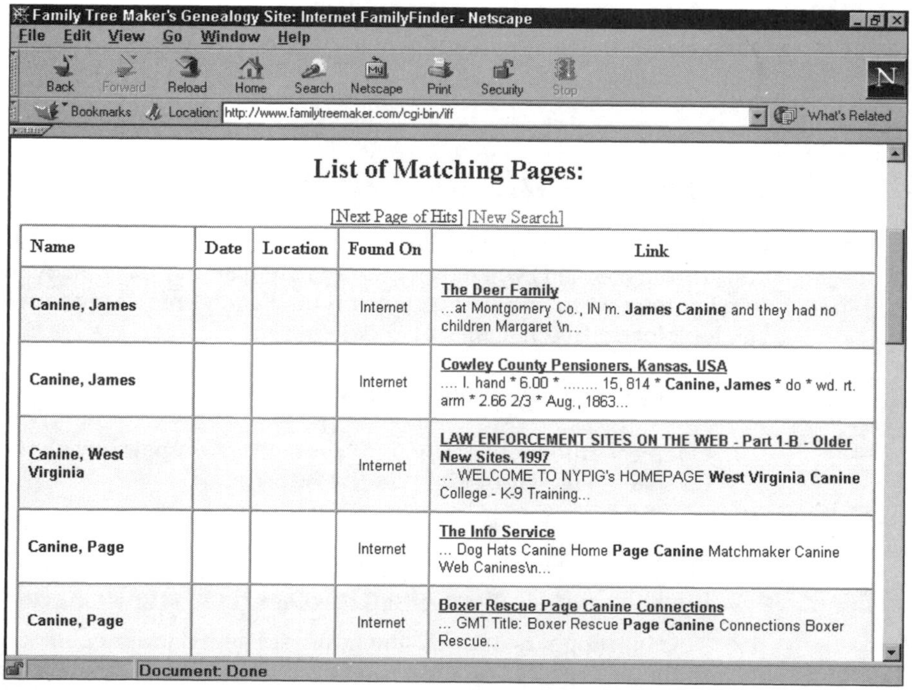

Figure 8-2: Internet FamilyFinder results for Canine.

Name	Date	Location	Found On	Link
Canine, James			Internet	**The Deer Family** ...at Montgomery Co., IN m. **James Canine** and they had no children Margaret \n...
Canine, James			Internet	**Cowley County Pensioners, Kansas, USA** .... l. hand * 6.00 * .... 15, 814 * **Canine, James** * do * wd. rt. arm * 2.66 2/3 * Aug., 1863...
Canine, West Virginia			Internet	**LAW ENFORCEMENT SITES ON THE WEB - Part 1-B - Older New Sites, 1997** ... WELCOME TO NYPIG's HOMEPAGE **West Virginia Canine** College - K-9 Training...
Canine, Page			Internet	**The Info Service** ... Dog Hats Canine Home **Page Canine** Matchmaker Canine Web Canines\n...
Canine, Page			Internet	**Boxer Rescue Page Canine Connections** ... GMT Title: Boxer Rescue **Page Canine** Connections Boxer Rescue...

6. **Select an underlined Web site link in the Link column to go to that site.**

   Keep in mind that by following a link, you may leave the Family Tree Maker Web site and go to a privately owned server. The Web page that appears may have a completely different look and feel. To return to the Internet FamilyFinder, you can use your browser's Back button.

Keep a few things in mind when using the Internet FamilyFinder. First, if you choose to search Internet pages, the results may include some extraneous pages that don't contain genealogical content. Although the search engine is designed to index genealogical sites, it also may index other pages that are linked from the genealogy pages (such as pages that genealogists have created for their other interests). Unfortunately, the search engine does not adequately filter out these pages in some cases. However, using this search engine generates fewer extraneous pages than if you use general search engines such as AltaVista or Lycos.

You may also receive a number of results from Family Archive CD-ROM indexes or the World Family Tree. These links don't lead you to the actual contents of the CD-ROM. Rather, they take you to Web pages where you can find out more about the CD-ROMs and how to purchase them. The Family Archive CD-ROMs and the World Family Tree are available for purchase only on CD, and you have to purchase the CD-ROM to see the full contents (which can be expensive depending on the number of results you get and individual prices of the CDs). The search just tells you that the name is on the CD-ROM. Many people are disappointed when they see this result, so we want to point this out ahead of time.

Secret Agents on the prowl

One really cool feature of the Internet FamilyFinder is the *Agent*. It notifies you (through e-mail) when the Internet FamilyFinder has discovered something of interest to you. The Agents on the FamilyTreeMaker.com Web site can look for up to ten names at once.

To use an Internet FamilyFinder Agent, follow these steps:

1. **Open the Internet FamilyFinder introduction page by choosing Internet⇨Find Individual on the Internet.**

   Or you can type **www.familytreemaker.com/iffintro.html** in your Web browser.

2. **Click the <u>Tell Me More About Internet FamilyFinder Agents</u> link.**

   This link appears in the Using Internet FamilyFinder column. It takes you to the Let Agents Work for You page, which provides a brief explanation of what Agents do.

3. **To set up an Agent, click the <u>Internet Family Finder Agent</u> link in the right-hand column of the page.**

   This link should take you to the Internet FamilyFinder Registration page, which has a series of fields on it (such as First Name, Middle Name, Last Name, Street 1, and so forth).You're required to provide this information about yourself if you want to establish a Family Tree Maker Online account, which allows you to use an Agent.

4. **Complete the fields in the form and then click Submit.**

   After you click Submit, the Internet FamilyFinder Agent page appears, which has the search form where you identify the surname or full name that you want the agent to look for.

5. **Type the name you want the Agent to watch for. You can enter the full name (First Name, Middle, and Last Name) or just the surname (Last Name field).**

   If you search for a name or surname that's too general (or common), you may receive a message telling you to make your query more specific. This usually means that you need to add a first name or middle name. Don't worry about using specific names because you can have up to ten Agents active at the same time.

6. **Select where you want the Agent to search (the Internet, User Home Pages, and so on) and then click the Search button.**

   When the Agent finds something that is of interest to you, it notifies you by e-mail and lets you know where to go to view the results.

You can also use similar technology to look for all the names in your Family File through the FamilyFinder Report. You can find more information on the FamilyFinder Report in our discussion of the Research Journal in Chapter 7.

Kinfolk in the Archive

A number of research aids have been produced for the genealogical community on CD-ROM. One series that has been around for a while is the Family Archive CD-ROM collection, which is produced by and available from Broderbund. To view them, you have to use your Family Tree Maker program — you can't just pop them in your CD-ROM drive and use them by them selves.

The Family Archive CD-ROM collection contains information on individuals for various time periods and locations. Most of the information is for individuals who lived in the United States and Canada. Here are some of the types of records covered by the series:

✔ Birth records

✔ Cemetery records

✔ Census microfilm CDs

✔ Land records

✔ Marriage records

✔ Military records

✔ Ship passenger lists

The CD-ROMs contain different amounts of information, depending upon the type of record that the CD-ROMs cover.

To search the collection, follow these steps:

1. **Choose Internet⇨Order Family Archive CDs.**

   Or you go to this Web site: `www.familytreemaker.com/cdhome.html`.

   Don't worry, you don't have to buy anything. You're just window-shopping right now. After you click the menu item, your browser opens to the page titled Family Archive CDs. The Search for CDs By box appears at the top of the page.

2. **Type the First Name, Middle, and Last Name of the individual you're looking for or enter the CD-ROM Number. Then click Go.**

   You may be wondering how you would obtain a CD-ROM number to enter. If you already ran an Internet FamilyFinder search (see "Using the Internet FamilyFinder," earlier in this chapter), it's a good possibility that the results contained hits from the Family Archive CDs. One of the information items provided with each Family Archive CD hit is the number of the CD-ROM (it shows up in the Found On column in the Internet FamilyFinder Report). Entering just the CD-ROM number takes you directly to the Web page that provides information specifically about that CD and allows you to skip Step 3.

   If you haven't already run an Internet FamilyFinder search and received a list of potential leads on the Family Archive CD-ROMs, you can search now for your ancestors among the CDs. Remember, you can search just on a surname. If you decide to do that, then simply leave the First Name and Middle fields blank.

   We decided to try to locate some references to Canine.

   The results page looks a lot like the page for the Internet FamilyFinder. It has the same five columns: Name, Date, Location, Found On, and Link. The difference is that it doesn't tell you the context of the name on the CD-ROM. So you can't determine whether that person is really someone you're looking for. Also, the dates listed in the second column usually follow the dates of the CD-ROM. In our case, some Canines were listed in marriage indexes, but the dates ranged from 1720 to 1926. That's a pretty wide range of years.

3. **Click an entry in the Link column to see a description of the CD-ROM.**

   At this stage, a lot of people are disappointed. They're expecting to see more detailed information about the individual, but instead, they see a general description of the CD-ROM and information on ordering it (see Figure 8-3). Keep in mind that the purpose of the index is to tell you the names that are on particular CD-ROMs. So in a way, this part of the site is really a product catalog. Yes, we, too, would like to see a little more information, but the company probably couldn't sell the CD-ROMs if it just put the information that we needed online.

   Most of the Family Archive CD-ROMs contain indexes to records found in archives and other collections. So even if you order a CD-ROM, more than likely it will list only where you can find the original record. The notable exception to this is the new line of Census Microfilm CD-ROMs. These CD-ROMs contain digitized images of microfilmed United States Census records. In particular, they currently cover selected states in the 1850 Census.

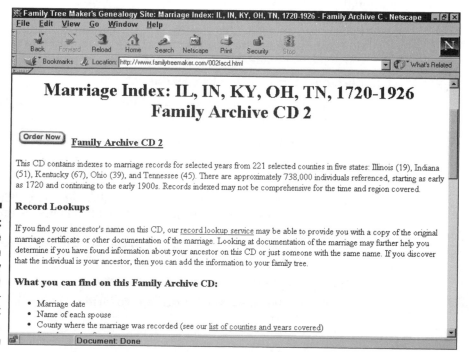

Figure 8-3:
The destination of Family Archive CD searches — the product description.

Take a Letter

Some days, we would like to have a secretary at home. He or she could do all the routine administrative tasks, freeing up our time to do more important things (like genealogical research). Unfortunately, the old family budget doesn't include funds for a secretary, so we're stuck doing administrative things ourselves. Fortunately, one area of the FamilyTreeMaker.com site performs some of the functions of a secretary for genealogists: the Create Letter section.

The Create Letter section allows you to create a letter to send to a relative (in case you don't have much to say). Here are the basic steps for filling out the letter:

1. **Choose Internet⇨Create Letter to a Relative.**

   Or go to this URL: www.familytreemaker.com/letters.html.

   You're magically transferred to the Help section of the FamilyTreeMaker.com site (that is, after your browser is launched). The Create Letters to Relatives and Government Agencies page should appear.

2. **Click the <u>Create a letter to a relative</u> link.**

   You can find this link in the right-hand column under Letter Links. This link takes you to another part of the FamilyTreeMaker.com site, the Online University. The title of this page is Form Letters and Other Aids. The portion of the page that we're interested in appears under Form Letters at the top of the page, although the rest of the page is helpful as well.

3. **Click the <u>Form letters in English</u> link.**

   You can construct form letters in five different languages: English, French, German, Italian, and Spanish.

   Our relatives are in the United States, so we select the English option.

4. **Click the <u>Form letter for requesting genealogical information from family members</u> link.**

   This form has a rather long title, don't you think? Anyway, clicking the link takes you to a copy of the form letter. The form letter is text only and has bracketed areas where you need to add information, as shown in Figure 8-4. Because this form doesn't generate a personalized letter, you need to follow a few more steps.

5. **Open your favorite Windows word processor.**

   It doesn't matter which word processor you use as long as it allows you to cut and paste.

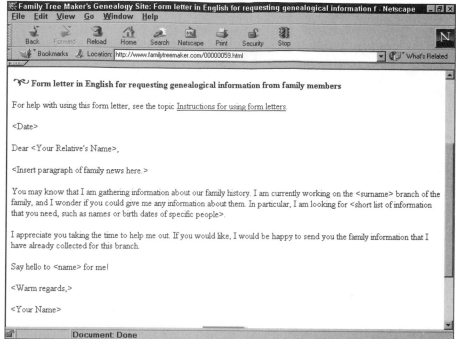

Figure 8-4:
An example
of the form
letter to a
relative.

6. **Press Alt+Tab to return to your Web browser.**

   Or select your Web browser from the Windows taskbar.

7. **Click on the Web page and drag the cursor until the text of the form letter is highlighted.**

   You may have to repeat this step a few times if your browser doesn't scroll, highlighting a different section of the letter's text each time.

8. **Choose Edit⇨Copy (or your browser's equivalent) to copy the page.**

   You can also press Ctrl+C for the same effect.

9. **Press Alt+Tab to return to your word processor.**

   Or select your word processor from the Windows taskbar.

10. **Choose Edit⇨Paste (or the equivalent) to paste the text in your word processor.**

    Pressing Ctrl+V also works.

11. **Replace the text in the brackets to meet your needs.**

12. **Print and mail the letter to the appropriate relative.**

    Don't forget to put a stamp on it. Maybe one of those fancy new eStamps would be nice.

Whew, that's a long list of steps. For shorter letters, you may find it easier to just retype the text using the form letter as a guide. Either way, the form letter can save you time when creating these letters, time that you can spend doing other research tasks.

After you have the form letter in a word processor file, save it and then use it as a template for future letters. That way you don't have to go through all of these steps each time you want to create a letter.

Help is just a click away

There's an old saying that you learn something new every day. Although you may not learn something new about your ancestors every day, you can find out about plenty of other resources that eventually may lead you to new information about your ancestors. If you're in the mood to find out a thing or two, FamilyTreeMaker.com has a section filled with How-To articles that can shed light on things that you may not have thought about before. Some prominent genealogists, as well as some Broderbund employees, wrote these articles.

Here are some examples of topics covered in the How-To articles:

- The Basics (organizing your research, the importance of given names, what is a first cousin, once removed)
- African American research
- Census record research
- Church record research
- Conferences and associations

- Documenting sources
- Family Tree Maker tutorials
- Immigration research
- Medical history
- Oral histories and family traditions
- Photographs
- Research techniques
- Reunions
- Technology

To access these articles, choose Internet⇨ Articles (or go to www.familytreemaker. com/backissu.html). In the index of How-To articles, you can pick whichever article sounds interesting. You also have the option of listing the articles by author or viewing only the newest articles. Links for these two options appear at the top of the How-To Articles page on the FamilyTreeMaker.com site.

Getting Your Message Out to Other Researchers

Say that you decide to start your own business. Maybe it's one of those Internet start-ups that will eventually be worth millions of dollars. Or perhaps it's just a small, home-based business that you operate in your spare time. Either way, you'll probably have to advertise your business to attract customers — it's a simple fact of business. Believe it or not, the same holds true for genealogists. A key to being successful is finding other researchers who can assist you (and whom you can assist) in putting all the pieces together. To find these genealogists, you need to advertise. One good way to advertise is to post messages on the World Wide Web, notifying people of the ancestors you're researching.

The GenForum section of the Genealogy.com site has one of the largest Internet message boards for genealogy. The various boards in the GenForum section allow you to post information on the surnames you're researching and the geographic areas that you have an interest in. They also discuss how to research effectively.

The concept behind the boards is pretty simple. You enter your information in a Web form, which is then posted on a specific message board on the GenForum server. When other researchers search the message board, they can read your message and reply to you by e-mail or by posting a response on the message board.

Finding a forum

Follow these steps to read the message boards:

1. **Choose Internet⇨Message Boards.**

   Or go to `genforum.genealogy.com/`.

   Selecting the Message Boards option launches your browser and takes you to the home page for the GenForum boards. At this point, you have several options, depending on what kind of search you want to perform.

   GenForum refers to its message boards as *forums*. Try to find a forum for a surname — that way you can see if anyone is looking for the same ancestors that you are. Unfortunately, no forums exist for Canine or Feline. So we have to look for the surname Helm.

2. **In the field under Forum Finder, type the surname you're looking for and click the Find button.**

In our case, we enter *Helm*. But feel free to enter a surname that interests you. If you feel like browsing the forums, you can also select a letter beneath the word *Surnames*.

If the surname you entered already has a forum, then your browser takes you to the forum's page, as shown in Figure 8-5. If not, you have the opportunity to apply for a new forum on the surname.

Don't worry if your surname doesn't have a forum. The GenForum section is constantly growing and adding surnames. You may also want to search the other forums to see if the name is included in a variant spelling or if someone else mentioned the name in a passing reference in another forum (see the next section for details).

3. **After you find a forum, read a message by clicking its link.**

   As soon as your browser loads the message board page, you should see a list of bulleted messages to choose from. You can also navigate to other pages of the message board if the messages don't all fit on a single page. If you don't want to read all the messages, you have the option to see the latest messages, today's messages, and any messages posted in the last seven days. These options are available in green script at the top of the page.

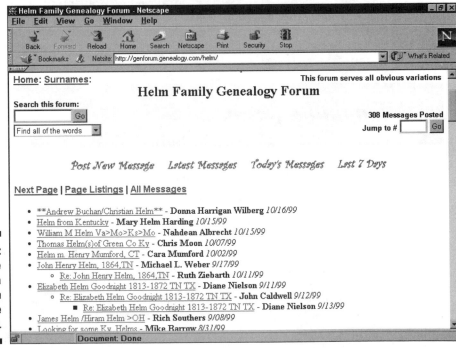

Figure 8-5:
An example of a GenForum message board.

Searching for the needle in the forum

Even if you find a forum for the surname that interests you, we suggest that you search all the GenForum boards to look for any other references to your ancestors. Here's how to do that:

1. **Scroll to the bottom of the GenForum home page.**

2. **In the Search All of GenForum field — which is in the lower-right corner of the screen — type the surname that interests you and click the Go button.**

   If you don't remember how to get to the GenForum home page, take a look at the preceding section. The search field for GenForum isn't obvious, so you have to be looking for it. If you look carefully, you can see it at the bottom right of the page with a yellow background (see Figure 8-6).

   You have the option to turn proximity matching on or off. *Proximity matching* means that if you type in two or more words, the search engine looks for instances in which the words appear close other. We suggest leaving this option selected (which is the default setting) unless you want to see all the pages that contain both the words *John* and *Smith,* rather than *John* and *Smith* next to each other.

   After you execute the search, a page returns with a list of items matching your search criteria, as shown in Figure 8-7.

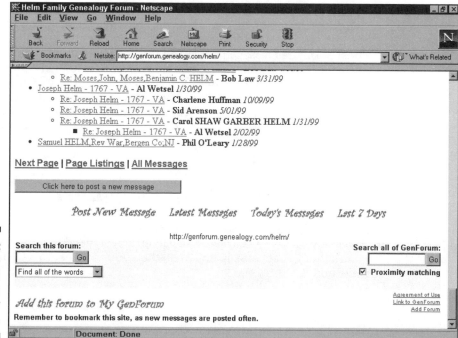

Figure 8-6:
The almost-hidden search form for GenForum.

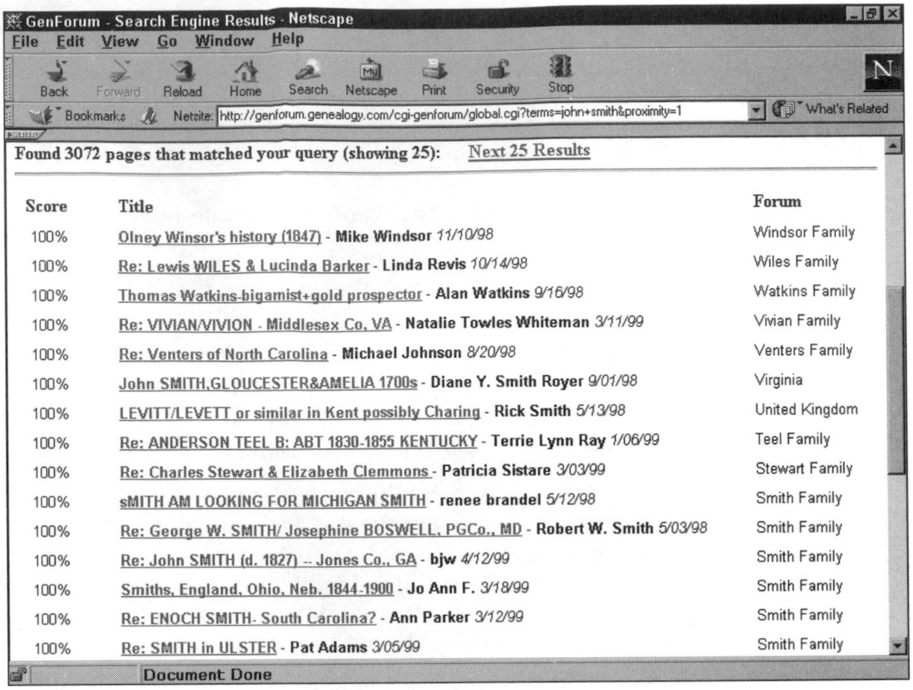

Figure 8-7:
The results
page from a
GenForum
search.

3. Click the link of a message that seems promising.

The results table has three columns containing Score, Title, and Forum.
The Score field shows you the likelihood that the result matches your
search. The Title field shows you the title of the message that was
posted on the message board. And the Forum field tells you what message board the message was posted to. The Forum field can be helpful in
figuring out whether the message may be relevant to you. If the Forum
name is not the same as the surname you entered, but it is a name that
you've found associated with your ancestor (perhaps the maiden name
of his wife), then the likelihood of finding valuable information may be
greater than the Score field indicates.

Posting a message to GenForum

Finding other researchers who have posted information to GenForum is only
half the story. As we say earlier in the chapter, you need to advertise the
ancestors that you're looking for. To do that, you can post to a GenForum
message board.

Posting to a message board is a pretty easy task; just follow these steps:

1. **Find a message board, or forum, that you want to post to.**

   If you're not sure how to do this, just follow the steps in the preceding section.

2. **Click the <u>Post New Message</u> link near the top of the message board page.**

   You should see some green text, just above the list of messages. The first one in the row is the <u>Post New Message</u> link.

   Clicking this link generates another page, which contains the fields that will generate your message. This page includes the Name, E-Mail, Subject, and Message fields, as shown in Figure 8-8.

3. **Fill out the appropriate fields and then click the Preview Message button.**

   Make sure that your message contains enough information for other researchers to determine if they can assist you. Include full names, birth and death dates and places (if known), and geographic locations where your ancestors lived (if known). For more tips on how to create effective messages, see our book *Genealogy Online For Dummies,* 2nd Edition (IDG Books Worldwide, Inc.).

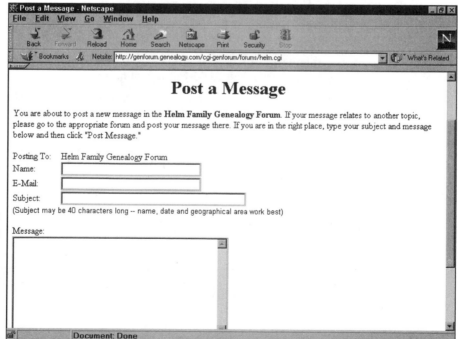

Figure 8-8:
Post a
message
with the
message
form on
GenForum.

Clicking the Preview Message button is an important step because you can see how the message will look when it's posted. This option can prevent you from posting an embarrassing message.

4. **If you're satisfied with the way that the message looks, click the Post Message button.**

   The Web site posts your message for the world to see.

It's a good idea to post to as many message boards as you feel are appropriate. For example, if you're looking for information on a particular ancestor, post a message not only to the message board for that person's surname, but also to the message board for his or her spouse's surname.

My GenForum, your GenForum

One last thing about GenForum that's sort of neat is that you can customize it to display links to all of your Family Pages. So if you're researching several families, you don't have to search for each family every time you enter. This feature is called My GenForum. Just follow these steps to use it:

1. **Locate a message board that you want to return to.**

   Follow the instructions in "Finding a forum" (earlier in this chapter) to locate a GenForum message board.

2. **At the very bottom of the message board, click the <u>Add this forum to My GenForum</u> link.**

   You can find this link beneath the search form in a green script (see the lower left corner of Figure 8-9 for an example of the link).

   Clicking this link generates a new Web page with a green column on the left. This column contains a link to the message board that you just added to My GenForum.

   To return to this page in the future, click the <u>My GenForum</u> link at the top of the GenForum home page (it's kind of an ugly yellow color, at least on our monitors).

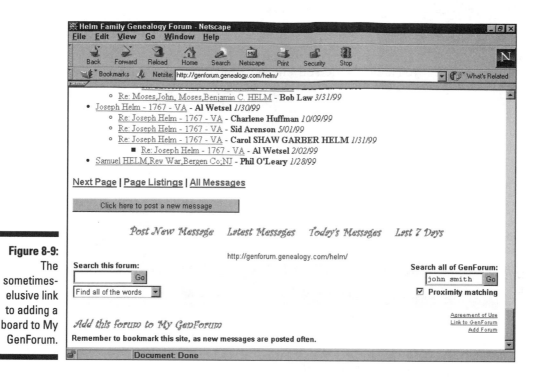

Figure 8-9:
The
sometimes-
elusive link
to adding a
board to My
GenForum.

Home on the Range: User Home Pages

One of the options you have, as a Family Tree Maker user, is the ability to post information from your Family File onto the FamilyTreeMaker.com Web site. This collection of information is generally known as the User Home Pages section. Not only can you eventually post your information here (see Chapter 12 if you're so inclined), but you can also find out if anyone else has posted information of interest to you.

To find other users' home pages, follow these steps:

1. **From Family Tree Maker, choose Internet⇨My Home Page.**

   Or go directly to `www.familytreemaker.com/users/index.html` in your Web browser.

   This action launches your Web browser and takes you to the User Home Pages. Don't worry that the menu option is labeled My Home Page if you haven't created one. The link is the same whether or not you have established a home page on FamilyTreeMaker.com.

2. **Type in your search criteria and click the Go button.**

You can find User Home Pages three ways. The first way is to do a full-text search of all the User Home Pages. The second way is to search by the last name of the person who created the page (this is good only if you know the person who authored the page). The final way is to browse through pages arranged by the author's last name.

The search type that is probably the most useful is the first one: the full-text search. It's the one that is labeled `Search home pages for any information`.

We decided to keep with our motif and search on the surname Canine. So we typed *Canine* in the Last Name field and clicked the Go button.

This action produced another Web page, showing the results of our search. It's the familiar five-column table that includes the Name, Date, Location, Found On, and Link fields. Notice that the Link column also includes the context of the first occurrence of the search term on the page. You can use this information to determine whether the link will be useful.

3. **Click an interesting link in the Link column.**

   This link takes you to the User Home Page where your search terms were found. Figure 8-10 shows an example of a User Home Page.

4. **Click your browser's Back button to return to the results page to look for further pages of interest.**

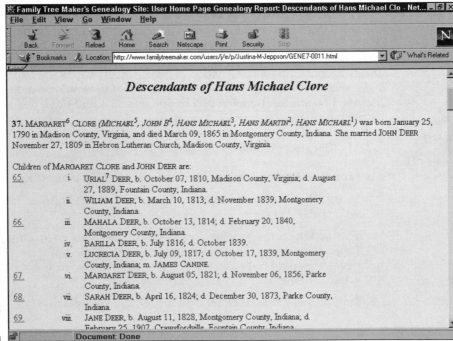

Figure 8-10: A User Home Page showing a descendant report.

A Bit of Security About Death

Okay, maybe we can't give you any security about death. But we can show you how to use the Social Security Death Index on the FamilyTreeMaker.com site.

The Social Security Death Index is an index of persons for whom Social Security death claims were filed with the United States Social Security Administration. It's a good resource for finding information about individuals who died after 1962. The information contained in the index includes Name, Social Security Number, Issue State (where card holders received their cards), Birth, Death, Death State, Last Known Residence, and Last Payment Location.

Searching the index is relatively easy, just follow these steps:

1. **Using your Web browser, go to the Social Security Death Index page at** www.familytreemaker.com/fto_ssdisearch.html.

   The search box contains a number of fields that you can use to narrow down your search. The index contains more than 55 million names, so enter as much information as you can (especially if you're working with a common name).

2. **Type the name of the individual you're searching for in the Last Name and First Name fields.**

   Neither field is required, so you can search just on a last name or just on a first name (although we don't recommend searching just on a first name). If you're not sure of the correct spelling, you can use the question mark in the place of a single letter (such as A?ril) and an asterisk in the place of multiple letters (such as Mat* to get all the variations of Matthew).

3. **(Optional) Select the Use Soundex option.**

   If you select this option, the search engine looks for names that sound like the name you entered, but are not necessarily spelled the same. Soundex searching tries to account for spelling mistakes or names that have changed over time. (For more about Soundex, check out Chapter 7.)

4. **Enter the birth and death dates in the appropriate fields.**

   If you don't know either, simply leave the dates blank. If you do a search with birth and/or death dates and do not get the results you were looking for, try the search again without the dates. On occasion, the dates are reported incorrectly in the index.

5. **If you know the person's Social Security number, enter it.**

   Remember to enter it without the dashes. If you don't know the number, just skip the field.

6. **Type in the state of death and the last-known zip code, if known.**

   Same rules as before. If you know it, enter it; if not, skip the field.

7. **Click the Search Now button.**

   We did a search on the name Canine, and Figure 8-11 shows the results. The search found 97 individuals with that surname.

8. **After you positively identify someone, click the <u>Write It</u> link to generate a letter requesting a copy of the application for the Social Security Card.**

   The letter fills in the necessary information that the Social Security Administration needs to fulfill the request. It also tells you the fee that needs to accompany the request.

The original application for the Social Security Card contains several pieces of information, including full name at birth (including maiden name), mailing address, age at last birthday, date of birth, father's full name, mother's full name, current employer's name and address, and the applicant's signature.

You may have to do several searches with different combinations of information before you find the person you're looking for. However, keep in mind that not all people have death claims filed, so your relative may not be in the index. And in some cases, names are misspelled, which also makes it difficult to find them (even with Soundex).

Figure 8-11:
Results from
the Social
Security
Death Index
search.

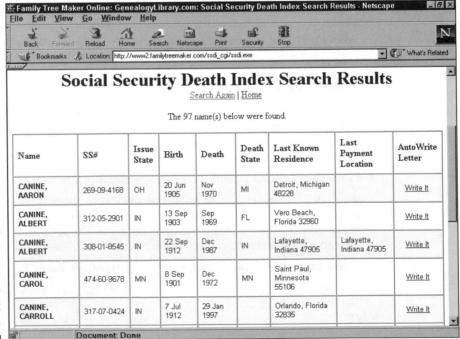

Social Security Death Index Search Results

Search Again | Home

The 97 name(s) below were found.

Name	SS#	Issue State	Birth	Death	Death State	Last Known Residence	Last Payment Location	AutoWrite Letter
CANINE, AARON	269-09-4168	OH	20 Jun 1905	Nov 1970	MI	Detroit, Michigan 48228		Write It
CANINE, ALBERT	312-05-2901	IN	13 Sep 1903	Sep 1969	FL	Vero Beach, Florida 32960		Write It
CANINE, ALBERT	308-01-8545	IN	22 Sep 1912	Dec 1987	IN	Lafayette, Indiana 47905	Lafayette, Indiana 47905	Write It
CANINE, CAROL	474-60-9678	MN	8 Sep 1901	Dec 1972	MN	Saint Paul, Minnesota 55106		Write It
CANINE, CARROLL	317-07-0424	IN	7 Jul 1912	29 Jan 1997		Orlando, Florida 32835		Write It

Letting the Research Directory Be Your Guide

When you start researching ancestors who lived in a state that you haven't previously researched, knowing a little about the resources available in that state is helpful. The Genealogy Research Directory, which is part of the FamilyTreeMaker.com site (`www.familytreemaker.com/00000088.html`), lists information on a variety of topics, including addresses that you need in order to retrieve records from state and county agencies.

The directory contains information on the following:

- ✔ **National resources:** This section includes information on the National Archives and Records administration, national historical and genealogical societies, and topics such as researching military records.

- ✔ **State resources:** State resources include addresses, hours, and holdings of vital records offices, state libraries and archives, and prominent genealogical societies.

- ✔ **County information:** County information contains the addresses and phone numbers for county courthouses in each state.

- ✔ **International, ethnic, and religious resources:** This section contains brief outlines of the types of resources available for researching these particular groups. The Ethnic area provides information on such groups as African-American, Asian Indian, Chinese, Filipino, Japanese, Korean, Native American, Vietnamese, as well as European and Central American ethnicities. The religious groups section includes information on the Anglican, Baptist, Eastern Orthodox, Jewish, Lutheran, Methodist, Mormon (Church of Jesus Christ of Latter-day Saints), Presbyterian, Puritan, Quaker, and Roman Catholic groups.

- ✔ **Genealogy dictionary:** This section contains the definitions for words commonly used in genealogical research and words that may not be common today. For example, here you can find the definitions for such popular words as codicil, holographic will, and quadroon.

- ✔ **Bibliography and suggested reading:** This section contains a list of books that were consulted when developing the How-To sections of the FamilyTreeMaker.com site.

Getting an education at the Online University

Do you want to learn about genealogy without leaving the comfort of your favorite chair? Here's your opportunity. The Online University located at `www.familytreemaker.com/university.html`, provides self-paced courses designed to teach you the basics of genealogical research at no cost. Currently, six online courses are available:

✔ **Beginning Genealogy.** This course has six lessons including Mapping the Course and Equipment for the Hunt, Vital Records, and Your Best Ally in the Hunt — The U.S. Federal Census.

✔ **Tracing Immigrant Origins.** The Tracing Immigrant Origins course has 12 lessons including Identifying the Immigrant, Reading the Place Name, and Modern Naturalization Records.

✔ **Tracing Immigrant Origins Part II (Post Civil War Immigrant Sources).** Lessons in this six-part course include Clues from Census Records, Dying to Be Found, and Enlisting the Help of Others.

✔ **Tracing Immigrant Origins Part III (Between 1820 and 1865).** This four-part series includes Enlisting the Military's Help, Compiled Records Via Your Computer, and U.S. Customs Passenger Lists.

✔ **Beginning Internet Genealogy.** This 16-part course features Online Reference Sites, Libraries in the Digital Age, and Search Engines — Sorting through the Web.

✔ **Internet Genealogy, Level 2.** This five-part series includes Help from Societies, Conducting Online Research, and The Mechanics of Writing Your Family History.

Each course consists of a series of Web pages with links that take you to the next page in the series. The Online University periodically posts new lessons and creates new courses.

Finding Out About Upcoming Events

One thing that you should do when you get the chance is to attend genealogical conferences, workshops, and fairs. These events are opportunities to find out new research methods, and network with other researchers who may be able to lend a hand to your research. So how do you find out about them?

A good source of information is the Upcoming Events section of FamilyTreeMaker.com. You can find the section by going to this address: `www.familytreemaker.com/othrevnt.html`.

The Upcoming Events page, shown in Figure 8-12, lists conferences and workshops that take place all over the world. The list is in date order and includes the name of the event, a link to the event's home page, the date of the event, and a brief description of what will be covered at the event.

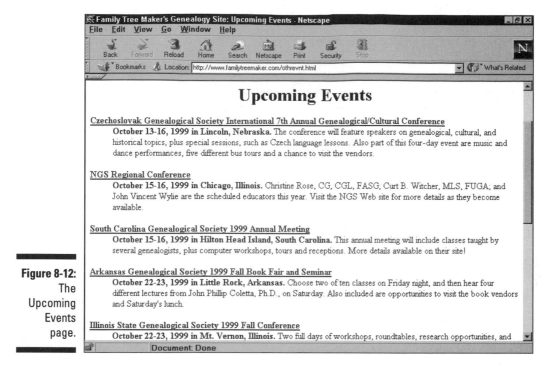

Figure 8-12:
The
Upcoming
Events
page.

Need a Research Assistant?

At some point in your research life, you may need the help of a professional — we mean a genealogist, not a psychiatrist. You may need help when you're researching ancestors who seemingly spontaneously generated themselves — that is, you can't find any records listing who those ancestors' parents were. If you find yourself in that situation, then you'll want to take a look at the Research Services available on FamilyTreeMaker.com.

To access this page, choose Internet⇨Research Services or type this address in your Web browser: `www.familytreemaker.com/gramain.html`.

The types of records that the professional researchers can look into for you include the following:

- ✔ Foreign census records
- ✔ United States census records
- ✔ Immigration records
- ✔ Military records
- ✔ Native American records

- Phone/city directories
- Foreign vital records
- United States vital records

The research services offered on FamilyTreeMaker.com can go beyond simple record lookups. These services include

- Searches in specific geographical areas
- Searches in specific publications
- Evaluation of existing research and recommendations on what to do next
- Research of your entire lineage (Now, where's the fun in that?)
- Extension of a family line
- Verification of family information

You can order these services online and pay by credit card. This kind of sounds like a commercial, but it's the truth. Keep in mind that your results with a professional genealogist may vary with the particular family line that you are researching. Some are just harder to find records on than others. There are no guarantees that the professional genealogist will be able to find what you need in every case.

Surfing the Web with the Genealogy SiteFinder

Don't even think that the fun stops with just the FamilyTreeMaker.com site. A lot more is out there on the wild and wooly Web. In fact, hundreds of new pages devoted to family history appear on the Web every month. The content and accuracy of these sites vary widely, as does the creativity of the person responsible for the resource.

So how do you find the sites that you need to conduct your research? One way is to consult a comprehensive list of links. A comprehensive list of links is a site that indexes genealogical links in some sort of categorized scheme. Some sites list links alphabetically, some list them by type of Internet resource, and others list them by subject.

The Genealogy SiteFinder section of the Genealogy.com site is an example of a comprehensive list of links. It's one that we're quite partial to because we maintain it. It's the second oldest and largest comprehensive list of genealogical links on the Internet, and it's organized by subject and includes abstracts stating the resources that are available at each site. Before getting too deep into the mechanics of the Genealogy SiteFinder, we describe what types of information that it classifies. That way you know what you're looking at.

Types of Internet resources

You can classify most of the genealogy resources available on the Internet into these categories:

- ✔ **Personal Web pages:** Personal Web pages are probably the largest group of resources available on the Internet. They can range from a list of the surnames that an individual is researching to full-blown family histories complete with online genealogy databases.

- ✔ **One-name studies and surname mailing lists:** One-name studies are groups that research any person who lived at any time with a given surname. They tend to have an international scope and welcome anyone who is researching the surname. Surname mailing lists are where groups of people join together to share information on individuals that have a common surname (including any variations of the surname).

- ✔ **Family groups and associations:** Many formal and informal family groups and associations have placed information about their organizations and genealogical data online. These groups usually focus on the descendants of a particular ancestor.

- ✔ **Geographically focused Web sites and mailing lists:** Many genealogists have posted Web resources for the places in which they live or research interests. Societies have also placed information online for their communities. Mailing lists have been established so that researchers can discuss resources that are available in particular geographic areas.

- ✔ **Transcribed records sites:** These sites are usually created and maintained by volunteers who transcribe the contents of a particular set of records, such as census records and passenger lists. Some commercial entities also have transcribed records and then placed them into online databases.

- ✔ **Sites containing digitized original records:** These sites contain scanned images of original records. Not enough of these sites exist, but more are coming online every day. These sites are established by government agencies and commercial entities.

- ✔ **Subscription-based sites:** You must pay a fee to access the genealogical data at these sites. Some sites charge a monthly, a quarterly, or an annual fee, whereas others charge on a per-view basis.

- ✔ **Supplies and services sites:** These sites sell all kinds of research aids and offer research assistance for a fee.

- ✔ **Other sites:** Of course, many other types of sites contain information that may be useful to genealogists, such as historical sites, map collections, and educational sites.

Structure of the Genealogy SiteFinder

The Genealogy SiteFinder is broken down into categories, with subcategories below them — similar to the structure of Yahoo! The major categories include

- ✔ Computers
- ✔ How-To and Help
- ✔ Media
- ✔ People
- ✔ Places/Geographic
- ✔ Supplies and Services

Searching the Genealogy SiteFinder

The problem with many links sites is that you have to think like the people who categorized the links. What happens if you don't think like they do? One unique thing that sets the Genealogy SiteFinder apart from other link sites is its search engine. You don't have to think like us in order to find the links that you need. Instead, you can conduct a search of the links and their abstracts to find the links that you're looking for — saving you time and aggravation.

Here is how to use the Genealogy SiteFinder:

1. **Use your browser to go to the Genealogy SiteFinder home page at** `www.genealogy.com/links/index.html`.

   On the right side of the screen is a yellow column containing a field labeled `Search Genealogy SiteFinder for the word(s)`.

2. **In the search field, type in the words that you're looking for and click the Search button.**

   The site displays a page with three columns. The first column contains the number of the result, the second column contains the link to the page where your search criteria is, and the third column shows you the likelihood that the page meets your search criteria and the size of the document.

3. **Click a link that looks interesting.**

   Underneath the link are several lines that show the context of the first appearance of your search criteria on the page. If you need more information to determine whether the page is useful, click the <u>Show Hits</u> link in the third column. This link takes you to another page that shows you the specific instances of your search criteria on the page.

If you don't find a link to the family you're researching, don't panic. That doesn't mean that no information on that family exists. It may simply mean that we haven't categorized the site yet. Plus, with the rapid expansion in genealogy sites, even if a site doesn't exist today, it may exist tomorrow.

Taking a Look at GenealogyLibrary.com

Another resource that we want to highlight is GenealogyLibrary.com. Genealogylibrary.com is a subscription-based service that is a companion site to FamilyTreeMaker.com and Genealogy.com. The site has over 1,900 online databases and over 200,000 census images from the 1850 Federal Census.

Materials on the GenealogyLibrary.com site include

- Bible collections
- Birth records
- Census records
- Court records
- Marriage records
- Tax records
- Family histories
- Local histories
- Obituaries

You can subscribe to the site on a monthly or quarterly basis. We suggest that you try it for a month first and see if it meets your expectations. If it doesn't, then you can always cancel it, and you're only out one-month's fee.

Putting All Your Eggs in One Basket

We know that most of you have heard the expression "don't put all your eggs in one basket." But, for the purposes of this chapter, we want you to ignore that advice. Yes, we're going against years of tradition — but as a genealogist, you really need to have all of your research information at your fingertips.

What we're suggesting is that you put references in your Family File (in Family Tree Maker) to all the information that you find on the FamilyTreeMaker.com site or Genealogy.com site. That way, you don't have to sift through a stack of printouts to find that one detail you discovered on the Web.

You can reference or cite the Family Tree Maker resources in a couple of different ways:

- ✔ You can use the Research Journal in Family Tree Maker to keep track of where you find various pieces of information. That way the next time you need to see the information again, you can go straight to it rather than have to search for that napkin you wrote down the Web address on (for more on using the Research Journal, see Chapter 7).

- ✔ You can use the Notes feature to record what you see on the site as well as record the maintainer's contact information. This way you don't lose the information if the site is taken down (which happens more often than you think).

- ✔ If you prefer to keep your notes in a word processor or in a spreadsheet that tracks your research progress, make sure that you attach your notes to the individual's Scrapbook page in your Family File. Then the next time you research that person, you can easily find your notes.

- ✔ And, of course, you can always use the Source-Citation functionality of Family Tree Maker to cite where you found information on the Family Tree Maker site (Ctrl+S).

  Even if you like to keep all your research information in electronic documents, it's a good idea to incorporate them into the Family File structure. That way you don't have to open five or six different word processing files to figure out which one contains the last reference to Aunt Betty.

The only caution with putting all your eggs in one basket is the chance that your Family File could become corrupted or deleted. To prevent the mental breakdown that this would cause, make sure that you routinely back up your Family File to a diskette, a Zip disk, a CD-ROM, or another method of storage.

Part III
Share and Share Alike

The 5th Wave — By Rich Tennant

"That's a lovely family tree. Now just remove Donald Trump, Cindy Crawford and Arnold Schwarzenegger."

In this part . . .

One of the cornerstones of genealogy is sharing what you discover with your family and fellow researchers. Family Tree Maker can help you share your information several different ways. This part covers how to generate and customize family trees and reports, as well as how to put them all together to form a family history book. Finally, you find out how to export your information from Family Tree Maker to share with other researchers.

Chapter 9

Trees, Trees Everywhere

● ●

In This Chapter

▶ Creating typical Ancestor and Descendant trees

▶ Working with unusual family trees

▶ Printing family trees

▶ Using family trees in other Windows programs

● ●

You don't have to be a tree lover to know that many different kinds of trees exist. Some are tall and sleek, and others branch out over a wide area. Some are well kept and pruned, and others grow out of control. The same is true with family trees. Some family trees are very detailed, whereas others contain only a little information. Either way, one of the most important things that you can do with genealogical software is to produce a graphical representation of your family tree.

As with actual trees, family tree reports in Family Tree Maker can take on many different shapes and sizes. In this chapter, we take a look at the different kinds of trees that the program produces, as well as tell you how to customize the look of the tree and the information that is presented in it.

Which Tree Should I Plant?

Before we discuss how to construct family trees, we want to go over the different types of family trees that are available in Family Tree Maker and some of their popular uses. Because the program offers five different trees — some of which have variations — we constructed handy-dandy Table 9-1, which has all the details. At first, the formats in the table may seem a bit foreign to you, but please keep reading. We go into each format in detail in the next section.

Table 9-1		Common Varieties of Family Trees	
Type	*Formats*	*Contents*	*Uses*
Ancestor	Fan, Standard, Vertical	Ancestors	Quick reference for research trips, illustrations in books
Descendant	Fan, Standard	Descendants	Quick reference for research trips, illustrations in books
Outline Descendant	None	Descendants	Text representation of a Descendant tree, compact reference for research trips
Hourglass	Fan, Standard	Ancestors, descendants	Birthday parties, anniversaries
All-in-One	None	Ancestors, descendants, unrelated individuals	Big picture of your research, good for locat ing incorrectly linked people and orphan trees

Climbing Your Ancestor Trees

What do you think of when you hear the term *family tree* or *genealogical report?* Most people think of a pedigree chart, or what Family Tree Maker calls an Ancestor tree. This familiar chart begins with a box for an individual that has two lines that connect to the individual's parents and so forth.

Ancestor trees show only the direct ancestors of an individual. That is, they show only parents, grandparents, great-grandparents, and so forth — you know, what would typically be called the bloodline. So, if you're looking for your wily siblings, cousins, aunts, uncles, nieces, or nephews — you won't find them in an Ancestor tree.

Varieties of Ancestor trees

Family Tree Maker can display Ancestor trees three ways, in Fan, Standard, and Vertical formats.

Fan format

The Fan Ancestor tree, shown in Figure 9-1, displays your direct ancestors in a circular shape — kind of like, well, a fan. Each subsequent ancestor is placed farther out from the center of the circle until all the ancestors are shown. The Fan format is particularly good if you want to show several generations and have limited room. It's also a nice alternative if you're just plain tired of looking at square pedigree charts.

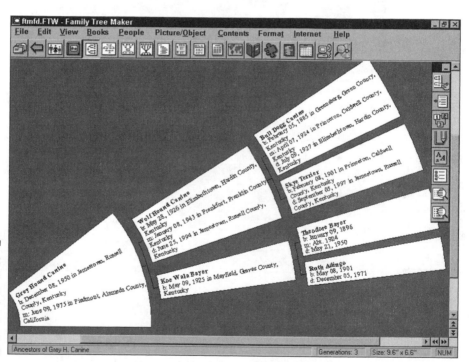

Figure 9-1:
An example
of an
Ancestor
tree in the
Fan format.

Standard format

A classic among family trees is the Standard Ancestor tree, shown in Figure 9-2. This report contains the typical rectangular boxes that are connected with branches. Each new set of ancestors is placed to the right of that couple's child (whether that child is you, one of your parents, one of your grandparents — you get the picture). The Standard tree offers a rather orderly appearance, for those of you that like to have things just so.

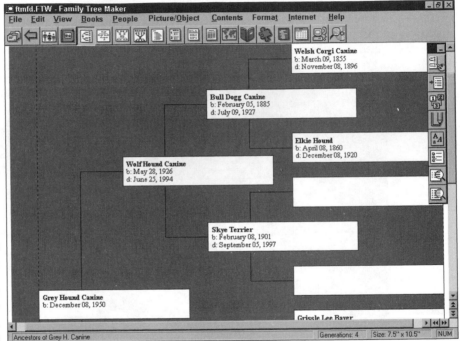

Figure 9-2:
The classic Standard Ancestor tree.

Vertical format

A variation on the Standard format is the Vertical Ancestor tree, shown in Figure 9-3. Each subsequent ancestor sort of floats above the preceding ancestor (that is, branches off from the top of the individual's box). Now that's an accurate depiction of the weight (or stress) that all these ancestors place on one person.

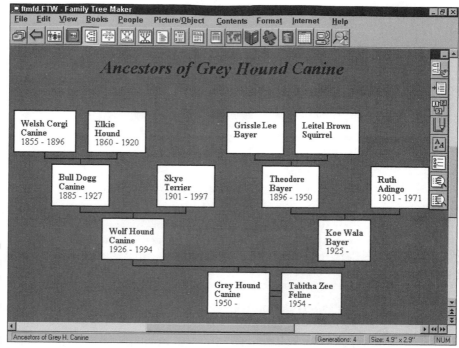

Figure 9-3:
The weighty
Vertical
Ancestor
tree.

Growing an Ancestor tree

We can't help you grow your family tree, but we can show you how to generate an Ancestor tree with Family Tree Maker. Follow these same basic steps to create all types of Ancestor trees:

1. **Open the Family Page of the person who is the focus of the Ancestor tree and click in the field where his or her name appears.**

   You can open the Family Page by clicking the tabs on the right side of the screen or by choosing the View⇨Index of Individuals. (For details on selecting a person from the Index of Individuals, see Chapter 3.)

   We decided to create a Fan Ancestor tree for our pal Grey Canine (we think it's rather appropriate to do a pedigree for him). Feel free to select someone who's already in your database. To select Grey, we open his Family Page and then click in the field where his name appears.

2. **Choose View⇨Ancestor Tree.**

   Or click the Ancestor Tree button. If you're looking at the default tool-bar, the Ancestor Tree button is the sixth button from the left (the white button with a blue chart on it). If you're using Version 7.0, it's the 5th button from the left and the 15th from the right.

   A pull-down menu appears, from which you can select the type of format for the chart.

3. **Choose a format for your tree.**

   Your choices are Fan, Standard, and Vertical. (To review what these for-mats look like, see the previous section, "Varieties of Ancestor Trees.") We select the Fan format for good ol' Grey's tree.

   After you choose a format, Family Tree Maker generates the report and displays it on-screen. A Cue Card for Ancestor Tree may pop up, offering help with the various customizing features. If you don't want the Cue Card to pop up every time you open an Ancestor tree, select the option labeled Click here if you don't want to see this Help Window again and then click OK.

4. **(Optional) Customize your Ancestor tree by using the series of eight buttons that appears on the side toolbar, as shown in Figure 9-4.**

   If you don't like the way that the tree looks or you just want to see more options, you can customize your Ancestor tree.

   You can customize your chart two other ways. The first way is to choose a feature to customize from the Format menu. A second, much faster way is to *right-click* on the chart (click the right mouse button while your cursor is on the tree screen) and choose a feature to customize from the menu that appears.

Figure 9-4:
Customize
your charts
with the
side toolbar.

5. **Verify that the chart includes the information that you wanted.**

   Sometimes the print inside the boxes on your screen is almost too small to read. A simple solution is to use the Zoom In and Zoom Out buttons located on the side toolbar. They're the last two buttons — see them? They're the ones with the clever magnifying glass icons.

6. **Print your completed report by choosing File⇨Print Ancestor Tree.**

   As a shortcut, you can also press Ctrl+P to execute the print command. (Of course, we're assuming that you have a printer hooked up to your computer. If you don't, then no matter how many keys you press, you won't be able to print your report.)

7. **If you want to change the focus of your tree to another individual listed on the chart, just double-click his or her box.**

   Family Tree Maker then transports you to that person's Family Page. At that point, repeat these steps from the beginning.

Crafting Ancestor trees

If you're a picky or artistic person who likes things to be different, you may not be crazy about the basic look of your Ancestor tree in Family Tree Maker. But don't fret! You don't have to settle for the status quo. Family Tree Maker enables you to customize the contents and format of your trees. But there's one little catch: The various elements that you can customize depend on the format of the tree you're working with. Some features apply to all Ancestor trees, regardless of format — we list them in the next section, "All trees." And under the appropriate format title, we list items that are specific to a particular tree format.

All trees

You can customize the following items on all three Ancestor tree formats (after you display the tree, that is):

- **Items to include in family tree.** You can include a variety of items in your family tree by clicking the second button on the side toolbar (the button with an arrow pointing at a sheet of paper). After clicking this button, the Items to Include in Ancestor Tree dialog box opens, as shown in Figure 9-5. You can include the items in the left column in your chart. The items on the right are currently contained in the tree. To add an item to your chart, highlight it in the left column and then click the button marked with a right-facing arrow. You can also change the font, set options, and change the order of appearance for each item.

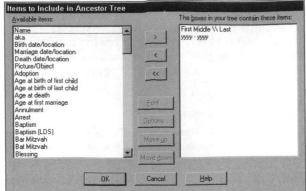

Figure 9-5:
The Items to
Include in
Ancestor
Tree
dialog box.

After you select an item to include, you may encounter an Options dialog box. This box allows you to customize the appearance of the item in the tree. Each item is unique in what you can customize, so you may not have the same options for all items. For example, the options for the Name item include the following:

- Format — you can format the name 13 different ways, such as First Middle Last, Last First Middle, or just plain Last

- Include Mr./Ms.

- Use Married Names for Females

- Use Aka if Available — if you select this, you have the option of using *also known as* in place of the name or inserting it between the middle and last name

- Last Name in All Caps

- Word Wrap

- Include Reference Number with Name

- Include Standard Number with Name

- Include Source — if you include sources, you also have the option to include the source label and include labels for empty source fields

To change the font, select an item in the right column and click the Font button. This action displays the Text Font, Style, & Size for Ancestor Tree dialog box. Here you can set the font face (such as Times New Roman, Courier, or Arial), size, style, color, and alignment by choosing from the appropriate drop-down list. After you're satisfied with the font (a preview of the font appears in the Sample box at the bottom of the dialog box), click OK.

Another item that you can change is the order in which the items appear in the box. To change the order, click an item in the right column and then click the Move Up or Move Down button until the item is where you want it.

✔ **Number of generations to show.** If you click the third button from the top on the side toolbar (the button with the numbers one, two, and three in little boxes), a dialog box appears, in which you can specify how many generations to display in your chart. Just type in the number of generations or use the up and down arrows to increase or decrease the number of generations. Then click OK.

✔ **Styles for Ancestor tree.** You can customize the way the boxes look by clicking the fourth button on the side toolbar (the button with a pencil drawing a line). The Styles for Ancestor Tree dialog box opens. It has three tabs — one for each of these styles:

  • **Boxes:** You can select a different box style for Females, Males, and Unknown Gender. Also, you can specify specific colors for the outline, fill, and shadows of the boxes. Figure 9-6 shows the Boxes tab of the Styles for Ancestor Tree dialog box. It contains the styles of boxes that are available for your family trees.

  • **Borders:** You can choose from several different border styles and even change the border color or the background color (see Figure 9-7).

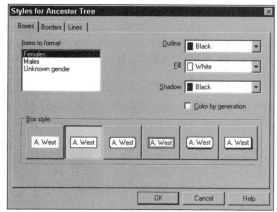

Figure 9-6:
The Boxes tab of the Styles for Ancestor Tree dialog box.

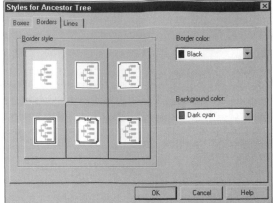

Figure 9-7:
The Borders
tab of the
Styles for
Ancestor
Tree
dialog box.

- **Lines:** This tab, shown in Figure 9-8, allows you to choose from three different line styles (for your branches). You can change the color of the lines, highlight a relationship between two individuals, and show non-natural parent/child relationships with dashed lines.

   One of the features that we like the most is the ability to highlight the relationship between two individuals. This feature is useful when creating trees to submit as proof of descendancy for lineage societies or when you want to show the descent from your original ancestor to yourself on very complex family trees.

You can maneuver among the three panels (layers) by clicking the tabs at the top of the box. Also, some of the options described in the three preceding bullets are not necessarily available for all your Ancestor trees. If a particular style is not available for a specific kind of chart, it is disabled in the dialog box.

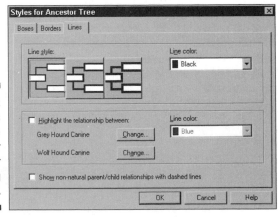

Figure 9-8:
The Lines
tab of the
Styles for
Ancestor
Tree dialog
box.

✔ **Text font, style, and size for Ancestor Tree.** The fifth button on the side toolbar (the button with the several styles of the letter *A*) allows you to change the font face, size, style, and color of the words appearing in the boxes in your report.

Similar to changing the font in your tree boxes, this setting allows you to change not only the contents of your boxes, but also the fonts of the report's title, the footnotes, and the generation labels.

Fan format

These customizable features are specific to the Fan format:

✔ **Format for Ancestor tree.** Clicking the top button on the side toolbar (the button with a finger pointing at two family trees) or choosing Format⇨Tree Format opens the Format for Ancestor Tree dialog box, shown in Figure 9-9. It allows you to set several options for Fan charts:

Figure 9-9:
The Format for Ancestor Tree dialog box for a Fan Ancestor tree.

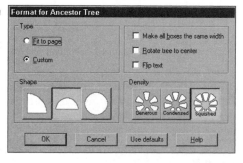

- **Type:** Your choices are either Fit to Page or Custom, which means that you can set the size of the chart to fit on a page or to your specifications.

- **Shape:** You can select one of three shapes for your chart: an arc, a semicircle, or a full circle.

- **Density:** You have three choices for how close together you want the individual boxes to appear on the report. These choices are Generous, Condensed, and Squished.

Generous spacing takes up the most paper. This setting is nice for charts that show just a few individuals. It's also a good idea to use this kind of chart when you're going to a family reunion — that way, relatives can write notes on the chart that you can later input into Family Tree Maker. Condensed spacing works well when you want to take a report with you on a research trip. If you're really pressed for space, then the Squished setting gives you just a little more room on a page.

To give you an example of the size differences among the three types of densities, we created a chart listing ten generations (not all the family lines reached the tenth generation in the tree, so the chart wasn't as large as a full, ten-generation chart). In our test, the Generous spacing option created a chart measuring 53.3 x 25.5 inches. With the Condensed setting, the chart measured 24.7 x 23.8 inches. And the Squished option created a chart measuring 24.5 x 19.2 inches.

Three other options are available in this dialog box. They include making all the boxes the same width, rotating the tree to center, and flipping text. You can select any of these options by clicking in the appropriate check boxes.

✔ **Options for Ancestor tree.** You can access this dialog box by clicking the sixth button on the side toolbar — the one with three check boxes and three lines — or by choosing Contents⇨Options. It offers only one option for Fan charts, which is to include (or not include) duplicate ancestors each time they appear.

Standard format

Here are the features that are specific to the Standard format:

✔ **Tree format for Ancestor tree.** Clicking the top button on the side toolbar (the button with a finger pointing at two family trees) allows you to set several features for standard charts, as shown in Figure 9-10. These features are

- **Type:** The choices are Fit to Page, Custom, or Book Layout.

- **Connections:** You can select one of three ways to connect your boxes to the branch lines: Detached, Overlap, and Fishtail.

   If you're feeling a bit detached from your family, then you may want to use the Detached connection setting. With this setting, your boxes don't touch one another and are connected with a line, sort of like a branch. Perhaps you're a little closer to your family, in which case, you'll want to use the Overlap setting. Here the boxes touch and slightly overlap one another. The final connection type is the Fishtail. Mysteriously enough, the positioning of the boxes takes on the shape of a fish — if you use your imagination. Each box aligns with the corner of the box in front of it.

- **Layout:** You have three choices for how close together you want the individual boxes to be on the report. These choices are Perfect, Collapsed, and Squished.

The Perfect setting creates the largest tree. Everything is evenly spaced, which is why we suppose it's perfect. The Collapsed tree is the middle bed — not too big and not too small. And at the other extreme is the Squished option, which creates the smallest tree. To show you the size difference, we created a ten-generation tree. With Perfect spacing, the tree measured 12.3 x 67.5 inches. The Collapsed tree measured 12.3 x 37.5 inches. And the Squished tree measured 12.3 x 30.3 inches.

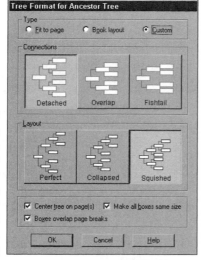

Figure 9-10:
The Tree
Format for
Ancestor
Tree dialog
box for
Standard
trees.

Three other options are available in this dialog box. They include making all the boxes the same size, centering the tree on the page, and allowing boxes to overlap page breaks. You can select any of these options by clicking in the appropriate check boxes.

✔ **Options for Ancestor tree.** You can open this dialog box by clicking the sixth button on the side toolbar — the one with three check boxes and three lines — or by choosing Contents⇨Options. This dialog box offers four options for standard charts: label the columns (such as Parents, Grandparents, and so on), include duplicate ancestors each time they appear, include the siblings of the primary individual, and include empty branches.

Filling in those empty branches

Everyone has some empty branches in their genealogy — unless they've traced their ancestors all the way back to Adam. And sometimes displaying these empty branches is a good thing.

We like to display empty branches when we print out an Ancestor tree. We then give copies of the Ancestor tree to relatives to see if they can fill in any of the gaps.

To set the option to display empty branches, follow these steps:

1. **Go to the Family Page of the person who is the subject of the tree.**

2. **Choose View⇨Ancestor Tree and then select a tree format.**

   Or click the Ancestor Tree button.

   We usually select the Standard tree format because that is what most people are used to seeing, and we don't want people becoming disoriented by the Fan format.

3. **After the Ancestor tree appears, click the Options button on the side toolbar.**

   Or choose Contents⇨Options.

4. **Select the Include Empty Branches option and then click OK.**

5. **Click the Format button on the side toolbar.**

   Or choose Format⇨Tree Format.

6. **Select the Make All Boxes the Same Width option and then click OK.**

   If you don't select this option, you'll have a bunch of small empty boxes that no one can write in.

7. **Click the Items to Include button on the side toolbar.**

   Or choose Contents⇨Items to Include.

8. **Highlight the life event for which you want to include a label in the blank boxes, and click the right-arrow button to copy it from the Available Items list to the list of items to contain.**

   This brings up an Options dialog box, enabling you to determine the format of the information and whether to include certain things. In the Include section, you determine the format for including dates, comments, and locations. The Labels section enables you to use field labels and set the format for those labels. And three options in the lower right of the dialog box enable you to Include Source Information, Display Only Preferred Dates/Locations, or use Word Wrap.

9. **Select the Include Labels of Empty Fields option and then click OK.**

   By default, Family Tree Maker has the labels turned off.

10. **Repeat Steps 8 and 9 for each of the life events (birth, marriage, and death) you want labels for on your Ancestor tree.**

If you just want to create a blank tree for relatives to fill out, display a tree and, when printing, select the Print Empty option. For more on how to print blank trees, see "Getting some output from your input," later in this chapter.

When you first start researching your family history, you may want to enter a few relatives' names in your Family File and then print out a standard Ancestor tree, making sure that you've selected the Display Empty Branches option for each of your relatives. Then the next time you're at a family reunion, pass out the Ancestor trees and have your relatives fill them out.

Vertical format

Here are the features specific to the Vertical format:

> ✔ **Format for Ancestor tree.** Clicking the top button on the side toolbar (the button with a finger pointing at two family trees) allows you to set several features for Vertical charts. These features include
>
> > • **Type:** The choices are Custom or Book Layout.
> >
> > • **Layout:** You have three choices for how close together you want the individual boxes to be on the report: Perfect, Collapsed, and Squished.
>
> Three other options are also available in this dialog box. They include centering the tree on the page, making all the boxes the same size, and allowing boxes to overlap page breaks. You can select any of these options by clicking in the appropriate check boxes.
>
> ✔ **Options for Ancestor tree.** You can access this dialog box by clicking the sixth button on the side toolbar or by choosing Contents⇨Options. You have three options for Vertical charts: label columns (such as Parents, Grandparents, and so on), include duplicate ancestors each time they appear, and include empty branches.

Falling from Descendant Trees

Another type of genealogical report that you're probably familiar with is the Descendant tree. This chart shows all of an individual's descendants (children, grandchildren, great-grandchildren, and so on.), usually laid out in neat little boxes.

Descendant tree types

Two types of Descendant tree reports are available in Family Tree Maker: the Fan format and the Standard format.

Fan format

The Fan Descendant tree, shown in Figure 9-11, displays an individual's descendants in a circular shape. Each subsequent generation is placed farther out from the center of the circle, until all the descendants are shown. The Fan format is a good option when you want to show information on several generations.

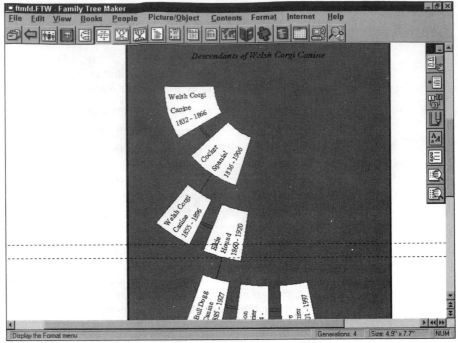

Figure 9-11:
An example
of a
Descendant
tree in the
Fan format.

Standard format

The Standard Descendant tree, shown in Figure 9-12, is probably what you're used to seeing. The subject of the report appears at the top of the screen, and the descendants' names appear in boxes connected with branch lines. As long as you're displaying just a few generations on the report, the Standard format is a nice clean report.

Creating a Descendant tree

Creating a Descendant tree is as simple as creating an Ancestor tree. Simply select the person who will be the focus of the Descendant tree. But instead of clicking the Ancestor Tree button, click the Descendent Tree button (it's the seventh button from the left, the white one with a red chart on it). If you're using Version 7.0, it's the 6th button from the left and the 14th from the right. As always, you can also choose View➪Descendent Tree. From there, you can select the type of format for your report (Standard or Fan, in this case), customize your Descendant tree, verify that the chart includes the information that you intended, and print your completed report by choosing

File⇨Print Descendant Tree. If you want to change the focus of your tree to another individual listed on the tree, just double-click that person's box to open his or her Family Page. At that point, you can start the process all over again.

Customizing Descendant trees

Customizing Descendant trees is a simple process. However, keep in mind that, like Ancestor trees, the things you can customize depend on the format you select. Some features apply to all Descendent trees regardless of format: the items to include, the number of generations to show, the styles for the descendent tree (boxes, borders, and lines), and the text font, style, and size for the Descendent tree. Other features apply to Fan Descendent trees, such as the actual format (type, shape and density) and the option to include (or exclude) duplicate ancestors each time they appear. Still other features apply to Standard Descendant trees, such as the format (type and layout), the option to include duplicate ancestors, and the option to label specific columns with terms such as Parents or Grandparents.

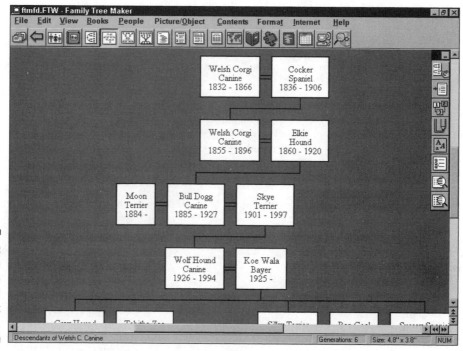

Figure 9-12:
The no-nonsense Standard Descendant tree.

Just an Outline Tree

At some point in your genealogical life, you will have compiled a great deal of information on at least one particular ancestor. You may end up entering data about hundreds of this ancestor's descendants and, at some point, want to print out a simple report of these descendants. (Such a report is particularly handy on research trips.) At that point, space becomes a problem. After all, you probably don't want to carry around 500 sheets of paper and try to assemble a traditional descendant chart that fills two rooms. (We question your sanity if you do want to do these things.) That's where an Outline Descendant tree can help.

An Outline Descendant tree, shown in Figure 9-13, doesn't fit most people's expectations of what a family tree should look like. In fact, it doesn't really look like a family tree at all. The Outline Descendant tree takes information from a normal Descendant tree and displays it in textual rather than graphical form. The report begins with a particular individual and then lists each descendant on a separate line. Each successive generation is indented on the page. If an individual has a spouse, the spouse appears on a separate line. Spouses also appear with a plus sign (+) in front of their names. Only one variety of the Outline Descendant tree exists.

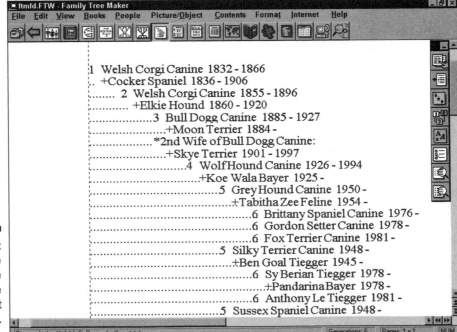

Figure 9-13:
An example
of the
Outline
Descendant
tree.

Creating an Outline Descendant tree

Creating an Outline Descendant tree is as simple as creating any of the other reports. Select the person who will be the focus of the Descendant tree, click the Outline Descendant Tree button (the tenth button from the left or, if you're using Version 7.0, the ninth button from the left — the one showing a piece of paper with indented lines), customize your Outline Descendant tree, verify that the chart includes the information that you intended, and print your completed report by choosing File⇨Print Outline Descendant tree. If you want to change the focus of your tree to another individual that is listed on the report, just double-click that person's name (in the tree) to go to his or her Family Page. At that point, you begin the process all over again.

Customizing Outline Descendant trees

So you don't like the way your Outline Descendant tree looks? We suppose you want some fancy bells and whistles that can change the look. Lucky for you, Family Tree Maker recognizes this fact and provides the necessary tools. Some of them may already be familiar to you. You can customize the items to include, the number of generations to show, as well as the text font, style, and size for the Outline Descendent tree. Given the very "untree"-like format of Outline Descendent trees, some unique customizing features are available to you. Such features are

✔ **Tree format for Outline Descendant tree.** Clicking the top button on the side toolbar (the button with a finger pointing at two family trees) allows you to set several features for Standard charts:

- **Indentation:** You can change the character that marks different generations' indentations. The default is a period (.), although you can use any character on your keyboard (such as #, !, or April's favorite, $). You can also control how much each generation is indented. The default setting is 0.30 inches.

- **Generation numbers:** In the default Outline Descendant tree, a number precedes each generation. This number tells you how far removed the person is from the subject of the report. You can choose to exclude this number, or you can change the generation starting number. The default starting generation number is one.

- **Size and spacing:** Here you can control the maximum height, in rows, for each individual. The default value is two. You can also designate the number of blank lines between individuals. The default is zero. And you can select an option to ensure that the report is always one page wide.

✔ **Individuals to include.** If you click the third button from the top on the side toolbar (the button with a green box containing three little people), you see a dialog box that allows you to specify who should be included in your report. The default setting is all descendants of the person for whom you want the report. However, you can set the report to show only the direct descendants between two individuals. You can also include siblings of direct descendants (should you select the Show Only Direct Descendants option).

✔ **Options for Outline Descendant tree.** To open this dialog box, click the sixth button on the side toolbar or choose Contents⇨Options. You have three options for Outline Descendant charts: Print Spouses, Include Duplicate Descendants Each Time They Appear, and Mark Individuals with Multiple Spouses.

Like Sands through the Hourglass (Hourglass Trees, That Is)

In the preceding sections of this chapter, we look at some family trees that display ancestors and others that display descendants. But that's not good enough, is it? You say you want to see both the ancestors and descendants of a particular person on one report? Just a little bit demanding, but if this is the case, Hourglass trees are your ticket.

We find that Hourglass trees are very useful for things such as birthday parties for relatives' celebrating milestones (such as 80th, 90th, 95th, or 100th birthdays). You can select the birthday boy or girl as the subject of the report and display his or her ancestors and descendants. Believe us, many of your relatives will be interested in your Hourglass tree (and that single contribution may get you out of clean-up duty).

Hourglass tree varieties

Two types of Hourglass tree reports are available in Family Tree Maker: the Fan format and Standard format.

Fan format

The Fan Hourglass tree (see Figure 9-14) shows an individual's ancestors and descendants in a circular shape. In the default report, the subject of the report appears in a circle in the middle. The ancestors branch out toward the top of the report, and the descendants branch out toward the bottom of the report.

Standard format

The Standard Hourglass tree, shown in Figure 9-15, is a combination of the Vertical Ancestor tree and the Standard Descendant tree (for more information on these types of family trees, see "Climbing Your Ancestor Trees" and "Falling from Descendant Trees," earlier in this chapter). The subject of the report appears in the middle box, with ancestors branching toward the top of the report and descendants toward the bottom.

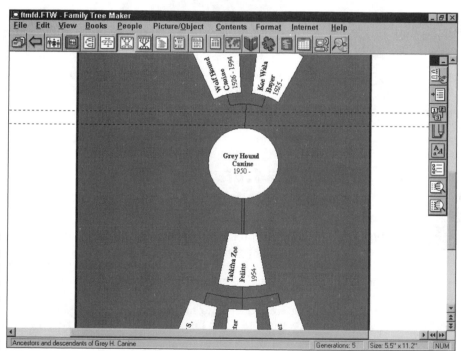

Figure 9-14: An example of the Hourglass tree in the Fan format.

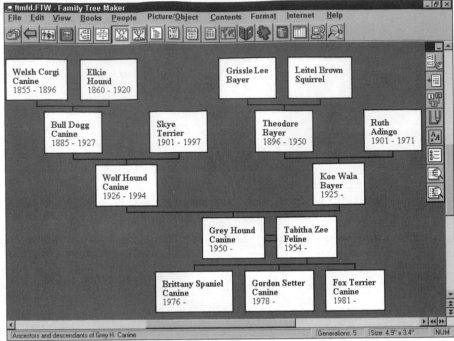

Figure 9-15:
The
Standard
Hourglass
tree.

Crafting an Hourglass tree

To create an Hourglass tree, select the person who is the focus of the Hourglass tree, click the Hourglass Tree button (the eighth button from the left or the seventh button from the left if you're using Version 7.0 — the one with a blue and red chart forming an hourglass shape), select the type of format for your report (Fan or Standard), customize your Hourglass tree, verify that the chart includes the information that you intended, and print your completed report by choosing File⇨Print Tree. If you want to change the focus of your tree to another individual that is listed on the tree, double-click that person's box to go to his or her Family Page. At that point, begin the process all over again.

Customizing Hourglass trees

Once more, with feeling! As you may have guessed, you can customize the old standbys on all of your Hourglass trees: items to include, the number of generations to show, the styles for your Hourglass tree (boxes, borders, and lines), as well as the text font, style, and size. For a Fan Hourglass tree, you can also customize the tree format (type, shape, density) and include duplicate ancestors when they appear. For a Standard Hourglass tree, you can customize the format (type and layout), choose to include duplicate ancestors, label columns, and include empty branches of the Ancestor tree.

Grouping Families Together

At some point in your career as the family historian, you will need to print some sort of document that identifies every person in your lineage (related or not, but entered in your database). How are you going to do that? Family Tree Maker to the rescue! If you really need the big picture (and we do mean *big* picture if you have a lot of people in your database), then the All-in-One tree is for you.

The All-in-One tree, shown in Figure 9-16, displays everyone from your Family File in one big family tree. It includes *everyone* unless you tell it not to — even individuals who are included in your database but are not related to you by blood, such as stepparents, stepchildren, life partners, and multiple parents (biological and adoptive). The default setting for Family Tree Maker is to include individuals who are not related or somehow tied to your family. However, you can change the settings so that these people are not included.

Try it, you might like it

The absolutely best way to figure out the ins and outs of the different family tree reports is to play with them. Don't be afraid to make changes to the default settings and to experiment with different chart looks. If you get nervous about messing with the default settings, then write them down before you make any changes. Also be aware that some dialog boxes have a button that resets the features to the default settings should your changes go awry.

Keep in mind that each family tree you create may look better with some additional formatting. So don't always try to use the same formatting (unless you're really attached to it) for large trees and small trees. Just like with real trees, the amount of foliage is often your guide to how to prune it.

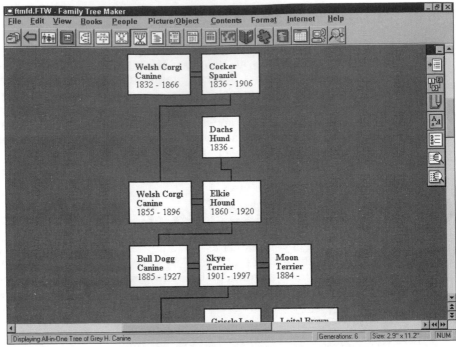

Figure 9-16:
Everybody
and their
dog is in the
All-in-One
tree.

One of the most useful things about this report is that it allows you to look at your research as a whole. You can use the tree to spot obvious problems with your research — such as children that are connected to the wrong parents. Also, it's handy for finding orphan trees — families that you've found information on but haven't connected to a specific member of your family.

Producing an All-in-One tree

You may know this routine. Select the person who is the focus of the All-in-One tree, click the All-in-One Tree button (the ninth button [eighth if you're using Version 7.0] from the left, the one showing a piece of paper with indented lines), customize your All-in-One tree, verify that the chart includes the information that you intended, and print your completed report by choosing File⇨Print All-in-One Tree. If you want to change the focus of your tree to another individual listed on the tree, double-click that person's box to open his or her Family Page. At that point, start the process again.

Customizing All-in-One trees

You're not crazy about the All-in-One tree's appearance? Then change it. As we explain earlier, you can customize the items to include, the number of generations to show, the styles for an All-in-One tree (boxes, borders, lines), as well as the text font, style, and size. You can also choose from a smorgasbord of other options. For example, you can choose to show unconnected step-family trees, show unrelated trees (including solitary unlinked boxes for people with no parents or children), display siblings in the order shown on the Family Page, or use a thicker line to set the primary individual's box apart from all the others.

Printing Your Family Trees

After Aunt Edna finds out that you've put together some good information on the family's history, she will undoubtedly want copies of some family trees. Unfortunately, she doesn't have a computer — and wouldn't even think of touching one, let alone buying one. So, you have to print out some family trees to avoid the wrath of the family.

Warming up to print

Printing a family tree is pretty straightforward, although you can customize some settings. For the most part, Family Tree Maker uses the Windows printer settings by default. If you want to change some settings for a particular tree, then you can adjust the printer setup options from within Family Tree Maker.

Keep in mind that if you adjust the print settings through Family Tree Maker, you change the setting for only a particular tree. If you create another tree, the print settings revert to the Windows settings (unless you previously changed the settings for that tree).

To change the print settings in Family Tree Maker, follow these steps:

1. **Create the tree you want to print in Family Tree Maker.**

   Before you can change any settings, you need to display the tree for which you plan to change the settings. Remember, you're only changing the settings for the tree that you're currently viewing.

   We decided that we wanted to change the print settings for the Ancestor tree. So, we generated the Ancestor tree for Grey Canine.

2. **Choose File⇨Print Setup.**

   The Print Setup for Ancestor Tree dialog box appears, as shown in Figure 9-17. Just in case you didn't already know it, the dialog box reminds you that the setup information applies only to the Ancestor tree. Okay, we think we've driven that point home.

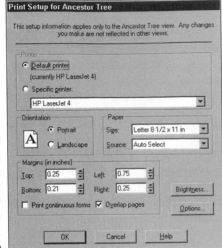

Figure 9-17:
The Print Setup for Ancestor Tree dialog box.

3. **Change any print settings that you want.**

   You can change a few different things from within this dialog box:

   • **Printer:** This option allows you to select the default printer or another printer from the drop-down list (assuming you have another printer and it is installed through Windows).

   • **Orientation:** Here you can select your paper orientation: portrait or landscape.

   • **Paper:** This option enables you to select the paper size (such as, 8.5 x 11 and 8.5 x 14) from this list, as well as define the source of the paper (Auto Select, Upper Tray).

   • **Margins:** You can adjust the top, bottom, left, and right margins by entering your desired margin (in inches) or by using the up and down arrows to increase or decrease the margins. You can also choose to print continuous forms (if your computer uses continuously fed paper) or overlap pages (if you want information at the margin of one page to be repeated on the next page) by clicking in the appropriate check boxes.

- **Brightness:** The Brightness button leads you to another dialog box that allows you to control the color brightness of all the pictures and objects on the tree.

- **Options:** This button leads you to a dialog box that allows you to configure more settings for the selected printer. You can configure resolution, dithering, intensity, graphics mode, fonts, and device options. These options are similar to some of the Windows printer settings. For more on these options, see the documentation that came with your Windows operating system or your printer manual.

4. **After you're satisfied with the settings, click OK.**

For the most part, you probably won't have to mess around with many printer settings, other than to fine-tune a chart here or there. But knowing how to do so may help you later.

Getting some output from your input

If you're familiar with Windows, you probably think that printing in Family Tree Maker is a no-brainer. Well, it pretty much is. But we want to take a minute to discuss a few printing options.

Say that you've displayed and customized an Ancestor tree and you're ready to print it. You can choose File⇨Print Ancestor Tree or press Ctrl+P. Either action opens the Print Ancestor Tree dialog box, shown in Figure 9-18. From this dialog box, you can specify the following settings:

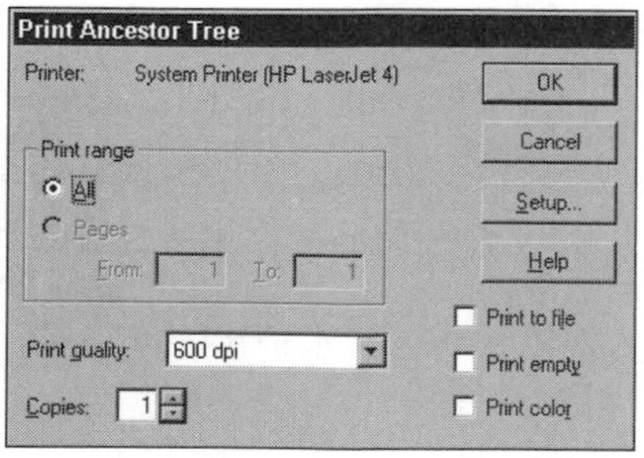

Figure 9-18: The Print Ancestor Tree dialog box.

- **Print Range:** You can specify whether you want to print all the pages of the tree or just a certain page range.

- **Print Quality:** Changing the print quality to a lower setting can save you ink when you're printing a large chart in draft form. Print quality depends on the number of dots per square inch that your printer can print. Refer to your printer documentation for more details on print quality.

✔ **Copies:** You can adjust the number of copies that you want to print. The default setting is one.

✔ **Setup:** The Setup button takes you to the Print Setup for Ancestor Tree dialog box (refer to Figure 9-17).

✔ **Print to File:** This option enables you to save the tree so that you can print it at a later date, which is handy if you have a large chart that you want to take to a printer or copy store to print on a plotter. Because the copy store probably doesn't have Family Tree Maker, printing to a file saves you the trouble of having to install Family Tree Maker on one of its computers. If you select this option, you're prompted with a dialog box when you print, requesting the name of the output file.

If you intend to use another printer to print the file, you must change the settings in the printer setup dialog box to match the destination printer.

✔ **Print Empty:** This feature allows you to print a blank tree. It's handy if you're going to visit relatives or going on a research trip without your computer and want to fill in some information on a tree.

✔ **Print Color:** This option allows you to print your tree in color (if you have a color printer, that is). If you don't have a color printer and you select this option, your tree will be printed in grayscale colors.

After you're satisfied with the print options, click the OK button. If your printer is connected and turned on, your tree should begin to emerge.

Planting Seeds of Your Trees: Using Family Trees in Other Programs

Wouldn't it be great if you could save your Family Tree Maker trees in your favorite word processor? That way, when you wanted to send the tree to family members who don't have Family Tree Maker, you wouldn't have to print it out and mail it to them. All you would have to do is send them the word processor file. Well, if this is your desire, then you'll be happy to know that Family Tree Maker can grant your wish.

To save a copy of a Family Tree Maker tree in another Windows program, you simply cut and paste the tree into the target program.

Say that you want to create a three-generation Ancestor tree and paste it into a Microsoft Word document (the word processor doesn't have to be Word — it can be any Windows word processor, spreadsheet, or database program, or whatever). Follow these steps to save the tree in another program:

1. **Create the Ancestor tree in Family Tree Maker.**

   Select the individual that you want to be the subject of the report and then click the Ancestor Tree button or choose View⇨Ancestor Tree. Then select the format type for the tree — Fan, Standard, Vertical.

   We want to create an Ancestor tree for Grey Canine. So, we select him and choose to create a Standard Ancestor tree.

2. **Customize the Ancestor tree for the right look.**

   You can customize the Ancestor tree by using the buttons on the side toolbar or by using the features in the Format and Contents menus.

3. **Choose Edit⇨Copy to create a copy of the Ancestor tree.**

   Or you can press Ctrl+C.

4. **Open the Windows program in which you want to paste the Ancestor tree.**

   If you already have the other program open, you can press Alt+Tab to switch to the other application, or you can click the appropriate program icon on your Windows taskbar.

   We open Microsoft Word and create a new document.

5. **After you're in the other program, paste the Ancestor tree into your document.**

   You can do this by using the Edit menu of your Windows program or by pressing Ctrl+V.

   We press Ctrl+V and insert the tree into the Word document.

   After you get the tree into your other Windows program, you may be able to work with it in other ways. Some programs may paste it as an uneditable picture, whereas other programs may allow you to use the Paste Special command in order to create an editable object. See the documentation that came with your Windows program for more information on its capabilities.

6. **Don't forget to save the document in your other Windows program.**

   Saving the document in your other Windows program doesn't affect the contents of your Family Tree Maker Family File. Keep in mind that this tree is simply a copy of your Family Tree Maker tree — so, feel free to experiment with it in your other Windows program.

The ability to copy your Family Tree Maker trees to other Windows programs opens up lots of possibilities, especially if you decide to publish your own family history book or share your information with others who don't have genealogical programs.

Chapter 10

News, Get Your News Here

*P*icture yourself as the publisher of a large newspaper (you can even imagine yourself with the patented vest and cigar, if you like). Every day, several reporters gather information in the community that they later assemble into articles. Just before the printing deadline, the editors put these articles together to form a complete newspaper. This collection of articles gives you — and your readers — a picture of what's going on in the world (okay, how good a picture they give is debatable — but the example serves its purpose).

The reports in Family Tree Maker serve a similar function to the reporters' articles. You (the publisher) ask Family Tree Maker (an editor) to come up with information about the contents of your database (the information gathered by reporters). Family Tree Maker generates reports based on the type of information that you request. You can then print out these separate reports and use them to assemble a picture of the status of your genealogical research.

This chapter looks at the many different reports that are available in Family Tree Maker, as well as details how to create them and customize them to suit your needs.

The Old Standards of Genealogy (Reports, That Is)

Once upon a time, the field of genealogy was very disorganized. When people wrote books about their family histories, they came up with their own ways of organizing and presenting the information. After a while, it was difficult to quickly skim through a book to see if it dealt with your ancestors. Sometimes just figuring out how the author organized the book would take hours. Around 1870, the editor of the *New England Historical and Genealogical Register* decided that he couldn't stand the chaos any longer. So he devised a system called the Register form — a common way for genealogists to structure their information — which was the first standard genealogy report.

Genealogy reports are different than family trees in that they contain much more detailed information on families and present it in a lot less space. If you're ever interested in publishing your genealogy, genealogy reports are something that you definitely want to look at. Family Tree Maker comes with three standard genealogy reports:

- Register
- NGS Quarterly (by the way, NGS stands for National Genealogical Society)
- Ahnentafel

Table 10-1 helps you keep the different standard reports straight.

Table 10-1	Types of Genealogy Reports	
Type	**Focus**	**Quirks**
Register	Descendants	Does not provide a number for individuals who do not have descendants. Those without descendants are excluded from the remainder of the report.
NGS Quarterly	Descendants	Assigns numbers for all individuals regardless of whether they have descendants. Those without descendants are excluded in the remainder of the report.
Ahnentafel	Ancestors	Uses mathematical relationships to assign numbers to individuals.

Registering your genealogy

If you didn't fall asleep during our introduction to standard genealogy reports, you know that the Register genealogy report gets its name from the *New England Historical and Genealogical Register*. The Register format report is a descendant-ordered report, which means that the report usually begins with the original ancestor (sometimes referred to as the *progenitor*) at the top and then works its way through the generations of descendants. In the case of the Family Tree Maker Register report, the report begins with the individual who is the subject of the Family Page and then lists that person's descendants, one generation at a time.

The goal of the Register report is to display your genealogical information in terms of a family unit, generation after generation. What does that mean? We can show you better with an example. Take a look at the report for Wolf Hound Canine (remember that's pronounced kah-neen) in Figure 10-1.

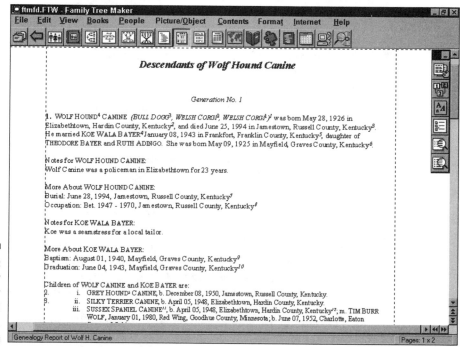

Figure 10-1:
Register
report for
Wolf Hound
Canine.

As you can see from the report, Wolf is a member of generation number one because the report begins with him. Each entry in the report can be divided into several parts, which are as follows:

- ✔ **Descent from original ancestor.** Notice the group of names listed in parentheses next to Wolf's name. They look something like BULL DOGG³, WELSH CORGI², WELSH CORGI¹. This is a quick view of the direct line of Wolf's male ancestors. A superscript appears after each line, showing which generation the individual belongs to. In this case, Welsh Corgi Canine is the original ancestor because he is designated with the superscript one.

  Of course, you're probably thinking that superscripts usually indicate footnotes or endnotes — that's common sense. Unfortunately genealogy reports depart from common sense and use superscripts to designate generations, as well as footnotes. So, you have to pay close attention to the style of the superscript to determine if it's a generation designation or a footnote/endnote marker. In Family Tree Maker reports, if the superscript is not italicized, it's a generation designator. If it is italicized, it's a footnote/endnote marker (such as the superscript that appears after the word *Kentucky* in the second line of Wolf's entry). The descent from the original ancestor is useful to see in reports that contain many individuals — especially individuals that have the same first name. It helps you keep track of who descended from which family line.

- ✔ **Vital information.** Immediately following the descent is the vital record information, such as the individual's dates and locations of birth, marriage, and death.

- ✔ **Spouse information.** Following the vital information are details on the individual's spouse. This information includes the spouse's date and place of birth and death.

- ✔ **Notes.** If you entered any notes in the Notes section of Family Tree Maker, they appear just under the spouse information.

- ✔ **Children.** The final part of the entry contains information on the children of the individual (if any). Notice the two sets of numerals in that part. In front of Grey Canine's name is an Arabic numeral *two* and a lowercase Roman numeral *i*. The first numeral is Grey's Register number, which is the paragraph number where you can find additional information on Grey's family in the report. The second numeral is Grey's birth order number. He was Wolf and Koe's oldest child, therefore he gets the coveted number one.

  Also, notice that poor Sussex Canine doesn't have an Arabic numeral. This is because Sussex did not have any children. In a Register report, any child who doesn't have descendants is not included in the subsequent generation of the report (we know that's not fair, but we didn't make the rules). So, all of Sussex's information is contained in the children section of his parent's entry.

Enough with the talk — follow these steps to produce a Register report:

1. **Select the person who is the focus of the Register report.**

   To select the individual, you need to go to his or her Family Page. You can get to the Family Page by clicking the tabs on the right side of the screen or by choosing View⇨Index of Individuals. (For information on selecting a person from the Index of Individuals, see Chapter 3.)

2. **Choose View⇨Genealogy Report.**

   Or click the Genealogy Report button. If you're looking at the default toolbar, the Genealogy Report button is the 11th button (or 10th if you use Version 7.0) from the left (the one with the blue piece of paper that has the numerals one and two on it). After you click this button, Family Tree Maker creates a Register report.

   A Cue Card for Genealogy Report may pop up, offering help with the various customizing features. If you don't want the Cue Card to pop up every time you customize a report, select the option labeled Click here if you don't want to see this Help Window again. Then click OK to continue.

3. **Customize your Register report.**

   If you don't like the way that the report looks or you want to see more options, you can customize your Register report by using the series of buttons that appear on the side toolbar shown in Figure 10-2.

   You can also customize your chart two other ways. The first way is to select a feature to customize from the Format menu. A second, much faster way is to right-click on the chart (click the right mouse button while your cursor is on the tree screen) and select a feature to customize.

   If you want to create another type of genealogy report, just click the top button on the side toolbar and select one of the other two types. You can also create another report type by choosing Format⇨Genealogy Report Format.

4. **Verify that the chart includes the information that you intended.**

   If you have trouble reading the Register report, feel free to use the Zoom In and Zoom Out buttons located on the side toolbar — they are the last two buttons. See them? They're the ones with the clever magnifying glass icons.

5. **Print your completed report by choosing File⇨Genealogy Report.**

   As a shortcut, you can also just press Ctrl+P to execute the print command. Don't forget to turn on your printer first!

Figure 10-2:
Customize
your charts
with the
side toolbar.

A Quarterly report

Another common type of standard genealogy report is the NGS Quarterly report, shown in Figure 10-3. The *NGS Quarterly* is the journal of the National Genealogical Society and has been in place since 1912. The NGS Quarterly report is similar to the Register report. In fact, it's so similar that the NGS Quarterly report is often called the Modified Register report. The main difference between the reports is that the NGS Quarterly report assigns a number to children who do not have descendants (even though they are not shown in the next generation). Some stylistic differences also exist, such as the type of print for names (small capital letters versus mixed case), but they are minor. Just like the Register report, the focus is on the family unit, and the report is descendant ordered. Also, similar to the Register report, each entry includes the descent from the original ancestor (indicated by superscript), vital information, spouse information, notes, and information on children.

Creating an NGS Quarterly report is as simple as creating a Register report. Just follow these steps:

1. **Select the person who is the focus of the report.**

2. **Click the Genealogy Report button.**

   It's the 11th button from the left (10th from the left if you're using Version 7.0), the blue one that has the piece of paper with the numerals one and two on it.

3. **After the report appears on your screen, click the top button on the side toolbar and select the NGS Quarterly option.**

   You can also choose Format⇨Genealogy Report Format.

4. **Verify that the chart includes the information that you intended.**

5. **Choose File⇨Print Genealogy Report to print your completed report.**

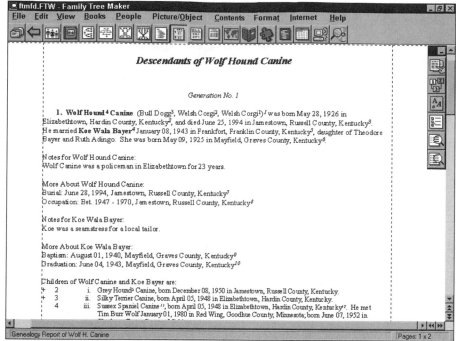

Figure 10-3:
NGS
Quarterly
report for
Wolf Hound
Canine.

An Ahnentafel by any other name. . . .

We think *Ahnentafel* is one of the scariest terms in genealogy. It sounds ominous, doesn't it? You may be thinking that your ancestor would be in trouble if she came down with Ahnentafel, but actually it isn't a disease. It's just another way of presenting genealogical information. Ahnentafel is a German word meaning *tafel of the ahnen* — oops, we mean tables *(tafel)* of the ancestors *(ahnen)*. You may also hear Ahnentafel called the *Sosa-Stradonitz System* because it was first used by a Spanish genealogist named Jerome de Sosa in 1676 and was popularized by Stephan Kekule von Stradonitz in 1896. Anyway, if you like math, you'll definitely like Ahnentafel.

An Ahnentafel report is an ancestor-ordered report that contains a method of numbering that shows a mathematical relationship between parents and children. Because it is ancestor ordered, each successive generation goes backward in time rather than forward (such as with the Register and NGS Quarterly reports). Here is how the Ahnentafel numbering works:

1. An individual is assigned a particular number: y.

2. The father of that individual is assigned the number that is double the child's number: 2y.

3. The mother of that individual is assigned a number that is double the individual's number plus one: $2y + 1$.

4. The father's father is assigned the number that is double the father's number: $2(2y)$.

   The father's mother is assigned the number that is double the father's number plus one: $2(2y) + 1$.

5. The mother's father is assigned a number that is double the mother's number: $2(2y + 1)$.

   The mother's mother is assigned a number that is double the mother's number plus one: $2(2y + 1) + 1$.

6. And so forth through the ancestors.

The mathematical relationship works the same way going forward through the generations — a child's number is one-half of the father's number and one-half (minus any remainder) of the mother's number. In the end, all males are even numbers, and all females are odd numbers — except for the individual who is the subject of the report (he or she is always the number one).

The spouses of the subject individual are assigned numbers as well. However, unlike the ancestors of the subject individual, their numbers are not calculated with a formula depending on the subject individual being assigned number one. Instead, they are simply assigned numbers in parentheses, and their numbers depend on the order of marriage. A first spouse is assigned the number (one). A second spouse would be (two). The third would be (three) — well, you get the picture.

You can more easily understand the Ahnentafel report by taking a look at the example in Figure 10-4. As you can see from the figure, the Ahnentafel report is a little different from the Register and NGS Quarterly reports. It begins with the subject individual (in this case, Wolf Hound Canine) who is number one. This number doesn't mean that Wolf is the progenitor of the Canines — remember this report is ancestor ordered. The report gives the vital information on Wolf, as you would expect, but it also gives information on his parents, Bull Dogg Canine and Skye Terrier.

Notice the numerals in front of each of Wolf's parents' names. These are their Ahnentafel numbers. Because Bull is Wolf's father, he is assigned the number two (because $2 \times 1 = 2$). Skye is Wolf's mother, so she is assigned the number three ($[2 \times 1] + 1 = 3$). An easier way to calculate Skye's number is to simply add one to her husband's number (because the spouse is always one number greater than the husband).

Following the information on Wolf's parents are details on his wife, Koe, and notes for both Wolf and Koe.

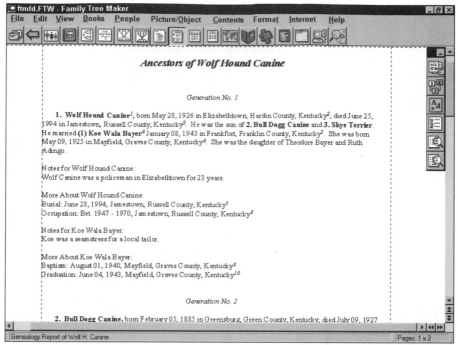

Figure 10-4:
Wolf
Canine's
Ahnentafel.

You can create the Ahnentafel report the same way that you create the Register and NGS Quarterly reports (see the preceding two sections).

Select the person who is the focus of the report and click the Genealogy Report button. (It's the 11th button from the left, the blue one that has a piece of paper with the numbers one and two on it.) After the report appears on your screen, click the top button on the side toolbar and select the Ahnentafel option (or choose Format⇨Genealogy Report Format). You can also use the View menu by choosing View⇨Genealogy Report. From there, you can verify that the chart includes the information that you intended, and print your completed report by choosing File⇨Print Genealogy Report.

Changing the Status Quo of Genealogy Reports

Face it, some people want things to look a certain way, and genealogy reports are no exception. Fortunately, you can customize some aspects of genealogy reports, although not to the same extent that you can customize the family tree charts (see Chapter 9). The following four sections look at the components of reports that you can change.

Genealogy report format

Changing the format of the Genealogy report is the same thing as changing the type of Genealogy report. You can change the format in one of three ways (which also work for any other customization feature):

- Click the top button on the side toolbar (the one with a finger pointing at two sheets of paper).
- Choose Format⇨Genealogy Report Format.
- Right-click on the Genealogy report and select the Genealogy Report Format option from the menu that appears.

After you perform any of the preceding three commands, a Genealogy Report Format dialog box appears on your screen. In this dialog box, you can select one of the Genealogy report formats that we discuss earlier in the chapter (Register, NGS Quarterly, or Ahnentafel).

Also notice that after you select a format, the style of the format appears in the Sample area of the dialog box. You can preview the font to see if it's what you want before executing the report. After you're satisfied with the report choice, just click OK, and the report magically appears.

Number of generations to show

One of these days, you'll want to produce a report showing all the descendants of one of your original ancestors. The problem is that Family Tree Maker's default setting is to show four generations in Genealogy reports. Unless your research hasn't gotten that far, four generations simply won't do. Fortunately, you can change the default setting three ways:

- By clicking the Number of Generations to Show button on the side toolbar (the second button from the top — the one with the numbers one, two, and three in little boxes)
- By choosing Contents⇨# of Generations to Show
- By right-clicking on the report and choosing — you guessed it — # of Generations to Show from the pop-up menu

After you enter the number of generations in the field (or use the up and down arrows to increase or decrease the number), the titles of the individuals who will be reflected in the report appear at the bottom of the dialog box.

Text, font, style, and size

This feature is for you creative types. You can change the font for each item that appears in your Genealogy report. More specifically, you can change the font face, the size, the style, and in some cases, the color and alignment of the font. The number of fonts and styles that are available depends on what fonts you have installed on your machine and whether these fonts come in the bold and italic varieties.

To change a font for an item, follow these steps:

1. **Select the person who is the focus of the report.**

2. **Click the Genealogy Report button.**

   It's the 11th button from the left (10th from the left if you're using Version 7.0), the blue one that has the piece of paper with the numerals one and two on it.

3. **Choose the report format by clicking the Format button at the top of the side toolbar.**

   Your choices are Register, NGS Quarterly, or Ahnentafel.

4. **Click the Text Font & Style button (third on the side toolbar).**

   This opens the Text Font, Style, & Size dialog box, which enables you to determine the text format. It contains a section called Items to Format, and several drop-down lists where you set the font, its size, style, and color.

5. **Select the item you want to change the look of from the Items to Format list.**

   You can change the appearance of the following items: Body, Children Listing, Title, Subtitle, Page Numbers, and End Notes.

6. **Set your preferences for the item by using the drop-down lists on the right side of the dialog box.**

   You can see a preview of the font in the Sample area at the bottom of the dialog box.

7. **After things look good to you, click the OK button.**

Options

The fourth button on the side toolbar (the piece of paper with three check boxes and three lines on it) allows you to specify further options for your report, which are as follows:

✔ **Include Individual Notes:** This option allows you to include or exclude the contents of the Notes section of the Family Page. Depending on the number of notes and their length, you may want to suppress the Notes if you only need quick reference information. For reports that you submit for publication, you may want to include all of your Notes. You can find out more about individual Notes in Chapter 2. The default setting in Family Tree Maker is to include individual Notes.

✔ **Include More About Facts:** You can choose to include (or exclude) the More About Facts. You can access this list of facts by clicking the More button next to a person's name on the Family Page. The list includes things such as baptism, census, burial, and degree dates. (For the low-down on More About Facts, see Chapter 2.) By default, More About Facts are included in reports. You can also display only the preferred dates and locations, which is the default setting. But you may want to deselect this option if you're going on a research trip and want to include all notes, even if they conflict with each other, or if you're creating a report for publication and want to include all angles of the story.

✔ **Include Marriage Notes:** This option allows you to include Marriage Notes, but doing so gets a bit tricky because two areas of Family Tree Maker contain marriage information. This particular option refers to the Notes section that you get to by clicking the More button near the marriage information on the Family Page and then clicking the Notes button on the right side of the screen. This Notes section is the free-form text screen, not the table of facts. For more information on Marriage Notes and how to use them, see Chapter 2. The default setting is to include Marriage Notes.

✔ **Include More About Marriage Facts:** This option allows you to include the other set of marriage information. You can access the facts by clicking the More button near the marriage information on the Family Page. These facts appear on the screen in three columns: Fact, Date, and Comment/Location. (You can find additional details on using these fields in Chapter 2.) Interestingly enough, Family Tree Maker does not include More About Marriage Facts by default. You have to specify that you want to include them. And if you decide to include them, you also have the option of including only preferred dates and locations.

✔ **Include Titles:** Sometimes, you may want to include the titles of individuals in your reports. This option is particularly useful if several people have the same name and you want to be able to distinguish between them. For example, if several people are named Wolf Canine but they all held different ranks in the military, including their titles helps you easily tell the difference between Captain Wolf Canine and Admiral Wolf Canine. You can add titles to your individuals by clicking the More button for the individual and clicking the Lineage button on the side toolbar (see Chapter 2 for more information). Family Tree Maker turns on titles by default.

✔ **Source Information:** The next section of the Options dialog box provides three options for including (or excluding) source information:

- **Include Source Information as Endnotes.** All the endnotes for all the individuals in the report appear at the very end of the report. If you have a lengthy report with many individuals and sources, including all of them at the end can make them hard to work with. The solution in that case is to use the option described in the next bullet.

- **Include Source Information as Inline Notes.** The source note appears in parentheses right after the fact is presented in the report. You don't have to wade through several pages to find the source of the fact. (We like to use this setting when we're going on research trips and need quick access to source information.)

- **Exclude Source Information.** You need to be careful when using this option. If you intend to submit any of your information for publication or share it with other genealogists, we strongly recommend that you do not use this option. We explain our reasoning, at length, in Chapter 6. Also, for more information on inputting source information, see Chapter 2.

✔ **Generation Numbering:** You can choose two options from here: Automatically Find the Oldest Ancestor or Assume the Primary Individual is the Immigrant Ancestor. If you choose the first option, Family Tree Maker searches your database file and then numbers individuals based upon how many ancestors are listed in the file. For example, if we generate a report on Wolf Canine, Family Tree Maker looks to see if Wolf has a father, grandfather, great-grandfather, and so on. If it finds that Wolf has a father and grandfather in the database, it assigns generation number one to the grandfather, number two to the father, and number three to Wolf.

If you select the option to assume that the individual is the immigrant ancestor, the numbering changes. If Wolf is the subject of the report, he is assigned generation number one even if he has a father and grandfather in the database. The father and grandfather are assigned generation letters instead of numbers. For example, Wolf's grandfather is assigned generation letter A, and Wolf's father is generation letter B.

Why would you choose this option? Say you have a database that contains ancestors who lived in America and their forefathers who lived in England. You decide that you want to generate a report on the generations that lived in America, so you want the generation numbers to reflect only those who lived in America. Selecting this second option allows you to label the first immigrant to America as generation number one. Any of that immigrant's ancestors who lived in England would have generation letters instead of numbers. At a glance, you can now tell whether or not an individual lived in America.

The options that we just described give you latitude in choosing what information you want in each report. Feel free to mix and match the selections to see which formats and options provide the information in a way that is best for you. Everyone thinks differently, so don't just stick with the default items of the report.

Ready-Made Reports

After a long, hard day, it's nice to have some premade meals that you can just pop into the microwave. Your kitchen doesn't get messy, and you don't have to put much thought into preparing the food. Similar to microwave meals, Family Tree Maker has some premade reports that you can generate for an easy and quick look at the data contained in your Family File.

These premade reports include the Kinship, Data Errors, Medical Information, Addresses, Birthdays of Living Individuals, Marriage, Parentage, Documented Facts, Bibliography, Alternate Facts, and special LDS reports.

In the following sections, we explore these different reports, and how to create, customize, and print them. Now pick up your plate, and get ready to make some reports!

Report types

Before we go too far in our discussion of the types of premade reports, take a look at Table 10-2, which lists the different report types and what they do. This table is a quick reference that you can use the next time you want to create a report.

Table 10-2	Your Premade Report Buffet	
Type	*Applies To*	*Function*
Address	All individuals	Shows the contents of the Address pages
Alternate Facts	All individuals	Shows the facts that are not designated as preferred facts
Bibliography	All individuals	Lists the sources you've used for information in your Family File

Type	Applies To	Function
Birthdays of Living Individuals	All individuals	Contains the date of birth and age at next birthday
Data Errors	All individuals	Provides details on missing information and logic errors in your Family File
Documented Events	All individuals	Gives you details on which events are documented and which are not
Kinship: Canon & Civil	One individual	Shows the relationship between the subject of the report and the rest of the individuals in the Family File (includes degrees of separation)
Kinship: Relationship Only	One individual	Only shows the relationship between the subject of the report and the rest of the individuals in the Family File
Marriage	All individuals	Provides details on who is married to whom, including past spouses
Medical Information	All individuals	Displays information contained in the Medical Information field on the Medical page
PAF: Incomplete Individual Ordinances	All individuals	Provides a list of individuals who are missing vital pieces of information for ordinances in the Church of Jesus Christ of Latter-day Saints
PAF: Incomplete Marriage Sealings	All individuals	Contains a list of individuals missing marriage or sealing dates, which are important to the Church of Jesus Christ of Latter-day Saints
Parentage	All individuals	Shows the parents for individuals in the Family File

Kinship: Canon & Civil

One of the neat things about genealogy is meeting people, online and offline, who are your distant cousins. The challenge then is to figure out exactly how they are related to you. Is this person your fifth cousin, twice removed? Third cousin, once removed? You can spend a lot of time trying to map out the relationship, or you can use the Kinship report in Family Tree Maker.

Figure 10-5 shows an example of the Kinship: Canon & Civil report. The report consists of four columns. The first column contains the individual's full name (last name, first name, middle name). The second column identifies the relationship of the listed individual to the individual who is the subject of the report. The third and fourth columns contain the canon and civil degrees of relationship, respectively.

The canon and civil degrees identify the degrees of separation (or steps) between two individuals who are related by blood. These degrees are used to determine whether two individuals who were related could legally marry — an attempt to sort out the problem of kissin' cousins.

Is Bev your second cousin or your first cousin, once-removed?

Are you tired of trying to figure out the exact relationship between you and one of your relatives? Aren't there times when doing so makes you want to pull your hair out — especially as you add more and more names to your database and your family grows?

Family Tree Maker wants you to keep your hair. It wants to make your life a little easier so it includes a Relationship Calculator. The Calculator figures out the relationship between two people and then tells you what that relationship is. It even throws in the canon and civil codes (see "Kinship: Canon & Civil" in this chapter).

Using the Relationship Calculator is easy. Simply choose People⇨Relationship Calculator, and the Relationship Calculator window appears. The top half of the window reflects the two individuals whose relationship is calculated in the bottom half of the window. You find Change buttons next to each of the names so that you can select other individuals. And the bottom half of the window reflects the relationship between the two individuals. It identifies the common term for the relationship — such as first, second, or third cousins and the times removed (if any) — and provides the canon and civil codes (numbers). Of course, there may be times when you want to know the relationships among many people. Changing the names over and over so that the Relationship Calculator can determine the relationships just isn't practical. But don't worry, Family Tree Maker still has you covered — with Kinship: Relationship Only reports, which we cover in more detail in this chapter.

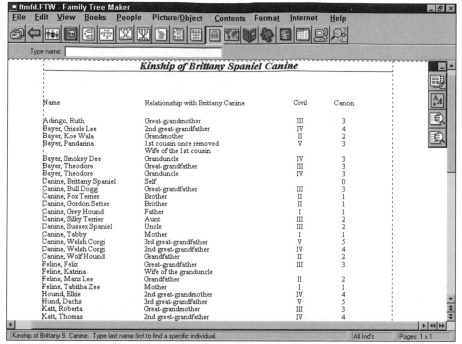

Figure 10-5:
A Kinship:
Canon &
Civil report
for Brittany
Canine.

The civil degree counts each step between two relatives as a degree. For example, two people who are first cousins — Brittany Spaniel Canine and Sy Berian Tiegger — share a common ancestor, their grandfather Wolf Hound Canine. The civil degree counts the number of steps between two individuals and their common ancestor — sort of like going up and down stairs to get from one room to another. In our case, Brittany is two steps up from her grandfather, Wolf. To get to Sy, you would then take two steps down. So the civil degree for Brittany and Sy is four.

The canon degree is figured a little differently. It counts only the number of steps between each individual and the nearest common ancestor. In our case, both Brittany and Sy are two steps from their common ancestor, Wolf. Therefore, the canon degree for Brittany and Sy is two.

Items that you can customize on the Kinship: Canon & Civil report are:

- **Text font and size:** Choose Format⇨Text Font, Size, & Style.

- **Border style:** Choose Format⇨Border Styles.

- **Title and footnotes:** Choose Contents⇨Title & Footnote.

- **Number of generations:** Choose Contents⇨# of Generations to Show.

For more information on each of these customizable items, see Chapter 7.

Kinship: Relationship Only

When you aren't really concerned with who is eligible to marry whom, a better report to run is the Kinship: Relationship Only report, shown in Figure 10-6. This report contains three columns: the full name of the individual, his or her birth date, and the relationship to the individual who is the subject of the report. You don't have to worry about any codes or degrees of relationship with this report.

One thing to keep in mind about both kinds of Kinship reports is that Family Tree Maker includes all children in Kinship reports, even if they are adopted, step, or foster children or if the status of the child is unknown. The only way to exclude children is to select the option labeled `Exclude this relationship from trees and kinship` on the Lineage page. You can reach the Lineage page by clicking the More button on the Family Page for the individual and clicking the Lineage button on the right side of the screen. (For more information on the Lineage page, see Chapter 2.)

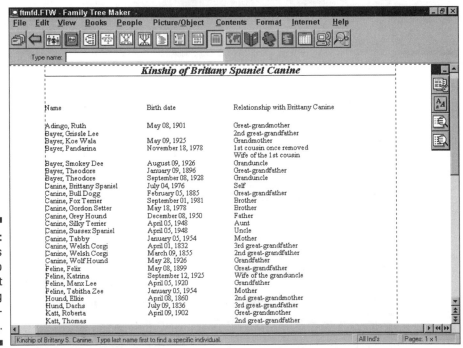

Figure 10-6: Brittany's Kinship report showing only relationships.

The items that you can customize for this report are the same as the Kinship: Canon & Civil report:

- ✔ **Text font and size:** Choose Format⇨Text Font, Size, & Style.
- ✔ **Border style:** Choose Format⇨Border Styles.
- ✔ **Title and footnotes:** Choose Contents⇨Title & Footnote.
- ✔ **Number of generations to show:** Choose Contents⇨# of Generations to Show.

If you want to find out more about these customizable items, see Chapter 7.

Data Errors

Nobody likes to be told they are wrong. But sometimes having someone point out errors is a good thing, especially when you're researching your genealogy. Honestly, it's true. In our haste as genealogists, we don't always cross every *t* and dot every *i*. The Data Errors report helps us sort out inadvertent errors, as well as tells us what gaps we need to fill in to make our research more complete.

The Data Errors report consists of three columns, as shown in Figure 10-7. The first column shows the full name of the individual where the error was found, the second is the individual's birth date, and third is the potential error. Family Tree Maker looks for several different types of errors. It tries to identify logic errors (a child being born before a parent), missing information (birth dates and marriage dates), and orphan individuals (individuals who are not listed as having any parents, children, or spouses).

 A handy feature of this report is that after the report appears on your screen, you can simply double-click the name of the individual in the report to go to that individual's Family Page. From there, you can correct or add any information.

Here are the items that you can customize for the Data Error, report:

- ✔ **Sort:** Choose Format⇨Sort. You can sort the individuals in the report by last name or birth date.
- ✔ **Text font and size:** Choose Format⇨Text Font, Size, & Style.
- ✔ **Border style:** Choose Format⇨Border Styles.
- ✔ **Title and footnotes:** Choose Contents⇨Title & Footnote.

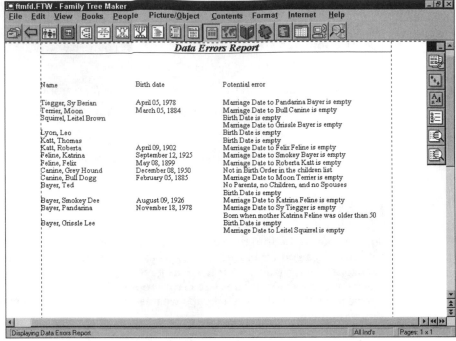

Figure 10-7:
Pointing
out your
mistakes —
the Data
Errors
report.

⤳ **Individuals to include:** Choose Contents⤳Individuals to Include.

⤳ **Include name capitalization errors:** Choose Contents⤳Options⤳
Include Name Capitalization Errors.

⤳ **Include empty birth and marriage date field errors:** Choose Contents⤳
Options⤳Include Empty Birth and Marriage Date Field Errors.

For more information on these customizable items, see Chapter 7.

Medical Information

For some researchers, medical information is very important. Whether you're
tracking down medical conditions or just getting insight into how people
lived and died, knowing about the ailments that afflicted your ancestors and
the injuries they sustained can provide you a window into the conditions
under which they lived.

Figure 10-8 shows an example of a Medical Information report. The report
consists of the individual's name, birth date, and medical information. Family
Tree Maker takes the medical information from the Medical Information field
on the Medical page. To get to the Medical page, click the More button of the
individual and then click the Medical button on the right side of the screen.

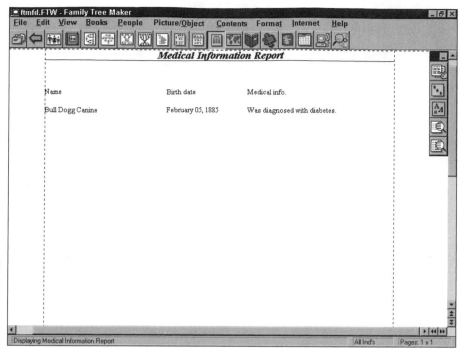

Figure 10-8:
A Medical
Information
report.

Oddly, the Medical Information report doesn't contain what we believe to be a key field on the Medical page — the cause of death for an individual. The report contains only the contents of the Medical Information field. So if you want to include a person's cause of death in your standard Medical Information report, make sure that you've included it in the Medical Information field.

As you may suspect, you can customize this report. These areas are

- ✓ **Maximum width:** Choose Format⇨Maximum Width. Here you can set the width of the columns and the spacing between the columns of the report.

- ✓ **Sort:** Choose Format⇨Sort. You can sort the individuals in the report by last name or birth date.

- ✓ **Text font and size:** Choose Format⇨Text Font, Size, & Style.

- ✓ **Border style:** Choose Format⇨Border Styles.

- ✓ **Title and footnotes:** Choose Contents⇨Title & Footnote.

- ✓ **Individuals to include:** Choose Contents⇨Individuals to Include.

See Chapter 7 for details on these customizable items.

Address

Your grandmother's 100th birthday is coming up, and your family wants you to create a large family tree as part of the decorations. But all the information in your database is not complete. To update it, you decide to send out some questionnaires to your relatives. Finding all those relatives' addresses is not a problem if you produce an Address report (assuming that you have entered everyone's address in Family Tree Maker).

The Address report (shown in Figure 10-9) contains three columns: the names of individuals, their addresses, and their telephone numbers. The address and telephone number information comes from the Address and Phone page. You can get to this page by clicking the More button for an individual and then clicking the Address button on the right side of the screen.

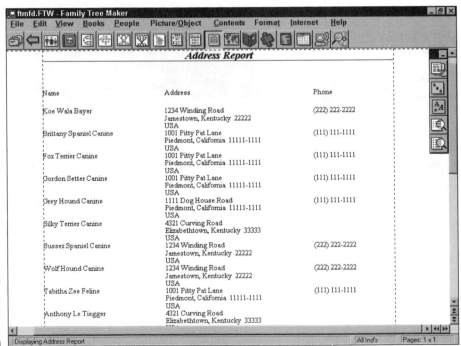

Figure 10-9: The Address report.

If you don't have an address for an individual when you're preparing a report, Family Tree Maker looks to see if that person's spouse has an address. If the spouse doesn't have an address, it looks for the parents' address. If the parents have an address, Family Tree Maker uses that address for the child in the report. So you need to double-check the address list to make sure that children who no longer live with their parents have the correct addresses.

The Address report has the same customizable options as the Medical Information report, which we describe in the preceding section.

Birthdays of Living Individuals

Are you tired of getting into trouble for not sending a birthday card to Aunt Betty? Are you not sure if it's her 81st or 82nd birthday? Now is the time to do something about it. The Birthdays of Living Individuals report, shown in Figure 10-10, is just the answer you're looking for. This report lists the individuals' names, birth dates, and ages at their next birthdays.

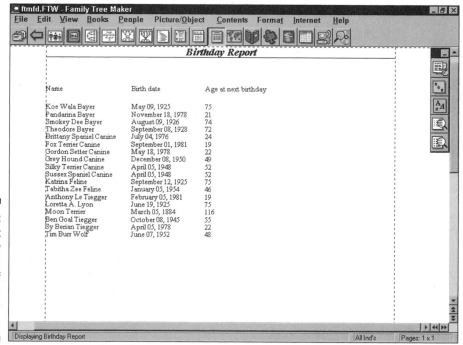

Figure 10-10: Never forget a birthday with the Birthday of Living Individuals report.

The same formatting options that apply to the Medical Information report (which we describe earlier in this chapter) also apply to the Birthdays of Living Individuals report.

Marriage

A Marriage report, shown in Figure 10-11, allows you to quickly review who is, or was, married to whom in your family. This report lists the husband and wife's names, their marriage date, and the relationship-ending status (such as death of one spouse and divorce).

The Marriage report shows all the spouses of a given individual. The relationship-ending status information comes from the More About Marriage page. You can see the information on this page by clicking the More button in the marriage area of the Family Page.

Here are the items that you can customize for the Marriage report:

- **Maximum width:** Choose Format⇨Maximum Width. You can set the width of the columns and the spacing between columns of the report.
- **Sort:** Choose Format⇨Sort. You can sort the individuals in the report by last name or birth date.
- **Text font and size:** Choose Format⇨Text Font, Size, & Style.
- **Border style:** Choose Format⇨Border Styles.
- **Title and footnotes:** Choose Contents⇨Title & Footnote.

If you have questions about customizable items, be sure to check out Chapter 7.

Parentage

Keeping track of children and their parents can be a challenge if you have a few hundred people in your database. But you can always refer to the Parentage report, shown in Figure 10-12, for a quick look at the parents of all the individuals. The report shows the name of the individual, both parents' names (if known), and their relationships to the child (natural, step, adopted).

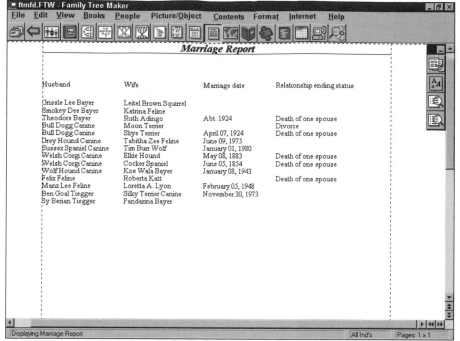

Figure 10-11:
The Marriage report contains all spouses, past and present.

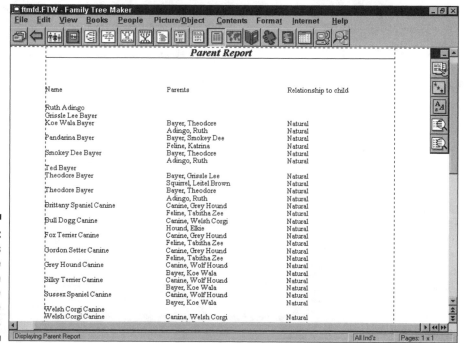

Figure 10-12:
See who is responsible for each child in the Parentage report.

The information in the Relationship to Child field comes from the Lineage page. You can find this page by clicking the More button for an individual and clicking the Lineage button on the right side of the page.

The options for customizing the Parentage report are the same as for the Marriage report, which we describe in the preceding section.

Documented Events

Sometimes, taking a step back and making sure that you're including the proper documentation of your family history is a good idea. The Documented Events report allows you to do just that. The default version of the report shows the individual's name, the event that has a source, and the source citation for the event.

Although the default version of the report is sufficient, we think that finding out the opposite of what the default report tells you is more helpful. You want the report to show which events are missing sources so that you can find the documentation. Fortunately, you can customize the report to show missing sources as well. Figure 10-13 shows the Documented Events report for individuals that are missing sources for particular events.

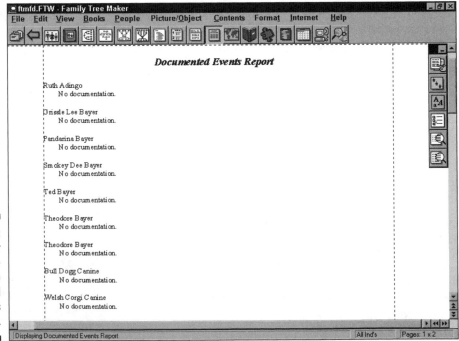

Figure 10-13: See your documentation with the Documented Events report.

Items that you can customize in the Documented Events report include

- ✔ **Text font and size:** Choose Format⇨Text Font, Size, & Style.

- ✔ **Title and footnotes:** Choose Contents⇨Title & Footnote.

- ✔ **Individuals to include:** Choose Contents⇨Individuals to Include.

- ✔ **Whom to report:** Choose Contents⇨Options⇨Whom to Report. You can list individuals and marriages with documentation or without documentation, or list all individuals regardless of documentation.

- ✔ **What to report:** Choose Contents⇨Options⇨What to Report. You can specify that you want to the report to list events and facts with documentation or without documentation, or list all facts and events.

- ✔ **Printed format:** Choose Contents⇨Options⇨Printed Format. You can determine whether your report shows the footnote format or complete documentation for each event.

For more information on customizing reports, check out Chapter 7.

Bibliography

Genealogical research is like anything else: After you've done it for a while, things all start to blur together. One way to get your focus back — without having to buy a new pair of glasses — is to create a bibliography of all the sources that you have used thus far. And, of course, Family Tree Maker has just such a report: the Bibliography report, shown in Figure 10-14.

The Bibliography report can serve several purposes. First, you can print out the report before going on a research trip so that you know which sources you've already covered. Also, if you need to refer to those sources again to confirm information, you have a handy list of them. The report can also show you what kinds of sources you've used. For example, if you're concerned that you have relied too heavily on secondary sources (see Chapter 1 for more on primary and secondary sources), you can run a Bibliography report to see the proportion of sources. Although the report does not specifically note which are secondary and primary resources, you should be able to tell at a glance whether you're using a birth certificate or another person's research as a source.

As with the rest of other types of reports, you can customize some aspects of the Bibliography report, including

- ✔ **Text font and size:** Choose Format⇨Text Font, Size, & Style.

- ✔ **Title and footnotes:** Choose Contents⇨Title & Footnote.

- ✔ **Individuals to include:** Choose Contents⇨Individuals to Include.

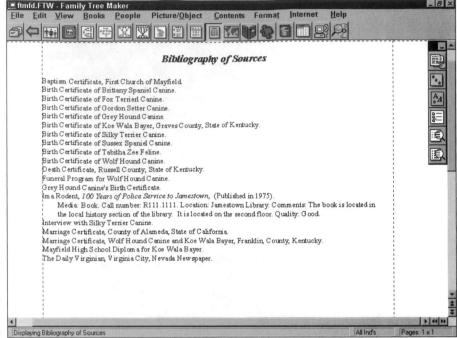

✔ **Report format:** Choose Contents⇨Options. You can show your report as a standard bibliography or an annotated bibliography. The standard bibliography shows the author, title, and publication information. The annotated bibliography includes the media of the source, the call number, the location, and the quality. For more on sources, see Chapter 6.

✔ **Source references:** Choose Contents⇨Options. Here you can choose whether to include footnotes without referenced sources in the bibliography.

Chapter 7 offers more specific information on customizing reports.

Alternate Facts

Occasionally, some of your sources may conflict with one another. One may say that someone was born on one day, and another source may say that the individual was born on a different day. In the absence of a birth certificate, you may not know which date is correct. To be thorough, you should note both sources as separate facts, each with a different date. Family Tree Maker requires you to set a preference for which fact is preferred. The other fact is then considered an alternate fact. The Alternate Facts report displays all the facts that are assigned alternate status, as shown in Figure 10-15.

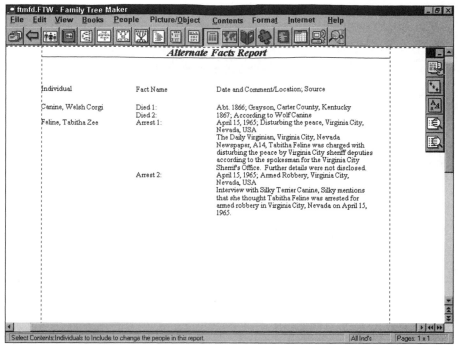

This report can serve as a checklist of items for which you still need to get primary sources, or it can be another source of confirmation. The report is particularly handy for planning research trips.

The items that are customizable for the Alternate Facts report are

- ✔ **Sort:** Choose Format⇨Sort. Allows you to sort the individuals in the report by last name or birth date.

- ✔ **Text font and size:** Choose Format⇨Text Font, Size, & Style.

- ✔ **Border style:** Choose Format⇨Border Styles.

- ✔ **Title and footnotes:** Choose Contents⇨Title & Footnote.

- ✔ **Individuals to include:** Choose Contents⇨Individuals to Include.

Page back to Chapter 7 for further customization information.

Reports Specific to LDS

Two Family Tree Maker reports are available to users who have configured the program to use the Church of Jesus Christ of Latter-day Saints (LDS) labels: the PAF: Incomplete Individual Ordinances report and the PAF:

Incomplete Marriage Sealings report. The first report shows which individuals are missing dates for birth or christening, death, baptism, endowment, and seal to parents. The second report shows each individual who is missing either a marriage or sealing date. Figure 10-16 shows an example of the Incomplete Individual Ordinances report.

Generating premade reports

After you decide what type of report you want, you're ready to generate it. Here are the basic steps to generate any report:

1. **If you're creating a Kinship report, select the person who is the focus of the report. If you're generating another kind of report, skip to Step 2.**

   The Kinship report is the only one that is based on an individual, so you need to position your cursor on that person's name to generate it. To select the individual, you need to go to his or her Family Page. You can open the Family Page by clicking the tabs on the right side of the screen or by using the Index of Individuals (choose View⇨Index of Individuals; see Chapter 3 for more information about navigating to Family Pages).

Figure 10-16:
The Incomplete Individual Ordinances report.

Name	Birth date	Death date	Baptism (LDS) date	Endowment (LDS) date
Adingo, Ruth	May 08, 1901	December 05, 1971		
Bayer, Grissle L.				
Bayer, Koe W.	May 09, 1925			
Bayer, Pandarina	November 18, 1978			
Bayer, Smokey D.	August 09, 1926			
Bayer, Ted				
Bayer, Theodore	January 09, 1896	May 21, 1950		
Bayer, Theodore	September 08, 1928			
Canine, Brittany S.	July 04, 1976			
Canine, Bull D.	February 05, 1885	July 09, 1927		
Canine, Fox T.	September 01, 1981			
Canine, Gordon S.	May 18, 1978			
Canine, Grey H.	December 08, 1950			
Canine, Silky T.	April 05, 1948			
Canine, Sussex S.	April 05, 1948			
Canine, Welsh C.	April 01, 1832	Abt. 1866		
Canine, Welsh C.	March 09, 1855	November 08, 1896		
Canine, Wolf H.	May 28, 1926	June 25, 1994		
Feline, Felix	May 08, 1899	September 23, 1975		
Feline, Katrina	September 12, 1925			
Feline, Manx L.	April 05, 1920	March 05, 1995		
Feline, Tabitha Z.	January 05, 1954			
Hound, Elkie	April 08, 1860	December 08, 1920		
Hund, Dachs	July 09, 1836			
Katt, Roberta	April 09, 1902	November 06, 1982		
Katt, Thomas				
Le Tiegger, Anthony	February 05, 1981			
Lyon, Leo				
Lyon, Loretta A.	June 19, 1925			
Spaniel, Cocker	May 06, 1836	December 25, 1906		
Squirrel, Leitel B.				
Terrier, Moon	March 05, 1884			
Terrier, Skye	February 08, 1901	September 05, 1997		

ftmfd.FTW - Family Tree Maker

File Edit View Books People Picture/Object Contents Format Internet Help

Displaying PAF Incomplete Individual Ordinances Report   All Ind's   Pages: 2 x 1

2. **Choose View➪Report.**

   Or click the Report button. If you're looking at the default toolbar, the Report button is the 13th button (12th if you're using Version 7.0) from the left (the one with the picture of a gray piece of paper that has blue lines printed on it). This action opens the last type of report that you created.

   A Cue Card for Report may pop up, offering help with the various customizing features. If you don't want the Cue Card to pop up every time you customize a report, select the option labeled `Click here if you don't want to see this Help Window again`. Then click OK to continue.

3. **Click the top button on the side toolbar.**

   Or choose Report➪Report Format.

4. **In the Report Format dialog box that appears, select a report type and then click the OK button.**

   (Or you can just double-click the report.) Family Tree Maker generates your selected report.

5. **Customize your report.**

   If you don't like the way that the report looks or you just want to see more options, you can customize your report by using the series of buttons that appear on the side toolbar.

   You can also customize your chart two other ways. The first way is to select a feature to customize from the Format menu. A second, much faster way is to right-click on the chart and choose a feature to customize from the pop-up menu that appears.

   If you want to create another type of report, just click the top button on the side toolbar and select one of the other types. You can also select another report type by choosing Format➪Report Format.

6. **Verify that the report includes the information that you intended.**

   You may want to use the Zoom In and Zoom Out buttons if you're having trouble reading the report. They are the last two buttons on the side toolbar — the ones with the clever magnifying glass icons.

7. **Print your completed report by choosing File➪Report.**

   As a shortcut, you can just press Ctrl+P to execute the print command. (Of course, we're assuming that you have a printer hooked up to your computer. If you don't, neither command will do you a lot of good.)

Reports, Made-to-Order

We've noticed that breakfast buffets have become rather popular in recent years. You go through the line and help yourself until you get to the eggs-made-to-order portion of the line. Of course, that's where the bottleneck always is. Someone in front of you just ordered some sort of spectacular omelet that seems to take hours to fix. Even with the bottleneck, the made-to-order egg section is a good concept. You get the kind of egg that you want, and it's usually hot. You'll find a similar concept in Family Tree Maker called the custom report. It allows you the flexibility of creating made-to-order reports that meet your research needs.

Generating custom reports

You can generate a custom report in the same way that you create the ready-made reports. Just click the Report button (the twelfth or thirteenth button from the left depending on which version of Family Tree Maker you're using — it has the picture of a gray piece of paper with blue lines printed on it) or choose View⇨Report. Either command produces the base report, which contains three columns: Name, Birth Date, and Death Date.

Now for the custom part. Say that we're going on a research trip to Kentucky to find information on the Canine family. We want to generate a report listing basic information that would be useful in the archives or library. Although knowing birth dates and death dates is nice, we need much more information to be able to use our research time most effectively. We need to know the birth and death locations, along with the sources of each. Knowing the dates of census returns and probate records is also helpful so that we can make copies of the originals.

Follow these steps to select information for the custom report:

1. **After the custom report appears on your screen, choose Contents⇨Items to Include in Report.**

   Or click the Items to Include in Report button (the second button on the side toolbar).

   Family Tree Maker displays the Items to Include in Report dialog box with two columns. The first column contains the items that you can display in a report. The second column lists the items that you have selected to be in the report (three default items will probably already be in this column — First Middle Last, Birth Date, Death Date).

   Say that we want to add the following items to our report: Birth Location, Birth Source Info., Death Location, Death Source Info., Census Date, Census cmt/loc, Census Source Information, Probate Date, Probate cmt/loc, and Probate Source Information.

2. **In the first column, select the item that you want to include.**

   We click the first item that we want in our report, Birth Location.

3. **Click the > button between the columns to move your selection to the second column.**

   Family Tree Maker copies the selected item to the second column.

   Because we selected Birth Location, an Options dialog box opens. Here we can choose whether to include only preferred information in the report. We decide to use all the information, so we deselect the option and click OK.

   A faster way to select items is to double-click each item that you want to include in the report instead of clicking the > button each time.

4. **In the second column, select the item that you want to position in the report. If you're happy where it currently is, you can skip to Step 6.**

   When the Birth Location was copied to the second column, it was placed beneath Death Date. If we generate the report, Death Date will be sandwiched between Birth Date and Birth Location. But we prefer to have all the birth information together. So we highlight Birth Location on the list so that we can move it under Birth Date.

5. **Click the Move Up button or Move Down button to reposition the item.**

   We click Move Up once and nestle Birth Location between Birth Date and Death Date. If we had moved it up too far, we could use the Move Down button to put it back in place.

6. **Repeat Steps 2 through 5 to move other items to the right column and to adjust the order.**

7. **After you have everything where you want it, click the OK button.**

   Presto, your report appears, and it should look similar to Figure 10-17.

8. **Customize the report any way you want.**

   You may not be thrilled with the way your report looks at first, but you can customize it (just like with the other reports). Customize your report by using the series of buttons that appear on the side toolbar on the right side of your screen (see the next section for more help).

   If you want to add or delete any information from the report, click the second button on the side toolbar and make the necessary adjustments.

9. **Print your completed custom report by choosing File⇨Report.**

   You can also press Ctrl+P to execute the print command.

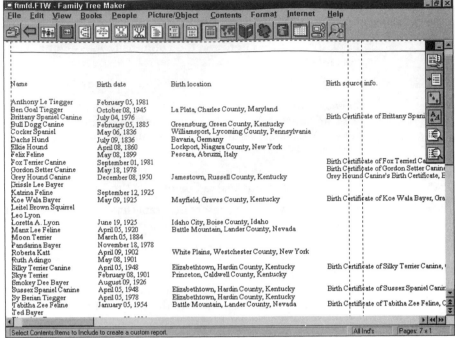

Figure 10-17:
Voilà, the
custom
report.

Sprucing up custom reports

Just as you can customize other kinds of reports, you can customize your
custom reports, too. Here is a list of the specific things that you can customize:

- **Maximum width for each column:** Choose Format⇨Maximum Width for
  Each Column. You can set the column width and spacing between
  columns for each column individually.

- **Sort:** Choose Format⇨Sort. You can sort the individuals in the report by
  two criteria that you used to generate the report (such as, sort by birth
  date and then by birthplace)

- **Text font and size:** Choose Format⇨Text Font, Size, & Style.

- **Border style:** Choose Format⇨Border Styles.

- **Title and footnotes:** Choose Contents⇨Title & Footnote.

- **Individuals to include:** Choose Contents⇨Individuals to Include.

- **Items to include:** Choose Contents⇨Items to Include.

One of the most important areas of customization (beyond Items to Include) is the Individuals to Include feature. This feature allows you to control exactly which individuals appear in your Custom report. By default, all individuals are included in the report. But sometimes, you just want information on a few individuals (especially for research trips to particular locations). To select just a few individuals, click the Individuals to Include button on the side toolbar (the third button from the top — it's green with little people on it). An Include dialog box opens, containing a button cleverly marked Individuals to Include. Click that button, and the Individuals to Include dialog box opens where you can select the individuals to include in the report. After you select the ones that you want, click OK.

Putting Your Family in a Group: Creating Family Group Sheets

One of the most useful reports in genealogical research is the Family Group Sheet. The Family Group Sheet contains information on a mother and father and their immediate children. Key information included in the Family Group Sheet is the birth, marriage, death, and burial dates for the mother and father; birth, marriage, and death dates for the children; and the names of the children's spouses.

Creating a Family Group Sheet is easy. Just go to the Family Page of the family that you want to generate the report for and click the Family Group Sheet button (the 11th button from the left in Version 7.0 — a button with a yellow sheet of paper on it). This generates the Family Group Sheet report.

You can customize a couple of things on the report. You can choose what items to include in the Family Group Sheet, and you can alter the text font and style. These options are accessible through the side toolbar on the right side of the screen.

Chapter 11

Writing Your Own Book

● ●

In This Chapter

▶ Selecting items to include in your book

▶ Determining the order of the contents of your book

▶ Printing your book

● ●

*A*h, the time has come for you to share your genealogical findings and general knowledge with others. After all, your annals of history are just as important for current and future researchers as those other books in the library, right? We think so.

The natural progression in genealogy is to publish a book of your findings after you've gathered a lot of information and supporting documents. Family Tree Maker makes this process easier.

Books are a great way to share your information, along with pictures and copies of documents. You can hand out books at reunions, send them to relatives as gifts (they make particularly nice birthday and holiday gifts), or distribute copies to local libraries and genealogical societies so that others can benefit from your research.

In this chapter, we take a look at the types of things that you can include in a Family Tree Maker book and walk you through the process of creating one.

Taking the First Step in Creating Your Book

At first, you may be a little intimidated at the thought of creating a book. Grandiose thoughts of writing a long narrative, selecting just the right photos to include, and putting everything together — not to mention finding a publisher — can be overwhelming. But what we're talking about is generating a book in Family Tree Maker, which isn't an intimidating process at all. You can pick and choose from items already in your Family File to create a book, and if you want, you can add more narrative.

Follow these steps to begin creating your book:

1. **Choose Books⊅New Book.**

   Or click the Books button — it's the 5th or 6th button from the right on the default toolbar, depending on which version of Family Tree Maker you're using.

   The New Book dialog box pops up, which contains two fields and three buttons.

2. **Enter a name for your book in the Book Title field.**

3. **Tab down and enter your name in the Author field.**

4. **Click OK.**

   A Cue Card for Books may pop up, which offers tips and highlights about creating your book. If you don't want the Cue Card to pop up every time you open a book, click in the check box that says Click here if you don't want to see this Help Window again. Then click OK.

   Behind the Cue Card, the Book view opens, as shown in Figure 11-1. From the list of Available Items on the left side, you can pick what you want to include in your book. On the right side is the Outline for your book, which initially contains only a Title Page. And between the two lists, these buttons appear:

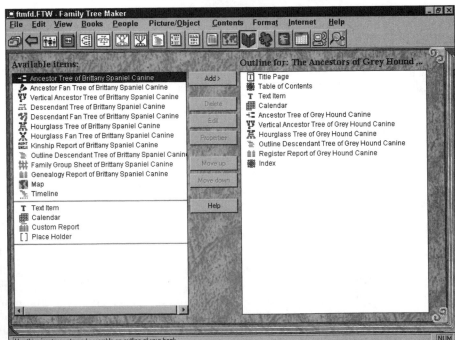

Figure 11-1:
The Book view in Family Tree Maker.

- **Add:** To add an item, highlight it on the Available Items list and click the Add button. The item then appears on your Outline.

- **Delete:** Highlight the item that you want to delete on the Outline and then click the Delete button. Family Tree Maker asks you to confirm that you want to delete it.

- **Edit:** Highlight the item that you want to edit on the Outline and click the Edit button. Family Tree Maker takes you to the item so that you can edit it. For example, if you choose to edit a family tree, Family Tree Maker takes you to that particular tree so you can edit it. To return to your book, click the Book button on the toolbar (the 5th or 6th button from the right on the default toolbar, depending on which version you're using).

- **Properties:** Clicking the Properties button opens the Item Properties dialog box, where you can change the name of the item, as well as mark that you want the item to begin a chapter and/or begin on an odd-numbered page. You can also designate to include a header or footer in this item. After you finish setting properties, click OK.

- **Move Up and Move Down:** You use these buttons to change the order of your book by moving an item in the Outline list. Just highlight the item and click the appropriate button, and you can see the item move up or down to other locations in your book.

- **Help:** Self-explanatory, right? This brings up Help.

You may think that these steps end midstream. That's because you're ready to start selecting and editing items to include in your book. In the following section, we walk you through this process and go into more detail about what's available. So keep reading. . . .

Selecting Items to Include in Your Book

Have you ever noticed that the narrative and illustrations (charts and photos) of a book are codependent? The narrative needs the illustrations to show the text visually. And the illustrations need the narrative to explain the images in detail. Your goal as you're creating your book is to successfully blend the narrative and illustrations so that the book is enticing to its readers. So if you want to create an impressive book, what you choose to include and where you place it are quite important.

You can choose from a variety of things when creating your book. On the left side of the Book view is a list of Available Items. You can select family trees, reports, a Family Group Sheet, a Timeline, narratives, a calendar, a Table of Contents, an Index, scanned photographs or documents, or almost anything that you've attached to your Family File with the Scrapbook feature.

What you choose to include depends on you. That makes sense, right? The book is a reflection of your personality whether you like it or not. If you're a picture-person (visually inclined), then you may want to include lots of charts and photos. If you're a give-me-the-facts kind of person, then you may prefer mostly text items and very few charts or pictures. If you're wishy-washy — well, good luck deciding what to include! Whatever your inclinations are, we recommend that you keep the reader in mind and try to have a variety of items in your book — don't overload it with just one or two types of items. Most readers enjoy a narrative that has an occasional illustration of some sort (whether it's a chart or a picture). We recommend that you always include a Table of Contents and Index (we cover these in more detail later in this chapter) so that readers can pick up your book and flip directly to the section that they're most interested in.

Enough with our aesthetic recommendations, we're ready to examine the items that you can include in your book.

A tree grows in your book

The Available Items list in the Book view begins with several family trees and reports for you to choose from. They are as follows:

- ✔ Ancestor Tree
- ✔ Ancestor Fan Tree
- ✔ Vertical Ancestor Tree
- ✔ Descendant Tree
- ✔ Descendant Fan Tree
- ✔ Hourglass Tree
- ✔ Hourglass Fan Tree
- ✔ Kinship Report
- ✔ Outline Descendant Tree
- ✔ Family Group Sheet
- ✔ Genealogy Report
- ✔ Timeline

(Check out Chapters 9 and 10 for detailed explanations about these trees and reports.)

Each tree and report on the Available Items list is specific to the person whose name field your cursor is in on the Family Page when you choose to go to the book view. For example, if our cursor is on Grey Hound Canine's name field on the Family Page when we click the Book button (fifth or sixth from the right, depending on the version of Family Tree Maker you're using), then the reports and trees in the Available Items list are specific to Wolf Hound Canine. So the Ancestor tree appears as `Ancestor Tree of Grey Hound Canine`.

Just because trees and reports on the Available Items list are limited to one individual at this time doesn't mean you can't include trees and reports for others in your database. To add a tree or report for another individual, you need to go to his or her Family Page and click the Book button. Say that after we selected a couple of trees for Grey Hound Canine, we decided to add a tree and report that focus on Ben Goal Tiegger. We go to Ben's Family Page using the Index of Individuals and then click the Book button. Now the Available Items list reflects trees and reports pertaining to Ben, from which we can choose.

To include a particular tree or report in your book, highlight it on the Available Items list and click the Add button. Family Tree Maker adds that item to the Outline list on the right. Then if you want to see or make any changes to the tree or report, highlight it on the Outline list and click the Edit button. (Or you can just double-click the item in the Outline list.) This action takes you to the tree or report, and from there, you can change or customize it. (For more information about editing and customizing trees and reports, check out Chapters 9 and 10.)

Gossip about Aunt Lola

You want your book to captivate your audience — you want it to be enthralling, right? (Well, you should at least settle for mildly interesting.) To make your book interesting, you need to provide more than just lists of names and dates and an occasional photo. You need to provide some color, some history, some oomph. How do you do this, you ask? Easy. Just tell some family stories — recall how a particular event in history impacted the lives of your ancestors, tell about the big family dinners that took place every third Sunday of the month at great-grandma's house, or explain why your parents decided to move to California.

You may have already entered some of this information into the Notes sections of the Family Pages. Or you may have already typed it in your word processor and attached it to a Scrapbook or two in your database. If so, it's relatively easy to cut and paste text from the Notes or to add a Scrapbook item to your book. But if you haven't typed your stories into Notes or your word processor yet, you may want to use the text item feature of the book.

The text item window, shown in Figure 11-2, is a mini–word processor in which you can type to your heart's content. You can type in anything that you want to include in your book — from stories about a particular relative, to the recipe of Grandma's famous carrot cake, to poems written by your Aunt Gertrude (as long as you have her permission to include them in your book, that is). And you can insert photos or other scanned images from your Family Tree Maker Scrapbooks so that the illustrations accompany the text that references them.

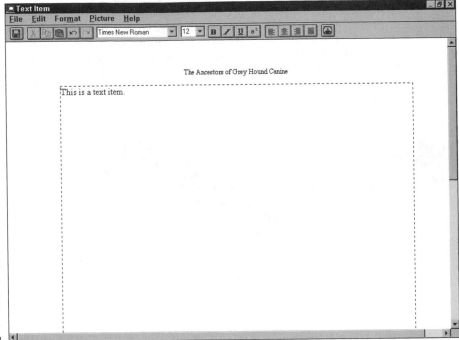

Figure 11-2:
The Text
Item
window is a
mini–word
processor.

Here's how to add and work with a text item:

1. **In the Book view of Family Tree Maker, select text item on the Available Items list.**

   The Add text item dialog box appears.

2. **Select the type of text item that you what to add.**

   Your choices are New Text, Introduction, Preface, Foreword, Dedication, and Copyright Notice.

3. **Click OK.**

   The type of text item that you're adding appears on your book Outline list. For example, if you selected Introduction, then that's what appears on the Outline list.

4. **Highlight the text item on the Outline list and click the Edit button.**

   Or you can double-click the text item on the Outline list.

   This action takes you to the text item where you can type your information.

5. **Format your text item and type in your text.**

   We look at formatting and other features of the text item word processing program in the next few sections.

6. **Close the text item by choosing File⇨Close.**

   You have to close the text item to return to the Book view and continue working on your book.

   If you haven't saved your text item, Family Tree Maker asks you if you want to do so before closing. Click Yes.

As with almost any word processor, the text item word processor allows you to change fonts, align text, add or delete page breaks, copy text, spell check, and print. In the following sections, we take a look at how to do these things so that your text item looks exactly the way you want it.

What a format!

Formatting a text item means picking a font and aligning text. You can change the formatting of a text item two ways: by using the Format pull-down menu or by using the toolbar. Yes, that's right — the text item word processor has a handy little toolbar at the top. It allows you to quickly perform any number of functions, including various formatting options.

The first of your formatting responsibilities is to pick a font. Your choice of fonts depends on the number and types of fonts installed on your computer. The more fonts that you have installed, the more choices that you have with Family Tree Maker. To select the font for your text item (or maybe just a portion of the text item), you can select from the Font drop-down list on the toolbar, or you can choose Format⇨Font and then select the font you want in the dialog box that appears.

After you choose a font face, you need to set the size of the font. Pick a size that's not too small to see but not so big that only one or two words fit on a line. A good default font size is 12. After you decide on your font size (or if you need to actually see some type in that size before deciding), you can select a size from the Front Size drop-down list on the toolbar, or you can choose Format⇨Size to make your choice.

Say you want to emphasize one statement in your text item to set it apart from the rest of the text. Formatting that statement in **bold** is a good option. You can either turn on the bold before typing your text (just be sure to turn it off after you finish), or highlight the text you want to emphasize (after you type it, of course) and choose Format⇨Style⇨Bold. You can use these same general commands for any Style type — **bold,** *italics,* <u>underline</u>, or super-script (which means the text is raised up a little from the rest of the text).

Last on the formatting front, but not least, is text alignment. If you're like April, your preference is to left-align anything that looks like a story (all the lines begin flushed to the left margin, and where the lines end on the right is jagged). If you're a die-hard newspaper enthusiast, you may prefer to fully-justify everything. Lucky for you, you can pick from left-justified, centered, right-justified, or fully-justified by choosing Format⇨Alignment or by clicking the appropriate button on the toolbar (the ones with the little lines on them).

Breaking pages

Whenever Family Tree Maker automatically inserts a page break in a text item, it displays the page break as a dotted line. This line enables you to easily see where one page ends and a new one begins. A similar thing happens when you manually create a page break in a text item — the only difference is that the line is solid black rather than dotted.

Why would you care where the page breaks are? You may want a particular paragraph to lead off a page that has a photograph, or you may not want a scanned document to be divided across two pages. Whatever your reason, you can manually insert page breaks wherever you want by following these steps:

1. **Position your cursor where you want to insert a page break.**

2. **Choose Edit⇨Insert Page Break.**

   If you inserted the break at the end of the text you typed, Family Tree Maker takes you a new, blank page. If you inserted the break somewhere within the text, it splits the page into two.

3. Fix any images that appear on two pages as a result of your page break.

Depending on where you inserted the page break, you may have cut across a photo or other scanned image. To fix the image, you need to drag it until it is entirely on one page. If you're not quite sure how to work with images, check out "A Picture Is Worth a Thousand Words," later in this chapter.

Just as you may want to add a manual page break, you may decide later that you don't want it there after all. That's your prerogative. Deleting a page break is as simple as creating one. All you have to do is position your cursor at the beginning of the page break and then press the Delete key on your computer keyboard. Voilà! The page break disappears.

Copying text

Imagine you're typing information about the Felines and you decide you want to include the story about how Grey Hound Canine and Tabitha Zee Feline met during the Bowlarama of 1975. You already included the story in your chapter about the Canines, but redundancy has never been an issue for you. So do you type the entire story again? No way. Why retype the story when you can copy it from the Canine chapter and paste it into the text item in the Feline chapter?

Follow these steps to copy and paste text in text items:

1. Go to the text item that has the text you want to copy by highlighting the item on the Outline list and clicking the Edit button.

The first text item appears.

2. Highlight the text that you want to copy.

You probably already know how to highlight text, but we'll go over it briefly — just in case. To highlight a block of text, hold down the left mouse button as you drag your cursor over the text.

3. Choose Edit⇨Copy.

Or press Ctrl+C. This step copies the highlighted text.

4. Close this text item by choosing File⇨Close.

If you made any changes to this text item and haven't saved them yet, Family Tree Maker asks you if you want to save the text item before closing. Click Yes.

5. **Go to the text item that you want to paste the text into by highlighting it on the Outline and clicking the Edit button.**

   The second text item opens.

6. **Position your cursor where you want to insert the text in the text item.**

7. **Choose Edit⇨Paste.**

   Or press Ctrl+V. Family Tree Maker then copies the text to the text item.

Spell checking

In this day and age, what would a word processor be without spell checking? We guess it would still be a word processor but not one that we'd use very often. In your haste to enter information, you'll undoubtedly make typos. Fortunately, a spell checker can catch at least some of the problems. So you'll be glad to know that Family Tree Maker has a spell checker for text items.

Here's how to use the spell checker:

1. **Open the text item that you want to spell check (if it's not already open) by highlighting it on the Outline list and clicking the Edit button.**

2. **Choose Edit⇨Spell Check Text.**

   Family Tree Maker begins spell checking your text item and opens the Spell Check dialog box. It consists of three parts: a Not in Dictionary field, which shows the misspelled word; a Change To field, which proposes the correct spelling and in which you can fix the spelling; and a list of Suggestions that you can scroll through to find a replacement. Four buttons appear on the right side of the box: Ignore, Change, Add, and Close.

   Click Ignore if you want to skip over the word. Click Change to change the spelling to whatever appears in the Change To field. Click Add to add the word to the dictionary. And click Close to close the spell checker.

3. **Fix the spelling of the word either by typing your own correction in the Change To field or by scrolling through the list of Suggestions and picking one.**

4. **Click the Change button.**

   This action fixes the spelling of that word, and Family Tree Maker starts looking for the next misspelling. If it finds another one, the Spell Check dialog box opens again, and you have the opportunity to fix the spelling.

   After the spell checker is finished, Family Tree Maker gives you the option of spell checking the rest of the text items in your Family File.

As with any spell checker, the Family Tree Maker spell check feature doesn't catch misused words that are spelled correctly. For example, if you mistakenly type *there* when you mean to use *their,* Family Tree Maker won't catch the error and alert you to fix the spelling. So you should always proofread your text items or, better yet, have someone else read through them — sometimes it helps to have another set of eyes look things over.

A calendar

One item that you may not ordinarily think about including in your book is a calendar, as shown in Figure 11-3. And yet it appears on the Available Items list and is a rather interesting addition to a book. It allows you to draw attention to birthdays and anniversaries without making the reader sort through a report.

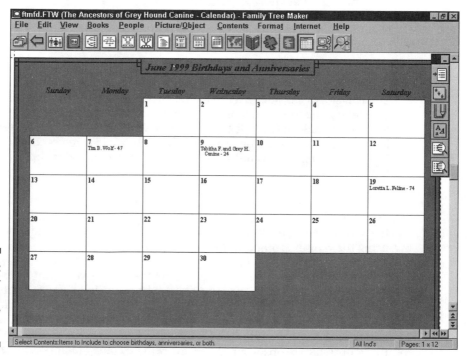

Figure 11-3:
A calendar generated with Family Tree Maker.

Just follow these two steps to insert a calendar in your book:

1. **Highlight Calendar on the Available Items list and then click the Add button.**

   Family Tree Maker adds it to your book Outline.

2. **Double-click Calendar on your Outline.**

   Or you can highlight it and click Edit.

   A Cue Card for Calendar may pop up, which offers tips and highlights about editing your calendar. If you don't want the Cue Card to pop up every time you open a calendar, click in the check box labeled `Click here if you don't want to see this Help Window again.` Then click OK.

   By default, the calendar includes the birthdays and anniversaries for everyone in your Family File. But you can customize it by using the side toolbar or the pull-down menus.

Now that you're in the Calendar view, you're wondering exactly what you can format, right? Read on to find out the details.

Items to include

You can select certain items to include and formats to use on your calendar by clicking the top button on the side toolbar. (Or you can choose Contents⇨ Items to Include in Calendar.) Family Tree Maker then opens the Items to Include in Calendar dialog box. This dialog box has three sections: Time Period, People, and Event Items to Include. It also includes three standard buttons: OK, Cancel, and Help.

In the Time Period section, you can set the Year and Month for your calendar. To set the year, click the up and down arrows next to the Year field (or type the year in the field). You can select all the months or just one month by using the Month drop-down list.

The People section enables you to select the format you want to use for names on your calendar. You can choose from the following formats: First Name, Middle Name, Last Name; First Name, Middle Initial, Last Name; Last Name, First Name, Middle Name; First Name, Last Name; First Initial, Middle Initial, Last Name; First Initial, Last Name; or Last Name. You can also select these options: Use Married Names for Female Family Members, Use Aka if Available (this one has the two subchoices: Instead of Name and Between Middle and Last Name), Last Name All Caps, and Print Only if Still Alive.

And in the Event Items to Include section, you can indicate — you guessed it — the events that you want to include on your calendar. Your choices are Birthdays, Anniversaries, or Both. Then you can select an option called Include Age for Birthdays and Years for Anniversaries. And guess what that option does — it's self-explanatory, right?

Individuals to include

Clicking the second button on the side toolbar opens a window where you can choose whether to include all the individuals in your Family File on your calendar or just selected individuals. (You can also open this window by choosing Contents⇨Individuals to Include.) Of course, if you choose to include only selected individuals, you need to click the Individuals to Include button and designate who you want to include.

Remaining buttons on the side toolbar

The remaining buttons on the side toolbar enable you to play around with the look of your calendar. The third button opens the dialog box that controls the box, line, and border styles. (Or you can choose Format⇨Box, Line, & Border Styles.) The fourth button controls text font and style. (Or you can choose Format⇨Text Font, Style, & Size.) And the last two buttons enable you to zoom in or out when reading your calendar.

Custom items for your book

So you want to get fancy, eh? Then you definitely want to include some custom reports. These are the reports that you create to your own specifications. Check out Chapter 10 for details on how to create and edit them.

To add a custom report, highlight it on the Available Items list and click the Add button. Then to actually customize it, double-click Custom Report on your book Outline or highlight it and click Edit. Family Tree Maker takes you to the report, which has a generic format until you customize it — it has the names of people in your database, their birth dates, and their death dates.

You can use the side toolbar or the pull-down menus to edit different parts of the report. The buttons on the side toolbar are the same as those for the calendar, so you can take a peek back at the preceding section to see what they are and what they do.

Focusing on the contents (Table of Contents and Index)

You may want to include a Table of Contents (shown in Figure 11-4) and Index (shown in Figure 11-5) in your book for several reasons. The most obvious one is that you want your book to look professional and impressive. Another is that you want your readers to be able to see at a glance what your book contains. This way they can quickly determine whether your book has information that may be pertinent to their research. The Index and Table of Contents also allows them to turn quickly to any information of particular interest. We are firm believers in using Tables of Contents and Indexes, mainly because those are the first sections that we look at when we pick up books.

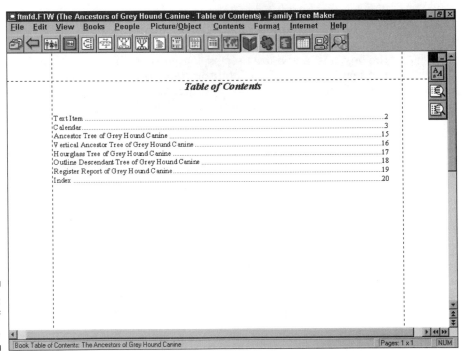

Figure 11-4:
A Table of
Contents.

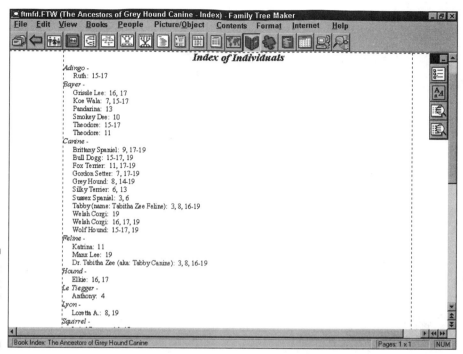

Figure 11-5:
An Index
compiled by
Family Tree
Maker.

Now for the really good news: Family Tree Maker does all the work for you in creating the Table of Contents and Index. All you have to do is add the items to your book Outline. (You can edit them a little, if you want.) Then Family Tree Maker reviews your book's contents and creates the Table of Contents and Index based on them. The Table of Contents reflects each of the items you've included in your book. If you change the title or name of an item (using Properties), the Table of Contents automatically updates to reflect the new name. The Index is a listing of names of people about whom you have information in your book and the pages on which the information appears. It's not a complete index — which means it doesn't list location names or other keywords.

The process for adding the Table of Contents and Index to your book is the same as for adding anything else that we discuss in this chapter. All you have to do is highlight the items on the list of Available Items and click the Add button. And, to edit them, you highlight them on the Outline and click the Edit button.

Technically, both the Table of Contents and the Index are Family Tree Maker reports. As such, they look a lot like the other reports, and you can change their font face and size. (You can also zoom in and out to see them more clearly.) You can customize several things in the Index by clicking the Index Options button on the side toolbar (it's the top button). This action brings up the Options for Book Index dialog box, which allows you to set the number of columns you want the index to have, as well as select the options to group first names together under the surname they share and to display index letters. Index letters are letters of the alphabet under which the surnames are categorized in the Index.

A picture is worth a thousand words

One of the easiest ways to spice up your book is to add a picture or two (or maybe more depending on the contents and length of the book). To add a picture, you need to have already stored it in one of your Family Tree Maker Scrapbooks. (We cover all the ins and outs of the Scrapbook feature in Chapter 4.)

After you have a picture in a Scrapbook, here's how you add it to your book:

1. **Go to the text item where you want to insert the picture by highlighting it on your book Outline and clicking Edit.**

   This step takes you to the text item.

2. **Place your cursor in the spot where you want to add the picture.**

3. **Choose Picture⇨Insert from Scrapbook.**

   The Individuals with Scrapbook Pictures dialog box appears, as shown in Figure 11-6. It lists all the people in your Family File who have Scrapbooks.

4. **In the Name field, enter the name of the person whose Scrapbook contains the picture you want (or scroll through the list and select the person) and then click OK.**

   The Insert Scrapbook Picture dialog box appears. It lists the Scrapbook items that are available for you to use. To preview the picture, select the Preview Picture option. If you want to include a caption with your picture, select the Display Caption with Picture option. And if, by chance, you selected the wrong person from the list of Individuals with Scrapbook Pictures, you can click the Select New Individual button at the top of this dialog box.

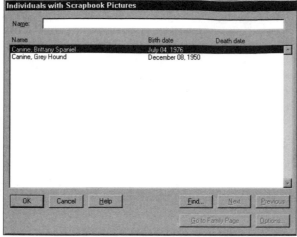

Figure 11-6:
The
Individuals
with
Scrapbook
Pictures
dialog box.

5. **Select the picture that you want to insert.**

Family Tree Maker inserts the selected picture in the location where your cursor is.

The picture may not look exactly as you expect it to look. It may be too big or too little, or it may not be positioned to your liking. If this is the case, just resize it or move it around. To change the size of it, choose Picture⇨ Size Picture and then set the width that you want the picture to be and click OK. To move the picture, simply click it and drag it to the location where you want it.

After you have your picture(s) in place in the text item, be sure to save the text item so that Family Tree Maker keeps it just the way you like it.

Mapping the way

If you're using Family Tree Maker Version 7.0, you have the option of including maps in your book. Including a map or two is a nice way to illustrate parts of your text items that refer to locations (that is, if you have any text items that mention places).

Including a map is as easy as selecting other items for your book. Just highlight Map on the Available Items list and add it to your Outline. Then double-click Map in the Outline (or highlight Map and click Edit) to get to the default map, which is of the United States.

The default map of the United States has marks for each of the places identified in your database. This means any place that's listed in a Location field on the Family Pages is reflected on the map. At some point, you'll probably want a map of something different. Never fear — side toolbar to the rescue!

The bottom five buttons on the side toolbar enable you to do some customizations that are standard in Family Tree Maker. In other words, they're the same things you can do for trees and reports. These buttons are Items to Include, Individuals to Include, Text Font & Style, Zoom In, and Zoom Out.

The top four buttons are specific to maps. The top button (Map Format) on the side toolbar brings up the Map Format dialog box, where you can select the layout of the map and indicate whether the map should have a legend. The next button (Map Size and Area) enables you to reset the map size and area that it displays — use the cursor (which becomes a crosshair) to crop the map to just the area you want. You use the third button (Change Map) to select another map. Your choices are Europe (political or shaded relief), North America (political), U.S. (shaded relief), and World (political or shaded relief). And the third button from the bottom of the side toolbar (Location Check) gives you a status report on the number of locations Family Tree Maker found for the particular area that the map covers — basically it tells you the number of locations it found for that area, as well as that it is going to mark the locations on the map for you.

After you get your map to look just the way you want it, be sure to save it.

Arranging or Rearranging Items

After you determine which items you want to include in your book, your next step is to place them in the order of your choice. You can do this two ways. The first is by highlighting the item in the Outline list and dragging the item to its new location. If you're not a fan of dragging, you can highlight the item on the Outline list and then use the Move Up or Move Down buttons to reposition it.

If you're having a little trouble deciding where things should go in your book, here are some helpful hints. Typically, the Title Page goes first, followed by the Table of Contents, and then the Introduction. And the Index should be the last thing in the book. And we suggest putting your chapters, reports, trees, and other items somewhere in the middle. Of course, these are just our recommendations, and you can put your book in any order you want.

Printing Your Masterpiece

You may be thinking, printing my book should be an easy process, right? You probably choose print from the File menu, or click a little printer icon, or something just as easy. Actually, it's not quite that simple if you don't want to use the default print settings for the entire thing. Say, for example, you prefer to have a particular tree printed with a portrait orientation, but the default is to print with a landscape orientation. The way Family Tree Maker is set up, each item in your book has its own print settings, so if you want to change the way something is printed, you need to go to that item and make the necessary alterations on a piece-by-piece basis. Here's how:

1. **Highlight the item on your Outline and click the Edit button.**

2. **Choose File⇨Print Setup and change any settings that you desire.**

   The basic setup includes designating the default printer, the orientation of the paper (landscape or portrait), the paper size and source, and the margins.

3. **Go back to the main Book view and choose File⇨Print Book.**

   Family Tree Maker uses the individual item settings to print the entire book.

Of course, if the default print settings meet your needs, then you can simply choose File⇨Print Book to print off a copy. Family Tree Maker then uses the defaults for each of the items in your book.

If you want to share a particular text item with someone, but you don't want to print your whole book, you can print just that text item. Go to the item, highlight it on the Outline, click Edit, and choose File⇨Print.

Other Book-Related Options

The first time you use the Books pull-down menu, you'll notice that your options are quite limited. In fact, you have only one choice — to create a New Book. But after you create the book, most of the other options on the pull-down menu become active so you can use them. In particular, these options are what you use to open existing books or to delete books. Also, an option called Book Properties starts out disabled, but becomes active after you've created a book.

By clicking Book Properties, you can find out the lowdown about a particular book. It tells you the title of the book, the author's name, the total number of pages, the date it was created, and the date it was last updated. It also controls your book's page numbering. And if you select Book Header and Footer, you can choose what appears as the header and/or footer throughout your book and determine the font to use for both.

Chapter 12

Exporting Relatives With Your Computer

- -

In This Chapter

▶ Copying your Family File

▶ Creating a Web page

▶ Contributing to the World Family Tree

▶ Generating GEDCOMs

- -

*E*veryone has those days when they want to send some of their family members away — preferably to Timbuktu. Regrettably, that's not what we discuss in this chapter. Instead, we talk about exporting genealogical information that you've gathered about your relatives to another file or onto the World Wide Web. We discuss four ways to share your information with other researchers including copying Family Files, exporting to the World Wide Web, contributing to the World Family Tree, and creating GEDCOM files to share with other researchers.

The Many Lives of a Copycat

What do you do when you want to share a physical document with another genealogical researcher? We're willing to bet that you simply photocopy the item and send the copy to the other person. Are we right? You can also copy your Family File to share with another person, but in this case, you don't need a photocopier. All you have to do is follow these simple steps:

1. **Start Family Tree Maker. If you have more than one Family File, open the one that you intend to share.**

   Typically, you start Family Tree Maker by double-clicking its icon or by choosing Start⇨Programs⇨Family Tree Maker (in Windows 95 or 98).

2. **Choose File➪Copy/Export Family File.**

   The New Family File dialog box appears. This dialog box allows you to pick a name for the file and choose the format in which to save the file.

3. **In the Save In field at the top of the dialog box, select where you want to save the copy.**

   The Save In field is a drop-down list box from which you can choose where to save the copy of your Family File. You can choose from the various directories and drives on your computer. If you're saving the copy to floppy disk, select the appropriate disk drive, which is usually drive A. If you plan to e-mail the copy (as an attachment to an e-mail message), save the copy to your computer's hard drive.

4. **In the File Name field, enter a name for the copy of your Family File.**

   You should pick a name other than the one you use for your Family File. If you try to use the same name, Family Tree Maker will scorn you, and who wants that? Actually, you will receive an error message telling you to specify a different name.

   Say we're making a copy of the Canine/Feline Family File, which is named Canine.FTW. We pick a new name for the copy of the database: Canine and Feline.FTW.

5. **In the Save as Type field, select the file format from the drop-down list.**

   You can choose from various FTW (that's the extension for Family Tree Maker) files and several GED (GEDCOM) files. (We cover GEDCOM in "Creating GEDCOM Files," later in this chapter.) Assuming you're sharing the file with another researcher who also uses Family Tree Maker, choose whichever FTW file type applies.

   If the researcher that you are sharing with uses a Macintosh version of Family Tree Maker, select Family Tree Maker 3.0 for Win/Mac.

   We want to share our Canine and Feline file with Cousin Silky Terrier Canine who uses Family Tree Maker 5.0 for Windows. So we select the appropriate FTW option for Version 5.0 from the drop-down list.

6. **Click the Save button.**

   Family Tree Maker saves a copy of your Family File in the location you've selected.

Now all you have to do is delete from the file anything that you don't want to share with the other researcher and then send the file to that person.

You may be asking, "Why would I want to delete anything from the copy before sending it to someone else?" In one short answer — privacy. You don't want to invade people's privacy by sharing personal information about them or stories that may hurt them. Otherwise, you may spend the rest of your life in the familial doghouse. We recommend that you remove anything about living persons from trees, reports, books, Family Files, and other items that you plan to share with a third party, even if that third party is directly related to you. If your relatives are rather thick-skinned and don't mind that you share their names and places in the family with others, then your best bet is to privatize the file before copying it. But if your relatives are easily upset or may get hurt, you should withhold or delete the information before passing along a copy.

We cover two methods of hiding information in your Family File in the "When to withhold information" and "Keeping things private" sidebars, later in this chapter. But you can also delete information from the copy of your Family File. After you make a copy of your Family File, you can delete information from certain fields or even remove individuals and all of their information at one time.

Be sure that you do not delete anything in the primary file that you use for your research. We suggest that you check the file name in the title bar at the top of the screen to ensure that you are making changes to the correct file.

Follow these steps to delete a person from a Family File:

1. **Go to the Family Page of the person you want to delete.**

2. **Choose People⊏>Delete Individual.**

   A dialog box appears, asking if you're sure you want to delete this individual.

3. **Click Yes if you're positive that you want to delete this person from the file. Click No if you're not sure.**

   If you click Yes, Family Tree Maker removes this person and all of his or her information from your file.

We all make mistakes. So, if you happen to delete the wrong individual, you can get the information back if you act as soon as you make the deletion. To undelete an individual, choose Edit⊏>Undelete Individual or press Ctrl+Z.

Family Tree Maker automatically saves your work anytime you make a change or exit the program, so you don't need to manually save the file after you clean it up. All you need to do is eject the disk, write some contact information on it (in case the recipient has questions or for future reference), stick it in an envelope (preferably one designed for mailing disks), and send it to the other researcher. If you're e-mailing the file to the other person, just compose an e-mail message and attach the file.

A Personal Web Page: If You Build It. . . .

At some point, you're likely to want to share your information with global audiences and enable others to share information with you. One easy way to share your information is to post your data to a Web page. If you already have a personal Web page (through your Internet service provider account or through work), then consider putting your information there. If you don't have a Web page, Family Tree Maker can take care of it for you.

You've seen those bank and credit-card commercials offering exclusive privileges for members or card-holders. Well, as a member of the Family Tree Maker family, you have certain privileges, too. One such privilege is the ability to post your own Web page on the Family Tree Maker Web site. The site includes a section that is just for users. When you're ready to share your knowledge (well, genealogical findings anyway) with the world, just create a page using your software and upload it to the Family Tree Maker site.

Registering with Family Tree Maker Online

Please don't scream when we tell you this (we don't want to worry your spouse or roommate, you know), but registering your Family Tree Maker software with the company does not automatically register you to use portions of Family Tree Maker Online that are restricted to software users. You have to complete a Web-based registration form before you can create a User Home Page at the Family Tree Maker site.

We can hear you now: "Oh great. Another form to complete!" Relax — it's a simple and straightforward process. Just follow these steps:

1. **Hook up your phone line to your computer's modem.**

   Unhook the phone line from the phone that's nearest to your computer. Then plug that end of the phone line into your computer's modem; depending on whether you're using an internal or external modem, you plug the cord into the jack on the back of your computer or into the back of the external modem box.

2. **Start Family Tree Maker.**

   Double-click the Family Tree icon on your Windows desktop or use your Start button to start the program.

3. **Choose Internet⇨Go Online.**

   Your Web browser opens and goes to the Family Tree Maker Web site. If you've never used Family Tree Maker Online before, you need to complete the registration form that pops up. If you've just updated your Family Tree Maker software and have used the Family Tree Maker Online site before, then you need to verify information about your old account. Click whichever link best applies to your situation — New Family Tree Maker Online User or Verify Old Family Tree Maker Online Account — and then follow the online steps.

   After you've either registered or verified your information, the regular Family Tree Maker Online page will appear each time you go online by using the software.

   Our good friend Grey Hound Canine just bought Family Tree Maker 7.0 and is a brand-new user. We registered him to use Family Tree Maker Online.

4. **Click the New Family Tree Maker Online User link.**

   The Family Tree Maker Online Sign-Up page comes up. Scroll down until you see the fields that you need to complete in order to register.

5. **In the appropriate name fields, provide your First Name (required), Middle Name (Optional), and Last Name (required).**

   We enter *Grey* in the First Name field, *Hound* in the Middle Name field, and *Canine* in the Last Name field.

6. **In the appropriate address fields, provide your street address, city, state/province, zip or postal code, and country.**

   We enter Grey's address in these fields.

7. **Enter your phone and fax numbers in the Telephone and Fax fields, respectively.**

   In the Telephone field, we enter Grey's home phone number. He doesn't have a fax machine at home, so we leave the Fax field blank.

8. **Enter your e-mail address in the E-Mail Address field.**

   Grey's e-mail address goes in this field. We make sure to include the entire address — his user name, the @ symbol, and then the domain name. (A domain name is something like aol.com, uiuc.edu, or tbox.com.)

9. **If you want to receive occasional e-mail messages from Family Tree Maker and/or copies of the free *Family Tree Maker Magazine,* select the appropriate options near the end of the online registration form.**

   Grey loves to get e-mail and regular mail, so we sign him up to receive occasional e-mail messages and the magazine.

10. **Click Submit.**

    A new page appears, thanking you for registering. It tells you that your registration with Family Tree Maker is complete and that you now have access to all the online features. (If your registration is not successful, you receive a message to this effect with guidance on how to return to the form and complete it properly.)

Now wasn't that easy? And you were so worried. Of course, the next step is to create your User Home Page. But that process involves several steps, so we decided to give it its own section. Please keep reading. . . .

User Home Pages: Easy as 1-2-3

After you register to use Family Tree Maker Online, you can start creating your User Home Page. (If you haven't registered yet, take a look at the preceding section, which walks you through the process.)

Follow these steps to create your User Home Page:

1. **On the Thank you! page that appears after you finish registering to use Family Tree Maker Online, click the <u>Create Your Home Page</u> link now.**

   If you registered before and are returning to create your User Home Page, then go to the Web site at www.familytreemaker.com/ cgi-bin/_uhp_create.

   The Create Your Own Home Page Web page appears, as shown in Figure 12-1. It includes fields for you to provide information along with instructions on how to fill out the fields.

2. Enter a title for your home page in the Title field.

We like titles that are catchy but informative. Don't label your page something so generic or overwhelming that people won't want to visit it. So stay away from titles like *Smiths of the World* or *John Martin's Home Page*.

Say we're posting a User Home Page for good ol' Grey Hound Canine on which he plans to share all he knows about his ancestors. Without spending lots of time coming up with a title, we decide to call Grey's User Home Page *Howlin' My History: Some Canines from Pennsylvania and Kentucky.* This title is a catchy play on Grey's last name, but it also identifies the primary surname that the home page focuses on and the locations where Grey's ancestors lived.

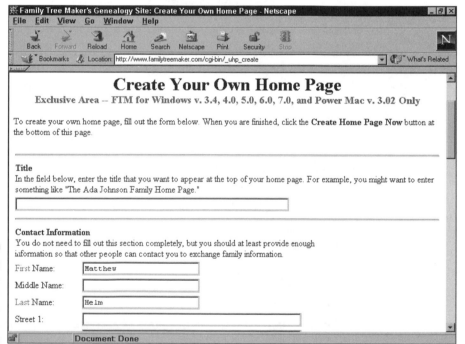

Figure 12-1:
The Create
Your Own
Home Page
Web page.

3. **In the Contact Information portion of the page, complete the fields for the types of information that you want to provide.**

   You can include your name, address, phone number, fax number, and e-mail address. Any field that you complete will appear on your page, so if you don't want people to have your address, don't provide it here. We recommend that you provide your name and e-mail address. This information enables visitors to contact you if they have questions or information to share with you.

   For our example, we enter Grey Hound Canine's information in the First Name, Last Name, and E-Mail Address fields.

4. **If you have another Web site, enter that URL in the URL field and enter a brief description of the site in the Description field.**

   Grey used to have one of those free Web pages, but because he didn't update it for a year, the provider banished him from its servers. Therefore, we don't enter anything in these two fields for Grey.

5. **In the Text box (it's a free-form box), enter any text that you want to appear near the top of your home page.**

   We recommend that you enter the surnames and locations that you're researching. That way, visitors to your home page can quickly determine if your page has anything to offer them or if they have anything to offer to you.

   For Grey's page, we enter two brief sentences — one identifying the surnames (and their locations) that Wolf is researching and one identifying the surnames that his wife is researching.

6. **Select a Style option to determine how your page will look.**

   This style will be used in part of the layout and the graphics on your page (things like the background or the images that separate sections of your page). Each style has links to samples so that you can preview what your page will look like before making your selection. Our only recommendation is that you try to pick something that isn't annoying to look at for very long.

   We like the Map style, shown in Figure 12-2, so we select it for Grey's home page.

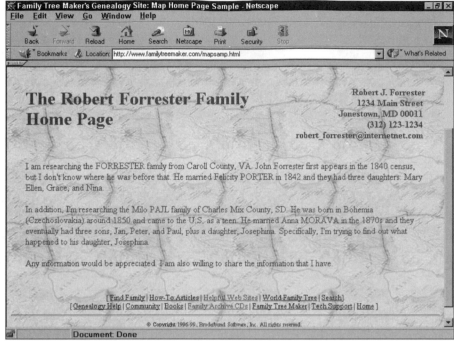

Figure 12-2:
The sample page where we can see the Map style prior to selecting it for Grey's User Home Page.

7. **Click the Create Home Page Now button.**

    If you leave something out that Family Tree Maker believes should be included, a page appears, identifying what is missing and giving you an opportunity to provide it.

    Family Tree Maker shows you a sample of what your home page will look like with the information you provided and the style you selected. This is your chance to change the look of your home page if you don't like it. Just click the Back button to return to the form that you completed and make any changes.

8. **If you like what you see on the sample home page, click the Create Home Page Now button.**

    Clicking the Create Home Page Now button from the sample page takes you to a page that tells you that your home page has been created. You can see your home page by clicking the <u>Here</u> link and then you can bookmark it.

After you create your User Home Page, you can always access it by choosing Internet⇨My Home Page. This action opens your Web browser and takes you directly to your User Home Page so you can view it or update it. If you want to share the address of your home page with others, you may want to jot down its URL. You can find it in the location field or address field of your browser. In our case, the URL is `www.familytreemaker.com/users/h/e/l/ April-Helm/index.html`.

Planting trees (and other things) on your Web page

One nice thing about using Family Tree Maker to put together your home page is that you can include any of the many charts, reports, and books you've already created. All you have to do is click a few buttons or open a few menus, and before you know it, you have an impressive Web site sharing your information with the world.

Here's how to add a family tree to your Web page:

1. **In Family Tree Maker, choose Internet⇨My Home Page.**

   This action takes you to your User Home Page on Family Tree Maker Online.

   Using Grey Hound Canine for our example, we see the page titled, *Howlin' My History: Some Canines from Pennsylvania and Kentucky.*

2. **Use the Alt+Tab key combination to return to Family Tree Maker.**

   You can also return to Family Tree Maker, while keeping your Web browser open, two other ways. You can use the Windows taskbar (which is usually at the bottom of the screen) or minimize your browser (by clicking the Minimize button in the upper-right corner of the screen — it's the one that looks like an underline).

3. **Choose Internet⇨Publish Family Tree to the Internet.**

   If Family Tree Maker isn't sure whether you're already online, a Publish Family Tree on the Internet dialog box opens, thanking you for trying to share your tree but reminding you to double-check your online status. If you're sure you're online, click OK.

   An Include dialog box opens, in which you can determine whether to include information about all individuals or only selected individuals.

4. **Select the All Individuals option or the Selected Individuals option. If you choose the latter, you must identify who you want to include by clicking the Individuals to Include button.**

We strongly recommend that you select the Selected Individuals option — and include information only about people who are deceased. You should be careful when posting any information to the Internet about living persons because it's an invasion of their privacy. For more about privacy concerns, see both sidebars in this chapter.

Because we don't want to include any information about Grey's living relatives, we select the Selected Individuals option. Then we click the Individuals to Include button and go through the list of people in Grey's database. We choose only those people that we know are deceased for inclusion in the tree.

5. Click OK.

A message box appears, telling you that Family Tree Maker is copying your information to your home page and asking if you want to contribute your information to the World Family Tree as well. (We talk more about the World Family Tree in the next section.) Answer No for now.

You then receive another message that your report has been successfully uploaded and should be available for viewing on your home page within so many minutes. After the tree is posted to your User Home Page, you can visit the page to see it. To see the tree that we posted to Grey's User Home Page, take a gander at Figure 12-3.

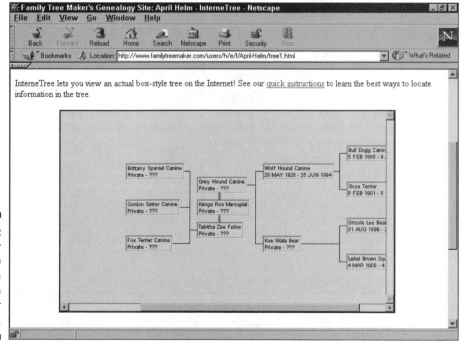

Figure 12-3: An Ancestor (pedigree) tree that we posted to Grey's User Home Page.

In some of the preceding steps, we touch briefly on protecting others' privacy. One way to do this is to go through the list of people in your database and mark only certain ones for inclusion in your online family tree (see the "When to withhold information" sidebar). Another way is to privatize your Family File before executing the command to publish your tree on the Internet. (We cover privatization in the sidebar, "Keeping things private," later in this chapter.) The only catch to privatizing is that it doesn't hide the names of your relatives — it only hides personal facts about them, such as dates and locations of births, marriages, and deaths.

Would you prefer to use reports or books rather than trees on your User Home Page? You're in luck — you can upload Family Tree Maker reports and books just as easily as you upload family trees. You follow similar steps to those for family trees (see the preceding steps), but instead of starting from the Family Page of the person who is the focus of a tree, you create the report or book in Family Tree Maker and customize it however you want. Then choose Internet⇨Publish Report to the Internet or choose Internet⇨ Publish Book to the Internet. Some of the formatting in your Family Tree Maker reports and books won't transfer to your home page, but for the most part, the documents will look similar.

When to withhold information

Situations may arise in which you want to withhold or suppress information about a person in family trees and reports that you create to share with others. The situations may be estranged relationships with parents, disowned children, out-of-wedlock births, or any number of other situations. Although you don't want to include this information on your tree or report, you don't want to delete it entirely from your database. So what do you do?

Family Tree Maker enables you to exclude some relationships from the family trees and reports that you generate. You can exclude the relationship between a person and his or her father, or mother, or both. Each relationship is handled separately.

You can find the option to exclude relationships with parents on the More About Lineage page. To open this page, go to the Family Page for the person whose relationship with his or her parents you want to exclude. Click the More button next to the person's name and then click the button for the Lineage page.

Selecting the option to exclude a relationship keeps Family Tree Maker from displaying it in family trees and reports, but it does not prevent the software from including the relationship in a GEDCOM file or your Family File in general. So, if you want to exclude a relationship from a GEDCOM file or a Family File, you must delete the relationship altogether.

Becoming Part of the World — The World Family Tree, That Is

Just as the ability to create and post your User Home Page is a benefit of membership in the Family Tree Maker family, so is the invitation to participate in the World Family Tree.

The *World Family Tree* is a large database (containing over 100,000 family trees) that Broderbund created to help genealogists share their information. It has been around since 1995 and continues to grow as more and more people contribute information to it. It currently has data about millions of individuals, but it is a source of controversy among some genealogical circles.

The folks at Family Tree Maker and Broderbund have taken quite a bit of flak about the World Family Tree because of its medium and availability. It's available only on CD-ROMs, and the CD-ROMs are not free, which angers many people. They don't understand how Broderbund can charge money for something that wouldn't exist without the contributions of others. Although we don't know what Broderbund would say about this issue, we do know that it takes money to create and maintain programs to handle all the information and make it accessible on the CDs, and it takes money to produce the CDs themselves. So if you contribute your genealogical information to the project, should you expect to receive a set of the CDs for free? We think not. (However, we must clarify that if you have the deluxe version of Family Tree Maker, it includes a set of the CDs — but not all of them.) Our advice is: If you feel uncomfortable about submitting your information, just don't do it. You can certainly share your information other ways, as we discuss earlier in this chapter, so there is no requirement to submit your information to the World Family Tree. Now that we've made our opinions known, we'll step down off our soapbox and get on to the nitty-gritty details of the World Family Tree.

How the World Family Tree can help you

If you're like us, you want to know exactly how something is going to benefit you before you'll spend your hard-earned money on it. So why should the World Family Tree be any different? It shouldn't.

The database known as the World Family Tree may help you make connections with others who share or are interested in some of the same family lines as you. It contains lots of information contributed by people from around the world. By connecting with others, you can get more information from other researchers and coordinate joint research, which can save you time and energy.

Aside from knowing the general benefits of the World Family Tree, wouldn't it be nice to know whether it contains information specific to your research without having to first buy the CDs? That's where the Internet FamilyFinder and the FamilyFinder Index come in. You can search the CDs by using the Internet FamilyFinder at the Family Tree Maker Web site or by using the FamilyFinder Index on CD (which comes with the deluxe version). Either utility identifies name matches and tells you which World Family Tree CDs have information that may be of interest to you.

How you can help the World Family Tree

Why would you want to contribute your family history to the World Family Tree if you don't get even one set of the CD-ROMs for your trouble? The primary reason is simple and self-serving: You want to connect with other researchers who are interested in the same family lines so that you can exchange information and coordinate research. Contributing your information to the World Family Tree gives other researchers one more way to find and contact you, much like if you posted your research findings on a Web page or provided a list of the surnames you're researching on a message board, newsgroup, or mailing list.

You do receive some other benefits for contributing your information to the World Family Tree. First, doing so enables you to store your findings in a location that is safe for the long term. If something would happen to the Family Tree Maker database and the records you keep at home, you can get a copy of the World Family Tree and pick up where your research left off, at the point where you shared or updated your contribution. That way, you don't have to start all over. Another benefit is that you can help others by enabling them to access your information. Not only can people today learn from your research, but future generations can, too, because your family tree becomes part of a database that will be archived at the Library of Congress.

Making a contribution

You can contribute your family history findings to the World Family Tree via the Internet, or you can save a copy to disk and mail it to Broderbund. Whichever method you prefer, exercise caution when sharing your file. Make sure that the data in your file is as accurate as possible and that you're not invading someone's privacy by sharing the information. In the following three sections, not only do we explore how to contribute your file, but we also go through a checklist of areas where you need to be careful.

Online donations

Contributing your genealogical information to the World Family Tree via the Internet is the easiest way to do so. Here's what you do:

1. **Start Family Tree Maker. If you have more than one Family File, open the one that you intend to share.**

2. **Choose Internet⇨Contribute to the World Family Tree.**

    The Your Rights as a Contributor to the World Family Tree dialog box appears.

3. **Read through the dialog box carefully and then click Yes or No, depending on whether you agree to contribute your information to the project.**

    The dialog box outlines your rights after you've contributed information to the World Family Tree. Primarily, it states that by submitting information, you give Broderbund your permission to reproduce and distribute your information in any form and that you give your permission for the company to use your name and contact information. It also addresses copyright, privacy, and compensation issues.

    If you click Yes, the World Family Tree Contribution dialog box appears (see Figure 12-4), in which you can provide your contact information.

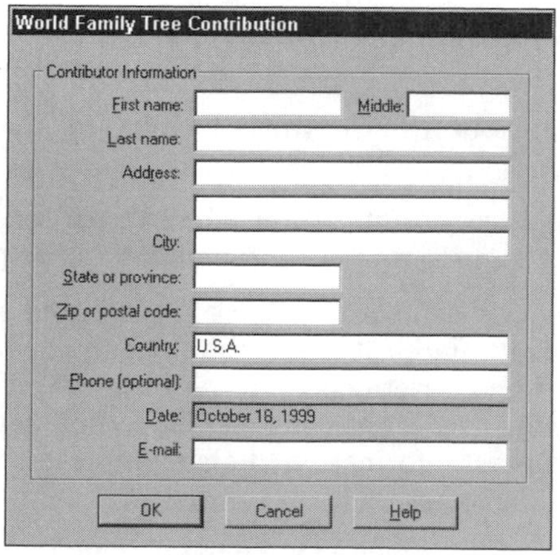

Figure 12-4: A dialog box in which you can provide your contact information to the World Family Tree.

World Family Tree Contribution

Contributor Information

First name: Middle:
Last name:
Address:

City:
State or province:
Zip or postal code:
Country: U.S.A.
Phone (optional):
Date: October 18, 1999
E-mail:

OK   Cancel   Help

4. **Complete all the fields in the World Family Tree Contribution dialog box.**

   This dialog box contains the following fields: First Name, Middle, Last Name, Address, City, State or Province, Zip or Postal Code, Country, Phone (optional), Date (autopopulating), and E-Mail.

5. **Click OK.**

   Your information is transferred to Family Tree Maker via the Internet.

May I have the disk, please?

You can contribute your genealogical information to the World Family Tree even if you don't have an Internet service provider or don't trust the Internet as a means for sharing information. All you have to do is use a floppy disk (either 3½ inch or 5¼ inch), which you then mail to Broderbund.

Follow these steps to create this disk:

1. **Start Family Tree Maker. If you have more than one Family File, open the one that you intend to share.**

2. **Choose File⇨Contribute to the World Family Tree.**

   A dialog box opens and asks you how you want to share your file. Your options are Online, Diskette, or Cancel.

3. **Insert a blank disk in your computer's floppy drive and select the Diskette option.**

   The Your Rights as a Contributor to the World Family Tree dialog box appears.

4. **Read through the dialog box carefully, then select Yes or No, depending on whether you agree to contribute your information to the project.**

   The dialog box outlines your rights after you've contributed information to the World Family Tree. Primarily, it states that by submitting information, you give Broderbund your permission to reproduce and distribute your information in any form and that you give the company permission to use your name and contact information. It also addresses copyright, privacy, and compensation issues.

   If you selected Yes, then a box appears in which you will direct your computer to store your contribution and provide contact information about yourself.

5. **Click the appropriate button for the destination of your World Family Tree contribution.**

Your choices are Floppy Drive (A:), Working Directory, and possibly other drives labeled as Floppy Drive. These other drives may include a Zip Disk or other removable media device. Family Tree Maker just calls them all Floppy Drives.

6. **Complete all the fields in the World Family Tree Contribution dialog box.**

   This dialog box has the following fields for you to complete: First Name, Middle, Last Name, Address, City, State or Province, Zip or Postal Code, Country, Phone (optional), Date (autopopulating), and E-Mail.

7. **Click OK.**

   Your information is copied to the disk.

8. **Take the disk out of your computer and label it with your name, your address, and the date.**

   The recipients can use this information to contact you if the disk is damaged or if they can't transfer your data from it for some reason.

9. **Put the disk in an envelope that's designed for mailing floppy disks and mail it to Broderbund Software, Banner Blue Division, World Family Tree Project, P.O. Box 760, Fremont, CA 94537-0760.**

Getting some exercise (exercising caution, that is)

Before you share your Family File with the World Family Tree project (or with anyone for that matter), you want to make sure that it's presentable. Here's a checklist of things to do before sharing your file:

- Make sure that you've documented the sources of your information by using the source citation features of Family Tree Maker (see Chapter 6 for details).

- Make a copy of your Family File and delete all the information about living persons. (You could privatize your file, but the World Family Tree would still contain names and genders of everyone listed in your database. Some people may not want even their names to appear on the CD-ROMs.)

- Run a Data Errors report on your Family File and try to fix any serious problems before sharing your information. We're not talking about making sure you have dates and locations for births, marriages, and deaths for every single person in your file (because you're likely to be missing at least a few). Instead, we're talking about fixing serious discrepancies that would cause others to question the integrity of your file — things like having a child's birth date after the death date of the mother, or a child's birth date prior to the mother's birth.

✔ Review your file and make sure that it doesn't contain anything that would be considered a violation of copyright law — that means no quotes in your book(s) or notes that are not attributed to the proper source.

✔ Use good taste when selecting items to include in the Family File that you're contributing. Don't include anything that can be considered defamatory, obscene, profane, or rude.

✔ Notify Broderbund if you move or change Internet service providers. This way, the company can keep its database of contact information as up-to-date as possible. It passes along your contact information to persons who inquire about your contribution to the World Family Tree. Having your current address enables the other researchers to contact you to ask questions about your data or to share their research information with you.

Creating GEDCOM Files

What is this GEDCOM stuff, anyway? It's the acronym for *Genealogical Data Communication,* but that really doesn't tell you much, does it? In plain English, a GEDCOM file is a text file that contains your genealogical information marked with a set of tags that other genealogical databases (which import the information) recognize and use to determine where to place the particular piece of information within their structures. It makes data translatable to different genealogical software programs so that you can easily share your family information with people who use genealogical software other than Family Tree Maker. The only requirement is that the other software supports GEDCOM.

In addition to creating GEDCOM files to exchange with other researchers, you can generate GEDCOM files to submit to larger cooperatives, which make the data from many GEDCOM files available to thousands of researchers worldwide via the World Wide Web and e-mail.

Creating a GEDCOM in Family Tree Maker is easy. You simply export your Family File to the GEDCOM format by following these steps:

1. **Start Family Tree Maker. If you have more than one Family File, open the one that you intend to share.**

   You can start the program by double-clicking the Family Tree Maker icon or by choosing Start⇨Programs⇨ Family Tree Maker (in Windows 95 or 98).

2. **Choose File⇨Copy/Export Family File.**

   The New Family File dialog box appears. This dialog box allows you to enter a name for the file and choose the format in which to save the file (GEDCOM).

3. **In the Save In field, select where you want to save the copy.**

   The Save In field is a drop-down list from which you can choose where to save the copy of your Family File. You can choose from the various directories and drives on your computer. If you're saving the copy to floppy disk, select the floppy drive, which is usually drive A. If you plan to e-mail the copy (as an attachment to an e-mail message), save the copy to your computer's hard drive.

4. **Type the new name for your GEDCOM file in the File Name field.**

5. **In the Save as Type field, select GEDCOM (*.GED) as the format by selecting it from the drop-down list.**

6. **Click the Save button.**

   The Export to GEDCOM dialog box appears, as shown in Figure 12-5. This dialog box enables you to set up the GEDCOM in a specific format.

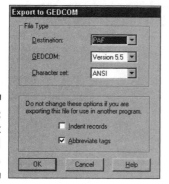

Figure 12-5:
The Export
to GEDCOM
dialog box.

7. **In the Destination field, select the destination software program to which you want to export the file.**

   If you don't know which program the other person uses, leave the field at its default setting: Family Tree Maker for Windows.

8. **In the GEDCOM field, select the version of GEDCOM to which you're exporting.**

   Most genealogical software is compatible with the most recent version of GEDCOM, so you're usually safe to keep the default setting. If you know that the person to whom you are sending your GEDCOM is using older software that supports an older version of GEDCOM, change the output settings to accommodate that person.

9. **In the Character Set field, select ANSI (which is the default) from the drop-down list.**

You can choose from four different character sets, including ANSEL, ANSI, IBMPC, and MACINTOSH. The default setting, ANSI, is the normal character set used by Microsoft Windows. If you are dealing with a lot of international characters, then you may want to use ANSEL as the character set.

10. **If you have a preference for how the GEDCOM output is formatted, select or deselect the Indent Records and Abbreviate Tags options.**

    If you select the Indent Records option, the records are indented rather than displayed in a straight list, flush left in the file. Indenting the records makes it a little easier to read through the GEDCOM when you open it in a word processor. Family Tree Maker indents lines based on the number code for the line. For example, all ones are flush left, twos are indented once, and threes are indented twice.

    If you select the Abbreviate Tags option, the GEDCOM tags are abbreviated rather than written in their entirety. For example, the tag *Header* would be *Head,* and the tag *Address* would be *Addr.*

11. **After you complete all the required boxes and are satisfied with the options that you have selected, click the OK button.**

After the file is exported to your hard drive, you can open it in a word processor (such as WordPad) and review it to ensure that the information is formatted the way you want it. Also, by reviewing it in a word processor, you can make sure that you've included no information on living persons and manually edit the information if you need to do so. After you're satisfied with the file, you can cut and paste it into an e-mail message or send it as an attachment.

Keeping things private

Sometimes in our haste and excitement to share the valuable, genealogical information we've collected, we forget that our databases and paper files may contain information about (or that affects) living persons. For example, your file may contain dates and locations of births and marriages for your kids, siblings, cousins, and so forth. It may also contain stories about your ancestors that are colorful but possibly embarrassing to some of your living relatives. We strongly recommend that you don't invade the privacy of these relatives by passing this kind of information along to other people.

You should act responsibly and remove any information about living persons from your database before sharing it. Actually, you don't really remove it from your primary database; you make a copy of your Family File and delete the information from the copy. Then you share the cleaned-up copy with others.

If your relatives don't mind your sharing minimal information about them with other researchers, you have another option for cleaning your file before sharing it. It's called privatizing your Family File. When you privatize your file, Family Tree Maker hides everything that you've entered about living persons except their names, genders, and places in the family (links to their parents and kids).

Here's how to privatize your Family File:

1. **Choose File⇨Preferences⇨Privatize.**

   The Privatize Information dialog box appears, which explains that privatizing hides information about living individuals in your Family File. Anything that is privatized won't show on the screen, and you can't print, copy, or export it.

2. **Select the Privatize Information option and then click OK.**

   Family Tree Maker privatizes your file and shows you a progress bar. After it's done, the Privatized File dialog box opens, informing you that Family Tree Maker doesn't privatize book items, so you need to manually remove or hide information about living persons in your book items.

3. **In the Privatized File dialog box, click OK.**

   After your file is privatized, the color of the Family Pages and your screen changes from yellow to green, and the file becomes *read-only*, meaning that you can't make any changes to it as long as it's privatized. The following figure shows an example of a privatized Family Page.

   To make your Family File active again so you can make changes and additions, choose File⇨Preferences⇨Privatize again.

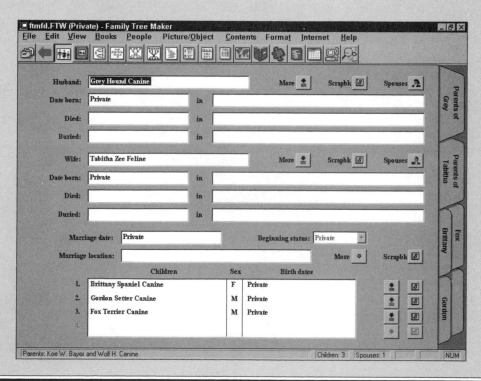

Part IV
The Part of Tens

The 5th Wave   By Rich Tennant

Hmm - this not good. Some Tarzan relatives on family tree, others swing from family tree.

In this part . . .

*I*n this part, you find out some ideas on how to make using Family Tree Maker more enjoyable. You discover some shortcuts that can save you time and some hints on how to avoid calling technical support. And, for those of you who have the deluxe version of Family Tree Maker, we cover the CD-ROMs that come with Version 7.0.

Chapter 13

Ten Things You Can Do to Reduce Stress

. . . .

In This Chapter

▶ Customizing Family Tree Maker

▶ Avoiding embarrassing situations

. . . .

Sit down in your chair. Now close your eyes. Breathe in, breathe out. Oops, wrong kind of book. Perhaps we can't reduce your overall stress (although we do recommend one of those chair back massagers — we find them quite helpful in times of stress), but we can give you some suggestions on things you can do with Family Tree Maker to make your research more enjoyable.

Bursting the Bubble

When you first begin using Family Tree Maker, the Bubble Help function (the little yellow tags that pop up when you place your cursor in a field or on a button) is a handy feature. It gives you information about the field that you're working in and helps you go along your merry way. After you've entered your 400th person in the database, this feature becomes, well, a little annoying to say the least. Fortunately, you can remedy the situation by shutting off Bubble Help. Simply choose File⇨Preferences⇨Help Tools. In the Help Tools dialog box that appears, deselect the Bubble Help option and then click OK. In this same dialog box, you can also get rid of Cue Cards, which can frazzle your nerves after you generate multiple family trees.

Finding Individuals in the Family File

Most people use only a fraction of the capabilities of the Find Individual function — which you access by choosing Edit⇨Find Individual. You can search on a number of fields beyond just the name of the individual, including all the fact fields, dates, places, and sources. You can also use a number of characters to refine your search. Table 13-1 contains a list of these characters.

Table 13-1	Characters for the Search
Character	*Function*
=	Finds the location of empty fields. Just enter the equal sign in the For field, and Family Tree Maker finds the first instance where that field is empty in a Family File.
>	Finds dates that occurred after a given date. For example, enter **>9/24/1765** to find fields that contain a date after September 24, 1765. This will also find dates that are specified as After September 24, 1765.
>=	Finds dates either on or after a given date. For instance, enter **>=2/4/1902** to find dates that are on or after February 4, 1902.
<	Finds dates that occur before a given date. For example, enter **<1/1/1808** to find a field that contains a date before January 1, 1808.
<=	Finds dates either on or before a given date. For instance, enter **<=11/27/1832** to find dates that are on or before November 27, 1832.
..	Finds a range of dates. It can also be used in combination with the greater than, less than, or equal signs. For example, to search for dates between September 1, 1897 and December 21, 1984, enter **>9/1/1897..<12/21/1984**.
?	Finds dates that are entered as Unknown or with the question mark symbol.
!=	Finds the location of fields that contain information. It's sort of the reverse of searching with just the equal sign.

Using the Find Individual command can save you time that you would otherwise spend browsing through pages or generating specialty reports. The best way to figure out all its features is to experiment with it.

We're Not All Purfekt, So Use Spell Check

Nothing is more embarrassing than displaying a well-designed wall chart at a family gathering and then having to listen to the peanut gallery snickering about your spelling. So our advice is to spell check your files often by choosing Edit⇨Spell Check. Depending on where you are in the Family File, you can spell check everything or just a particular section of the file.

You can customize several aspects of the Spell Check function. If you choose File⇨Preferences⇨Spell Check, you can select these options: Ignore Known Names, Ignore Capitalized Words, or Ignore Words with Numbers. If you frequently use abbreviations for things such as locations, you may want to select the Ignore Capitalized Words option. Select the Ignore Words with Numbers option if you don't want the spell checker flagging reference numbers as being mispelled. When you're spell checking your Family File, you may want to select the option to add names that Family Tree Maker does not normally recognize. That way you don't have to keep approving the use of the name every time that you perform a spell check.

References of the Numerical Kind

In Chapter 10, we talk a bit about genealogical numbering systems and how to use them in reports. Yes, we can hear you nodding off already, but numbering systems can be very useful for organizing your files. You can set Family Tree Maker to automatically assign reference numbers to individuals and to marriages by following these steps:

1. **Choose File⇨Preferences⇨Reference Numbers.**

   The Reference Numbers dialog box appears.

2. **Select how you want both the individual and marriage numbers set up.**

   The available choices are Numbers Only, Prefix Plus Numbers, and Numbers Plus Suffix.

By setting up automatic numbers, you don't have to constantly try to synchronize your offline numbering system (the numbers that you use on your paper files, that is, if you use a numbering system) with your online system. Just let Family Tree Maker assign the numbers and then adjust your offline system to match them (that is, if you don't already have a good offline system; if you do, you probably want to set Family Tree Maker to match your numbering system).

Next Category: Dates and Measures

Believe it or not, many genealogists get snippy about how people write dates. That's right, they have nothing better to do than quibble about whether the day should precede the month or vice versa. If you want dates to appear your way, Family Tree Maker allows you to specify your date preference. All you have to do is choose File➪Preferences➪Dates & Measures. You are greeted with a friendly dialog box that allows you to set preferences for both dates and measures. For dates, you can set the order as month-day-year or day-month-year. You can also specify a particular date style. Here are your choices:

Month	March	Mar	3	03
Separator	[a space]	/	-	.
Day	5	05		
Range prefix	Bet.	Btn		
Range separator	-	to	and	&

Other things that you can configure include

- The cutoff year for double dates. Double dates occur because of the correction of the Gregorian calendar in 1750.

- The labels that are used to indicate *About.* You can use *Circa* instead of *About* if you choose.

- The label for the word *in.*

- The type of measurement. You have two choices: English or Metric.

If you want to generate reports and family trees for submission to a journal that has a specific rule about dates, you should definitely set your date preference to match it. Otherwise, you may spend a lot of time correcting the dates in reports.

Face Up to Your Errors

Periodically run a Data Errors report to ensure that your data is clean. You should definitely run this report before generating family trees and reports for publication and before producing information for the family reunion. You can generate the Data Errors report by choosing View➪Report. After the custom report screen appears, choose Format➪Report Format and then select the Data Errors option. For more specific instructions on generating the Data Errors report, see Chapter 10. This report has saved us from some silly data errors and typos, and can help you as well.

Update Your Research Journal

One of the keys to maintaining your research momentum is to document the research that you have done and list the things that you still need to find. Keeping your Research Journal up-to-date is especially important if you don't research your genealogy every day. The journal can help you identify what you were doing the last time you were researching and keep you focused with the To Do list. To view the Research Journal, choose View⇨Research Journal. For the lowdown on using the Research Journal, see Chapter 7.

Customize Your Toolbar

Many people like to have things their own way. In fact, we wish that we could change some of our computer applications to be organized the way that we think rather than the way that the programmer thinks. One thing that you can have your own way in Family Tree Maker is the toolbar. The toolbar is one of the greatest time savers in Family Tree Maker. You can use it to run reports or create family trees quickly and to navigate through the program efficiently. These processes can be even quicker if you rearrange the buttons on the toolbar in the order that you want them.

You can customize the toolbar by following these steps:

1. **Choose File⇨Preferences⇨Toolbar.**

   The Customize Toolbar dialog box appears. The dialog box has two columns: one for available buttons and the other for what is currently on your toolbar.

2. **If you want to include a button on your toolbar, simply click the object in the Available column and then click the button marked with the greater-than sign (>).**

   Family Tree Maker moves the object into the Your Toolbar column, and it should now appear on the toolbar.

3. **If you want to change the order of a button, select a button in the Your Toolbar column and use the Move Up and Move Down buttons to position it where it suits you.**

4. **When you are satisfied with the order of your Toolbar, click OK.**

Change the Color of the Family Page

Say that you hate all things yellow — that color just grates on your nerves. So it's no surprise that you don't like the yellow background color of the Family Page. Fortunately, you can change it. However, we don't recommend that you attempt to do so unless you're experienced in changing settings in initialization files and you know something about color values. Before completing the following steps, we suggest that you read over them first and make sure that you know how to do them. If you have any doubts, don't try to change the color. Instead, work through your problems with the color yellow and find a way to peacefully coexist with it.

If you have experience in changing initialization file settings, you can change the background color by changing the Family Page Color entry in the Family Tree Maker initialization file. Here's how:

1. **Choose Help⇨System Information.**

   This action launches the System Information dialog box, which contains useful information for diagnosing problems and provides you with an inventory of your hardware.

2. **In the Run drop-list at the bottom of the screen, select FTW.ini.**

   After you select FTW.ini from the list, the Windows Notepad launches and displays the FTW.ini file.

3. **Locate the Options section in the FTW.ini file.**

   If your FTW.ini file looks like ours, it is the second section.

4. **Add a line in the Options section that designates the new colors that you want for your background.**

   The line that you should add is

   ```
   FamPagColor=A,B,C
   ```

   A, B, and C represent the color values for Red, Green, and Blue, respectively. For example, if we wanted to make the background a pale blue color, we would add the following line to the Options section of the file:

   ```
   FamPagColor=191,223,225
   ```

   To get the correct Red, Green, Blue (RGB) values, you need to use a graphics program that can show you the values, or you can use the Appearance tab of the Display settings in the Windows Control Panel.

Do not change any other lines in the FTW.ini file. If you do, the results are unpredictable.

5. **Save the FTW.ini file by using the Windows Notepad application.**

After you save the file, you can close the Windows Notepad application. The changes will take effect the next time that you start the Family Tree Maker program.

If you ever need to go back to the default background color, simply remove the line from the FTW.ini file.

Feeling a Bit Private?

Genealogists try to balance genealogy with privacy, especially when they share information. Many embarrassing details of living individuals' lives have been broadcast on the Internet and shared with hundreds of people with just a click of a button. To avoid this pitfall, we strongly recommend that you privatize your Family File before you generate any reports or family trees, or export information for another researcher. Believe us, doing so will save you a lot of grief later on. To privatize your file, choose File➪Preferences➪ Privatize Information. This action opens the Privatize Information dialog box. To privatize your entire file, select the Privatize Information option and click OK.

After you click OK, the screen changes a bit. First Family Tree Maker seems to be loading the Family File again. Then the screen changes to a green background for the Family File. A dialog box opens, informing you that Family Tree Maker doesn't automatically privatize the information in books. It recommends that you look over the text items in your book to see if you want to keep anything private. Clicking OK closes the dialog box. If you're looking at a Family Page for a living individual, you'll notice that the Birth, Death, Marriage, More About Facts, and Medical fields are marked private. Also the Notes page is grayed out entirely, not revealing any information.

While the Family File is in the Privatization mode, you cannot make any changes to the file. In effect, it becomes a read-only file. The only way to make changes is to shut off the privatization mode in the Privatize Information dialog box.

If you generate any reports or family trees, or export individuals, all the appropriate fields should be marked private. Just in case, we recommend that you double-check everything you plan to share to make sure that you don't disclose any confidential information.

Chapter 14

Ten Bonuses in the Deluxe Package

*T*he Deluxe version of Family Tree Maker 7.0 comes with 20 CD-ROMs that can assist you with your research. This chapter covers the contents of those CD-ROMs.

You can access all the Deluxe package CD-ROMs in the same way. Rather than repeat the steps over and over again throughout this chapter, we walk through them in the FamilyFinder Index example, and then you can return to the other CD-ROMS when you need to.

FamilyFinder Index

The FamilyFinder Index has been a staple of the Family Tree Maker Deluxe set for quite a while. It spans three CD-ROMs and contains an index to all the Family Archive CD-ROMs sold by Family Tree Maker, which contain nearly 200 million names. The individual Family Archive CD-ROMs include many different types of records and are composed of indexes and some original records.

Here are the steps to use the FamilyFinder Index (and any other Family Tree Maker CD-ROM):

1. **Start Family Tree Maker.**

   Double-click the Family Tree Maker icon on your Windows desktop or use the Start button to initiate the program file.

2. **Insert a FamilyFinder Index CD-ROM into your CD-ROM drive.**

3. **Click the View CD button.**

   This button is the farthest to the right on the default toolbar. It's the one with a magnifying glass looking at a CD. Or you can choose View⇨FamilyFinder⇨View CD.

   Surprisingly, no matter which CD-ROM you load in your computer, the word FamilyFinder appears as the choice on the View menu.

   A Family Archive License Agreement pops up if this is the first time you've used a Family Archive CD. We suggest that you read the agreement before clicking OK.

   Next, a Cue Card for FamilyFinder may appear. It gives you various tips about using the FamilyFinder Index. If you don't want to see this Cue Card every time you open the FamilyFinder Index, select the option labeled, Click here if you don't want to see this Help Window again. Then click OK.

   The FamilyFinder Index display resembles a book. The initial page of the Index briefly introduces the contents and explains how to search the Index. You can use the tabs on the right side of the page to navigate the Introduction, the contents list of the Family Archive CD-ROMs, and the Index search page. The other way to search the Index is to use the Search Expert feature. That's the path we follow in these steps.

4. **Click the Search Expert button in the upper-right corner of the screen.**

   This button is the one that has a picture of a book and a detective with a magnifying glass on it. When you click this button, the Search Expert dialog box appears. You can either search for someone in your Family File or someone who is not in your Family File.

5. **Click the button entitled** Search for Someone from your Family File.

   A list of names from your Family File appears. You can quickly get to an individual by typing that person's name in the Scroll to Name field.

6. **Click a name to select it and then click the search button to start the search.**

   The search button has a picture of a magnifying glass sitting in front of a group of books. The button's name is something like `Start search for Grey Hound Canine in all archives` (assuming that you clicked Grey Hound Canine's name). After clicking the button, you see a progress meter on the screen and then a list of results. If no results were found, you receive a message saying that no results were found, along with some recommendations on how to search effectively.

7. **Select a record from the results page and click the Information button.**

   Oddly enough, if you double-click the result, you see an ad about how to buy Family Archive CDs, instead of information about the result itself. To find out more information about the result, click the small button with the letter *i* in a blue circle at the bottom of the screen. The More About dialog box then appears, containing brief index information on where the individual is located on the Family Archive CD-ROM.

8. **Click OK to close the More About dialog box.**

   You can continue searching or select another Family Tree Maker feature.

Before purchasing a Family Archive CD, make sure that you know what's really on the CD-ROM. Some CD-ROMs are merely indexes to original records. Others contain transcribed genealogical works. And still others contain scanned images of original documents. Often, people are disappointed to find out that the CD-ROM contains only an index rather than copies of original records.

Social Security Death Index

Two CD-ROMs that have accompanied Family Tree Maker for quite some time contain the Social Security Death Index (SSDI). The SSDI is a database of over 60 million names of deceased individuals whose families received Social Security death benefits. Each record contains the Social Security number, the place of issue of the Social Security card, the birth date, the death date, the last residence, the zip code of the last residence, and the primary location associated with the zip code (such as a town and state). If you find someone who is a match in the database, you can use the information to request a copy of the original application for that individual's Social Security card from the Social Security Administration. The CD also contains names and addresses for vital records repositories in each state.

You can copy any information that you find in the SSDI directly to your Family File by clicking the small button at the bottom of the page, titled Copy information about [Name of Person] to your Family File.

The SSDI is a good place to get some hints for birth and death dates. However, be aware that some of the information contained in the database is incorrect. So rather than viewing the contents as gospel, use the database to get leads about where to look for primary records such as birth and death certificates.

Birth Records

The CD-ROM *Birth Records: United States and Europe, 900–1880* — which is included in the Deluxe package — contains information about over 1.8 million people. It is an index of birth records that appear on all the CD-ROMs produced by Automated Archives (the predecessor of the Family Archive CD-ROMs) through December 1993. Each entry includes the name, the date of birth (sometimes it's just the year between 900 and 1880), the location of birth, and the original CD from which the information was obtained.

Marriage Records

Another CD that comes with the Deluxe version of Family Tree Maker 7.0 is *Selected U.S. and International Marriage Records, 1340–1980*. It contains information about 1.4 million people from the United States and 32 other countries. Over 500 years of marriages are represented on the CD. A professional genealogist, Bill Yates, spent 34 years collecting the data from various sources, including electronic databases, biographies, family group sheets and pedigree charts, letters, Bible records, and wills.

Biographies and Genealogies

The Deluxe package includes two CD-ROMs that contain biographies and genealogies — one for the mid-Atlantic region of the United States from 1340 to 1940 and one for the South from the 1500s to the 1940s. The CDs contain biographical information, transcribed and abstracted records, private correspondence, and narratives from various books. The types and amounts of information vary, depending on which source you're reviewing.

The sources contained on the mid-Atlantic CD are

- *A Collection of Family Records with Biographical Sketches Bearing Name Douglas*
- *By the Name of Emerich, Emerick, Emmerich, Emrich, and Emrick*
- *Captain Mathew Dill and Mary of Monaghan Settlement and Descendants*
- *Genealogical Record of the Condit Family Descendants of John Cunditt, a Native of Great Britain Who Settled in Newark, N.J.*
- *Genealogy of the Dutton Family of Pennsylvania*
- *Stephen Banks Leonard*
- *The Emmons Family*
- *The Descendants of Adam Mott of Hempstead, Long Island, N.Y.*
- *The Dolman Compendium*
- *The Schell Family*
- *Tristram Dodge and his Descendants in America*

These are the sources that are included on the Southern CD:

- *Annals of the Fowler Family*
- *Biographical Genealogies of the Virginia-Kentucky Floyd Families*
- *Correction Sheet for the Genealogy of the Cloyd, Basye, and Tapp Families*
- *Genealogical and Historical Notes on Culpeper County, Virginia*
- *Genealogy of the Folsom Family*
- *Henry Duke, Councilor, His Descendants and Connections*
- *History of Kentucky, The Blue Grass State*
- *Our Ellsworth Ancestors*
- *Richard Clarke of Virginia, 1732–1811*
- *The Foard Family*
- *The Futrell Family in America*
- *The Origin and Descent of an American Van Metre Family*

Local and Family Histories

The *Local and Family Histories: New England, 1600s–1900s* CD-ROM is similar to the biographies and genealogies CDs for the mid-Atlantic and Southern states described earlier in this chapter. The main difference is that this CD also contains histories about localities and people. The information on this CD comes from local and family histories for geographic locations and residents of the New England area of the United States. It contains data on over 50,000 people and their families. You can find out about the people who lived in New England between the 1600s and 1900s, as well as find out what their lives and their communities were like.

These sources are included on this CD:

- *A History of the Town of Sullivan, New Hampshire (Volumes I and II)*
- *Edson Family History and Genealogy, Volume II*
- *Genealogical Records of Descendants of John and Anthony Emery of Newbury, Massachusetts*
- *History and Genealogy of Deacon Joseph Eastman of Hadley, Massachusetts*
- *History of Brookline, New Hampshire*
- *History of Ellenwood — Wharton and 20 Allied Families*
- *History of Pembroke, New Hampshire*
- *History of the Dudley Family*
- *History of the Town of Bristol, Grafton County, New Hampshire (Volumes I and II)*
- *Memoir of Samuel Endicott With a Genealogy of His Descendants*
- *Record of the Descendants of James Ensign and His Wife, Sarah Elson*
- *Some Descendants of John Endecott, Governor of Massachusetts Bay Colony*
- *The Downers of America, With Genealogical Record*
- *The Dudley Genealogies and Family Records*
- *The Descendants of Thomas Durfee of Portsmouth, Rhode Island, Volume II*
- *The Eaton Family of Nova Scotia*
- *The Edmister Family in America*
- *To the Descendants of Thomas Dickinson, Son of Nathaniel and Anna Gull Dickinson of Wethersfield, Connecticut and Hadley, Massachusetts*

Military Records

The *Military Records: U.S. Soldiers, 1784–1811* CD-ROM contains digital images of a card index to service records for 21,000 volunteer soldiers. These soldiers were from 22 states and territories of the United States. Each index card image contains the soldier's name, state or territory where he enlisted, rank, company, regiment, and battalion. If you find a card that has information about one of your relatives, you can contact the National Archives to get a copy of the actual service record.

Land Records

Do you have ancestors from Alabama, Arkansas, Florida, Louisiana, Michigan, Minnesota, Ohio, or Wisconsin? Did they live in one of these states sometime between 1790 and 1907? If you answer yes to these questions, you should definitely search through the *Land Records: AL, AR, FL, LA, MI, MN, OH, WI, 1790–1907* CD-ROM. It contains land records from the Bureau of Land Management's General Land Office. The CD-ROM has references to over 1.6 million people in the legal land descriptions and transfer of ownership property records. In addition to providing names, locations of land, measurements, and dates of purchase, the CD-ROM has document numbers and other information that you need in order to get copies of the original land records.

Passenger and Immigration Lists

If you're looking for information about an ancestor who immigrated to the United States through the port of Boston, then you'll want to review the *Passenger and Immigration Lists: Boston, 1821–1850* CD-ROM that accompanies the Deluxe version of Family Tree Maker 7.0. It is an index of some 161,000 people who arrived in Boston between 1821 and 1850. Each entry includes the immigrant's name, age, gender, arrival date, country of origin, and occupation. You can also find information about how to obtain copies of the actual immigration records.

World Family Tree

The World Family Tree is a huge database of information that researchers from around the world have shared with Broderbund just so that Broderbund can share it with you. Currently, it has data about millions of individuals.

The Deluxe version of Family Tree Maker 7.0 includes some of the World Family Tree on CD-ROM. You get *European Origins (Volume E1)* and *Volumes 1 through 5 (Pre-1600 to the Present)* on CD-ROM. For information about using the World Family Tree in your research and contributing your genealogical findings to it, check out Chapter 8.

Chapter 15

Ten Things That Can Save You Time

In This Chapter

▶ Editing shortcuts

▶ Finding people quickly

▶ Scanning directly into Family Tree Maker

*F*or most people, genealogy is a hobby that they do in their spare time. Even though it's called spare time, all of your time is valuable, and you want to make the most of it. Using Family Tree Maker enables you to do just that — organize your research and prepare for your next research trip so you can spend the bulk of your alleged spare time getting some actual research done. In the spirit of using Family Tree Maker to save time, we want to give you some shortcuts. And . . . here they are.

Using Keyboard Shortcuts for Editing Commands

After you really get the hang of entering information about your ancestors, you'll want to be able to move and edit information quickly. We suggest that you use the keyboard shortcuts for editing your information rather than the menu bar. Using keyboard shortcuts is usually more efficient because your hands are already on the keyboard (assuming that you're typing at the time). Stopping your typing to use the mouse can eat up some time, especially if you're doing the same editing command over and over again. Table 15-1 lists keyboard shortcuts that can save you time.

To use a keyboard shortcut, simply hold down the keys listed under the keystroke column in Table 15-1 simultaneously. For example, to copy text to the clipboard, hold down the CTRL and C keys at the same time.

Table 15-1	Editing Shortcuts
Keystroke	*Function*
Ctrl+C	Copies the selected text to the Windows Clipboard.
Ctrl+X	Cuts the selected text and places it on the Windows Clipboard.
Ctrl+V	Pastes text that is currently on the Windows Clipboard into your Family File.
Ctrl+Z	Either undoes or redoes the last editing command.
Alt+ Backspace	Undoes the last editing command.

Of course, using the good old Backspace key (which backs up and deletes one character), Delete key (which deletes one character to the right and is sometimes labeled Del on your keyboard), and Insert key (which switches between the Insert and Overwrite modes) also saves you time.

Using Navigational Shortcuts

Some navigational shortcuts may save you time. (Although we must admit that using the mouse to perform some of these functions is sometimes faster.) Table 15-2 lists these handy-dandy shortcuts.

Table 15-2	Navigational Shortcuts
Keystroke	*Function*
Tab	Moves your cursor to the next field on the page.
Shift+Tab	Moves your cursor to the previous field on the page.
↑	Moves your cursor to the field above the one that you are currently in.
↓	Moves your cursor to the field below the one that you are currently in.
←	Moves your cursor left one character.
→	Moves your cursor right one character.
Ctrl+←	Takes your cursor to the previous word.

Keystroke	*Function*
Ctrl+→	Takes your cursor to the next word.
Home	Moves your cursor to the start of the field that you are currently in.
End	Moves your cursor to the end of the field that you are currently in.
Ctrl+Home	Moves your cursor to the Husband field. If you are in the list of children, this takes you to the first child in the list.
Ctrl+End	Moves your cursor to the first empty field in the list of children.
Page Up	Moves your cursor up the list of children.
Page Down	Moves your cursor down the list of children.
F4	Transports you to the Family Page of the parents of the person occupying the Wife field on the current Family Page.
F5	Transports you to the Family Page of the parents of the person occupying the Husband field on the current Family Page.
F6	Transports you to the Family Page of the highlighted child in the list of children.
F8	Transports you to the Family Page of the next sibling of the husband or wife (depending upon which field you are in).
Alt+F8	Transports you to the Family Page of the previous sibling of the husband or wife (depending upon which field you are in).

Inserting Sources

Hopefully, you create many sources when you enter information into Family Tree Maker. (If you're confused about why you should enter sources, flip back to Chapter 6.) Rather than choosing View⇨Sources (or using the keyboard shortcut ALT+V+U) every time you want to enter a source, you can simply press Ctrl+S after you're in the field that you want to source. The Source Citation dialog box then opens right up.

Finding the Other Mate

Ah, the flipping-through-multiple-spouses dilemma. Well, if you're typing along and you don't want to remove your hand from the keyboard to use the mouse, you can quickly open the Spouses dialog box by pressing the F3 key. From there, you can select which spouse you need to work with.

Locating Individuals Fast

Sometimes you want to enter information on someone who is four or five generations removed from the person whose Family Page you're on. In this case, using the Index of Individuals is quicker than clicking the Family Page tabs several times. But who wants to use the pull-down menus to get to the Index? Not you! You're speedy. Well, chill speedy. You can open the Index of Individuals dialog box at any time by pressing the F2 key. Then type in the name of the individual (last name, first name) or click the Find button to search for an individual based on his or her name.

Scanning Directly into Family Tree Maker

One new feature of Family Tree Maker is the ability to scan a picture or download a digital photo directly into the program. This feature saves you time (possibly a lot of time) because you no longer have to scan the image into another program and import it into Family Tree Maker as an OLE object. To scan or download a picture, choose Picture/Object⇨Insert Picture from Scanner/Camera and follow the prompts. (Make sure that your scanner hardware and software is installed, compatible, and configured correctly before choosing this option; also make sure that the scanner is turned on.) For more on scanning, see Chapter 4.

Cleaning the FamilyFinder Report

Perhaps you've decided to delete your FamilyFinder report and start all over again. To do this, just run the Delete FamilyFinder Report utility by pressing Ctrl+Alt+Shift+↓. (Really, this shortcut sounds more complicated that it is — unless you have really short fingers.) You receive a message asking you to confirm that you want to delete the report. Click Yes to continue. After the report is deleted, you return to the Family Page. For more on the FamilyFinder report, see Chapter 8.

Using OLE Objects

Transcribing records can take an awfully long time. So sometimes attaching the record to the Scrapbook in Family Tree Maker is a better idea. To attach a record to the Scrapbook, you need to embed an Object Linking and Embedding (OLE) object into Family Tree Maker. You can do this by opening the Scrapbook and then choosing Picture/Object⇨Insert Object. For more on OLE objects, see Chapter 4.

Help Is Only a Button Away

If you've worked with Windows for awhile, you may already know that you can press the F1 key at any time to get context-sensitive help for the field that your cursor is in (at least if the software is written to Windows standards). You can get help with menu bar commands by clicking the menu bar, high-lighting the command that you have a question about (using the ↑ and ↓ keys), and pressing the F1 key. You can also get help with the buttons on the screen by pressing Shift+F1 (which turns the cursor into an arrow with a question mark) and clicking the button for which you have a question.

Exit, Stage Left

Okay, perhaps you don't really need to know how to make a speedy exit from Family Tree Maker — unless the battery on your notebook is about to go dead and you're tired of hearing the warning beeps. But just in case a need ever arises, isn't it nice to know you can make a quick exit from Family Tree Maker by pressing Alt+F4? We think so, too.

Chapter 16

Ten Ways to Avoid Calling Tech Support

*Y*ou've had a hard day at work. Now it's time to come home, relax, and do one of your favorite things. You kick off your shoes and find a comfy chair to prepare for your evening's activity. Then you pick up the phone and dial that nice, toll, technical support number. The automated voice answers, and you're in luck — all the technical support personnel are busy with other calls, but they'll be with you just as soon as they can. The music begins. You know the kind — it's nice and relaxing with the intermittent announcement that your call is important. You sink down into your chair, knowing that you'll become increasingly frustrated waiting on hold for 45 minutes. Sound familiar?

No one likes to call technical support. But occasionally, you can't figure out how to do something, and you don't know where else to turn. If you're working with Family Tree Maker, you can turn to this chapter of this book. This chapter includes a few troubleshooting tips that we hope will alleviate your need to call technical support (although you still may have to make the dreaded call for some special problems). So relax your dialing fingers — or at least set them on your keyboard — and read on.

Back Up! Back Up! Back Up!

Probably the best way to avoid having to call technical support is to make frequent backups of your Family Files. That way if something does go wrong with your Family File, you can always replace it with the backup.

If you work with your Family Files often, we recommend that you back up your files regularly on a certain day of the week (if you use your Family File several times a week) or on a specific date of the month (if you work with it only a few times a month). Also, remember to rotate the media that houses your Family File backups — that is, keep four or five sets of backups in case you need to reconstruct some information from the past.

To back up your Family File, follow these steps:

1. **Choose File⇨Backup Family File.**

   The Backup Family File dialog box appears.

2. **Select where you want the backup file created.**

   The Backup Family File dialog box lists the drives where your backup file can be created. You can choose to back up your file on removable media such as a floppy drive or on your hard disk drive. To make a selection, click the radio button for the location or click the Change Filename or Directory button.

   If you have another form of removable media — such as a Zip or Jaz drive — it may show up in the dialog box as a floppy drive or not show up at all. If the drive letter of your removable media device does not appear in the dialog box, then click the Change Filename or Directory button and choose the correct drive letter.

3. **Click OK when you're ready to back up the file.**

   After Family Tree Maker starts backing up the file, the progress meter appears on the screen. After it reaches 100 percent, another dialog box appears, telling you that the file has been backed up successfully.

   If you're trying to back up the Family File to a removable media source (such as a Zip or Jaz drive), you may run into an error if the disk is not completely blank. The backup program is designed to back up to floppy disks, not removable media drives, so it expects the disks to be blank. To get around this error, we back up our file to the hard disk first and then copy it to the removable media.

4. **Click the OK button when the file is successfully backed up.**

   You then return to the Family File page. You can find the backup file in the location that you specified. It has the same filename as your Family File and has an extension of FBC. For example, if my Family File is named helm.ftw, the backup file would be helm.fbc.

Make a practice of storing a copy of your backup files offsite. Keep a copy in your safe-deposit box (if you have one) or send a copy of your backup file to another researcher or a relative for safekeeping. That way, a natural disaster or fire won't destroy all your hard work.

Test Your Backups

We admit it. Sometimes we're not the most trusting people in the world. So occasionally we try to restore our backups before shutting down Family Tree Maker. This way we have the security of knowing that our backup files will work the next time that we need them. To restore a backup file, follow these steps:

1. **Choose File⇨Restore From Backup.**

   The Open Backup Family File dialog appears, with a list of files that have backup extensions.

2. **Select the backup file from the list of files.**

   This action opens the New Family File dialog box.

3. **Type a new name for your Family File in the File Name box and then click OK.**

   After the backup is restored, Family Tree Maker opens the first Family Page in the new file.

Family Tree Maker doesn't allow you to name the new file the same name as the old Family File unless you have the Startup Preferences set to allow the replacement of existing files (which is not the default setting). To change the setting, choose File⇨Preferences⇨Startup and select the Allow Replacing Existing Files option.

Automatic Backup

Making periodic backups of your Family Files goes a long way in protecting your data. But what happens if something jumbles your Family File before you have a chance to back up the file? Well, lucky for you, that's where the automatic backup function comes in. By default, the automatic backup function in Family Tree Maker is set to *on*. This function backs up your Family File every time you exit Family Tree Maker or open up a new Family File. The automatic backup file is saved with the FBK extension.

Some people disable the automatic backup function because it doubles the amount of disk space used by Family Files. You're taking a risk if you disable this feature. If your Family File becomes corrupted the next time that you open it and you did not manually back up the Family File, you may be out of luck.

To see if Family Tree Maker is set to automatically back up the Family File, simply choose File⇨Preferences⇨Startup. The Startup dialog box contains the option to automatically backup the Family File. If this option is selected, then the automatic backup is enabled.

Scanning That Disk

ScanDisk is a utility that comes with Microsoft Windows. When you run it, it examines your computer's drives for errors and then repairs them. Most people run ScanDisk when they may have a problem with their hard drive, and frequently ScanDisk runs by itself when the computer is not shut down properly. However, we recommend that you periodically run ScanDisk to protect the integrity of your Family Files, especially when they're large and used frequently. To run ScanDisk, do the following:

1. **Click the Start button on the Windows taskbar and choose Programs⇨Accessories⇨System Tools⇨ScanDisk.**

   This action launches the ScanDisk program.

2. **Select the drive that you want to scan and select the level of testing that you want ScanDisk to perform.**

   Two levels of scanning appear in the Type of Test section. For routine scanning, we suggest using the Standard setting. However, if you suspect a problem, then use the Thorough setting.

   If you aren't interested in all the gory details of ScanDisk, you may want to deselect the Automatically Fix Errors option. Otherwise, ScanDisk prompts you to confirm that you want to correct an error.

3. **Click the Start button when you're ready to roll.**

   The amount of time it takes ScanDisk to complete its tasks depends on the size of the disk it's scanning and how many errors it encounters. While you're waiting, you can see its progress at the bottom of the dialog box. If ScanDisk encounters any errors, it either fixes them automatically or prompts you for action.

4. **If ScanDisk finds no errors, it opens the ScanDisk Results dialog box. Click the Close button to exit ScanDisk.**

   The ScanDisk Results dialog box provides some statistics about the disk that was scanned.

Not only is running ScanDisk a good idea for keeping your Family Tree Maker files straight, but it's also a good thing for all of your programs (that way none of your important files become corrupt). Periodically running ScanDisk should keep all of your magnetic media in good shape — whether you have floppy disks, hard disks, or removable media.

Compacting Files

If you're running low on disk space or just want to keep your Family File neat and trim, then you should periodically compact your Family File. We also recommend doing this before you back up your Family File. When you delete pictures from your Family File, the size of the file does not always decrease, because Family Tree Maker is holding that picture slot open in case you decide to replace the deleted picture. It's just wasted space. To get back that precious space, open the Family File and press Ctrl+Alt+C. You then see a progress bar run across the page, and you return to the Family Page. That's all there is to it.

Checking Your Family File

Some undocumented utilities (at least they don't appear in the user's manual) that come with Family Tree Maker can help you keep your Family File healthy. One of these utilities is the Family File Checker utility. This utility searches your Family File for file integrity errors and then displays descriptions of the errors.

To run the utility, do the following:

1. **After you're in the Family File, press Ctrl+Alt+Shift+↑.**

   This step requires some keyboard acrobatics, but it does work. The Family File Checker dialog box opens.

2. **Click the Start button.**

   You should see a progress bar go across the screen. If the Family File contains no errors, the No Errors message appears. If the file does contain errors, a list of errors appears. Follow the prompts from Family Tree Maker to continue with the File Check.

3. **Click the OK button to exit the utility.**

   If you find errors in your Family File, you should run the File Fixer utility, described in the next section.

Fixing Your Family File

Fortunately, if your Family File has some problems, you can fix some of them with the Family File Fixer. The Family File Fixer utility attempts to correct the most common problems with Family Files (such as errors that occur when the Family File is not exited properly). You can run the utility by pressing Ctrl+Alt+Shift+←. This action opens the Family File Checker with File Fixer dialog box. Click the Start button, and the utility tries to fix the problems with the Family File. If this doesn't work, you probably need to bite the bullet and contact Family Tree Maker technical support.

Hidden Utilities

A few other hidden utilities can help your Family File stay healthy: the Cache Check and Index Check utilities. The Cache Check and Index Check utilities look at the integrity of the Cache and Index. Problems with these two areas can result in slowing the performance of Family Tree Maker. To run the Cache Check, press Ctrl+Alt+Shift+Home, and to run the Index Check, press Ctrl+Alt+Shift+End. If no problems are found in your Cache or Index, a small dialog box appears, telling that the search is complete. Just click the OK button to continue working with your Family File.

Defragmenting Your Drives

Each time that you use your computer, many files are created, modified, and deleted — a lot of them are temporary files that you never see. Over time, all of this hard disk usage takes its toll. Files become fragmented, or separated, on the hard disk. The result is a longer access time for your files, which eventually slows down the performance of your computer. Although defragmenting your drives does not have as great an impact on your Family Files as some of the other utilities that we mention in this chapter, it's something that you should do periodically to keep all your programs running smoothly.

To defragment your drive, follow these steps:

1. **Click the Start button on the Windows taskbar and choose Programs⇨Accessories⇨System Tools⇨Disk Defragmenter.**

   The Windows Disk Defragmenter program starts, and the Select Drive dialog box appears.

Run the Disk Defragmenter only when you won't be working with the disk for a while. Otherwise, the defragmentation will take forever to complete.

2. **Select the drive that you want to defragment.**

   You can choose from any of the drives that are available to your computer.

3. **Click OK to begin defragmentation.**

   After the program begins defragmenting, you see a progress bar and three buttons at the bottom of the defragmenting dialog box. You can use these buttons to stop, pause, and show details. If you want to see a graphical representation of what's going on with the hard drive, just click the Show Details button. After the defragmentation is complete, another dialog box appears.

4. **Click Yes to quit the defragmenter.**

   If you want, you can defragment another drive by clicking No. If you're finished, then go ahead and click Yes.

The amount of time it takes to defragment the disk depends on how large the disk is. If you have a large hard drive, you may want to take a break and let the defragmenter do its thing.

Splitting Up Your Family

We hope you realize that we don't seriously mean you should split your family apart. We're talking about splitting your Family File.

Even with all the space-saving things that you can do, you may eventually run into problems caused by the fact that your Family File has become too large and unwieldy (such as slow performance from Family Tree Maker, or difficulty backing up the files to one piece of media). The solution may be to split your Family File into two or more smaller Family Files. For example, once upon a time Matthew's Family File became too large, so we split it into four separate Family Files. Each Family File contained one of the family lines of his grandparents. This made the files much more manageable and allowed us to have just the information that we needed when we made research trips. You can split your Family File by creating a report containing the individuals that you want to include in the new Family File. For a step-by-step example of exporting individuals to a new Family File, see Chapter 12.

Part V
Appendixes

The 5th Wave   By Rich Tennant

"According to these reports, I'm related to Pee-Wee Herman."

In this part . . .

Here you find out how to install — and if you need to do so, uninstall — Family Tree Maker. You also find a glossary with definitions of words that we use in this book and terms that are generally used in genealogy.

Appendix A

Installing the Program

• •

*I*f you haven't installed Family Tree Maker yet and you're looking for a little guidance, then you're at the right place. This appendix goes over what you need to know to install the program. Also, we point you to some technical support resources that you can use if things don't go so smoothly. But think positive and get started.

Having the Right Stuff

To run Family Tree Maker on your computer, your computer needs to meet certain minimum requirements. The creators of Family Tree Maker recommend that you have the following:

✔ A 486 or faster central processing unit (CPU)

✔ Microsoft Windows 95 or higher operating system

✔ 8 megabytes (MB) of random access memory (RAM), although 16 MB is highly recommended

✔ 20MB of free disk space

✔ A CD-ROM drive (The CD-ROM drive must be connected to your computer — it can't be a CD-ROM drive accessible over the network.)

✔ A monitor with a 640 x 480 display (higher resolutions also work) with at least 16 colors (256 and higher colors supported)

✔ A Microsoft-compatible mouse

Remember that these are the very minimum requirements. If you plan to store pictures, video, and sounds in the program, then you'll need more RAM and free disk space.

Let's Install It!

You're ready to install the Family Tree Maker program. We know the excitement is building, so grab the Family Tree Maker CD-ROM marked *Installation Program* and place it into your CD-ROM drive on your computer. Here are the rest of the steps for completing the installation:

1. **If your CD-ROM drive supports autorun programs, you see the Family Tree Maker Auto Run/Install dialog box. Click the OK button to begin the install.**

   If you don't see this dialog box, then go to Step 2.

   If you do see the dialog box, skip to Step 5 after you click OK.

2. **Choose Start⇨Run.**

   This action opens the Run dialog box, which contains the Open box and three buttons marked Open, Cancel, and Browse.

3. **Type** D:Setup **in the Open box.**

   The letter *D* represents drive letter D. Your CD-ROM drive may be assigned a different drive letter. If so, substitute your drive letter for the *D*.

4. **Click the OK button to begin the install.**

   This action starts the Family Tree Maker installation program. You first see a small graphic that looks like a picture of the Family Tree Maker software box, and then you see a screen with a blue background.

5. **Read the Welcome dialog box and then click Next.**

   After you click Next, the Software License Agreement dialog box appears.

6. **Look over the license agreement and click Yes.**

   The Choose Destination Location dialog box opens. The default install directory is C:/Program Files/FTW. If you want to change the installation location to another location, click the Browse button and select a different directory.

7. **Click Next after selecting the installation destination.**

   You now have the chance to select two optional components to install along with the Family Tree Maker program: the Genealogy How-to Guide (which gives you some tips to help your genealogical research) and ClickArt (some clip art that you can add to your family trees). If you don't want to install either option because of space or other concerns, you can always access them directly from the CD-ROM.

Also notice that the bottom of the dialog box shows you the amount of space that is required for the installation and the amount of disk space that you have available. If you don't have enough disk space to complete the installation, then you need to go to Windows Explorer and free up some space by deleting files that you no longer need.

8. **Select the Optional Components that you want to install by clicking in the check boxes next to their names. Then click the Next button.**

   The Select Program Folder dialog box now appears. You can choose to place the program icons in an existing folder (a list of current folders is in the scroll box at the bottom of the dialog box) or in a new folder (the default name for the new folder is Family Tree Maker).

9. **Click the Next button.**

   You should see the program start installing on your computer. The progress bar across the middle of the screen shows you how much of the install is completed. You'll also see some snazzy ads telling you about Family Tree Maker features while you wait. When the program is done installing, the Select Browser dialog box appears.

10. **Select the Web browser that you want Family Tree Maker to launch when accessing Internet content and then click the Next button.**

    If you have a Web browser installed on your machine, you should see it listed in the dialog box. If you have more than one browser, you need to select which browser to launch. After you click the Next button, the Question dialog box opens.

    Family Tree Maker supports the following Web browsers: America Online 3.0 or higher, AT&T WorldNet Service 3.0 or higher, Microsoft Internet Explorer 3.0 or higher, and Netscape Navigator 3.0 or higher.

11. **Click Yes to Enable Brodcast or click No to disable it.**

    No, that's not a misspelling you're seeing there. It really is called Brodcast — as in Broderbund broadcast.

    The dialog box offers you the opportunity to enable Brodcast, which is a program that keeps you informed of new product features, free offers, and news. If you don't want to enable this, just click the No button. After you make a selection, the Setup Complete dialog box appears.

12. **Click Finish to complete the installation.**

    This action opens the Registration dialog box that allows you to electronically register the product. If you don't feel like registering at this time, click Register Later.

If you choose to register now, follow the dialog boxes and complete the appropriate fields. After the registration is complete, the installation program closes.

By registering the product you will receive information on updates and program upgrades. You will also receive the free Family Tree Magazine.

 If you have problems installing Family Tree Maker, check to make sure that you don't have other programs running in the background on your computer. Other programs may conflict with the install. One of the major culprits of bad installs is anti-virus software. So, if you have anti-virus software running on your computer, it's a good idea to shut it down before attempting the install.

A Call for Help

If you run into trouble during the installation or have any problems using Family Tree Maker, here are some resources that you can use to get help:

✔ The User's Manual that accompanies the Family Tree Maker product has a troubleshooting section in the back. It covers issues such as installation problems, Family Tree Maker Online problems, printing problems, error messages, display problems, computer problems, CD-ROM problems, and print setup problems.

✔ You can contact technical support representatives at 510-794-6850 on Monday through Friday from 7:00 a.m. to 5:00 p.m. Pacific time. Note that this is not a toll-free number, and you will accumulate long-distance charges on your telephone bill. You may also encounter long waits during times of high call volume. So you may want to consider using some of the other resources before calling the technical support number.

✔ The Interactive Automated Help System is available 24 hours a day at 510-794-6850. The number has prerecorded instructions that take you through the troubleshooting process. If you require additional instructions after going through the automated system, you leave your name and fax number so that customer service representatives can fax the instructions to you.

✔ Technical support information is also available on the Family Tree Maker Web site at www.familytreemaker.com/supptop.html. This area of the site includes Frequently Asked Question files and user message boards. Family Tree Maker technical support people monitor the message boards.

> ✔ If you can't get answers from any of the preceding methods, you can try posting to the soc.genealogy.computing newsgroup. Some people feel that the genealogy newsgroup receives too many Family Tree Maker posts, but you should feel comfortable posting to the newsgroup, especially if you haven't received answers by using the other methods listed.

Uninstalling Family Tree Maker

At some point, you may want to uninstall Family Tree Maker. Before uninstalling the program, make sure that you back up all your Family Files in the rare case that they are accidentally deleted. Here are the quick steps to uninstall the program:

1. **Choose Start⇨Settings⇨Control Panel.**

   The Control Panel appears.

2. **Double-click the Add/Remove Programs icon.**

   This action opens the Add/Remove Programs Properties dialog box. The dialog box contains three tabs: Install/Uninstall, Windows Setup, and Startup Disk. We are interested in the Install/Uninstall tab.

3. **Select Family Tree Maker from the list of programs to be automatically removed.**

   A list of programs appears at the bottom of the dialog box. Scroll through the list until you find Family Tree Maker and then highlight it. After you select Family Tree Maker, the Add/Remove button is activated.

4. **Click the Add/Remove button.**

   A dialog box appears, asking you to confirm the deletion of the Family Tree Maker program. Click Yes to proceed or No to cancel.

5. **Click Yes.**

   The uninstall program called unInstallShield begins to uninstall Family Tree Maker. Along the way, it may ask you if a shared file should be removed. Unless you're absolutely positive that no other program is using it, you should not remove the file — otherwise you may unintentionally disable another program. At the end of the uninstall process, a message appears, stating that the uninstall was successfully completed.

6. **Click the OK button.**

After you click the OK button, the Add/Remove Programs Properties dialog box reappears. If you're finished deleting programs, click the Cancel button. Then you can close the Control Panel by clicking the Close button (the small *x*) in the upper-right corner of the window.

The Family Tree Maker program group should no longer appear on your Start menu, and any Family Tree Maker icons should be deleted from your desktop.

Appendix B

What Does This Mean? (A Glossary of Terms)

• •

Abstract: A brief overview or summary of what a document or Web site contains.

Administration: Handling of the estate of a person who died *intestate.*

Ahnentafel: A well-known genealogical numbering system. Ahnentafel is a method of numbering that has a mathematical relationship between parents and children. The word itself means *ancestor* and *table* in German. It's also referred to as the *Sosa-Stradonitz System* of numbering.

Albumen print: A type of photograph that was produced on a thin piece of paper coated with albumen and silver nitrate and usually mounted on cardboard; typically taken between 1858 and 1910.

All-in-One tree: A tree that lists everyone contained in the *Family File,* regardless of whether they are related.

Ambrotype: A type of photograph that was printed on thin glass and usually had a black backing; typically taken between 1858 and 1866.

Ancestor tree: A tree that runs horizontally across a page and identifies a primary person (including that person's name, date and place of birth, date and place of marriage, and date and place of death), his or her parents, and then each of their parents, and so on until the chart runs off the page. Also called a *Pedigree chart.*

Ancestor: A person from whom you are descended.

Archive: A physical location where historical documents and records are stored.

Attach: To link together two records in the *Family File* based upon a child-parent relationship.

Banns: See *marriage banns.*

Baptismal certificate: A certificate issued by a church at the time of baptism; sometimes used to approximate birth in the absence of a birth certificate.

Bibliography: A list of books or other materials that were used in research; also a list of books or other materials that are available on a particular topic.

Biographical sketch: A brief written account of a person's life.

Biography: A detailed written account of a person's life.

Birth certificate: A legal record stating when and where a person was born.

Bookmark: A method for saving links to your favorite Web sites within your Web browser so you can easily return to them.

Bounce: When e-mail doesn't reach the intended party for some reason or another and is returned to the sender.

Bounty land: Federal land given to a person in exchange for military service or some other civic service.

Browser: See *Web browser.*

Cabinet card: A larger version of the *carte-de-visite* photograph; typically taken between 1865 and 1906.

Cache: A directory on your computer where your Web browser stores information about Web pages and images it has downloaded. This enables the browser to load that page faster if you visit it again within a specified period of time.

Canon Code: A code that explains the bloodline relationship in legal terms by identifying how many degrees of separation (or steps) are between two people related by blood. Canon law counts only the number of steps from the nearest common *ancestor* of both relatives.

Carte-de-visite: A type of photograph that was a small paper print mounted on a card; collections were usually bound together in photo albums. Typically taken between 1858 and 1891.

CD-ROM: Acronym for compact disk-read only memory; used in your computer's compact disk drive. A CD-ROM stores large amounts of information (including multimedia) that can be retrieved by your computer.

Census index: A listing of the people who are included in particular census records, along with references indicating where you can find the actual census records.

Census: The counting of a population undertaken by a government.

Cite: To name the source of some information and provide reference to the original source.

Civil Code: A code that explains the bloodline relationship in legal terms by identifying how many degrees of separation (or steps) are between two people related by blood; civil law counts each step between two relatives as a degree.

Civil records: Government documents that contain information on the civic duties of your *ancestors,* proceedings of municipal governments, or any other records of your ancestors' interaction with the government; often found in local and state archives or courthouses.

Civil registration: Primary record of a vital event in life: birth, death, or marriage; for the most part, originals are kept by local governments. Also called *vital records* in the United States and Canada.

Commercial Internet service provider: A company or organization that supplies access to the Internet for a fee.

Comprehensive genealogical site: A Web site that identifies a large number of other genealogical sites containing information on families, locations, or a variety of other genealogically related subjects.

Cookies: Pieces of information that are sent to your computer by other computers when you visit certain Web pages. Generally, cookies are used for navigational purposes or by commercial sites that want to rotate banner advertisements for you so that you don't get tired of the same old advertisement. They are also used to keep track of the personal preferences of a user on a particular site.

Copyright: The exclusive right of a creator to reproduce, distribute, perform, display, sell, lend, or rent his or her creations or prepare derivative works.

County clerk: The clerk of the county court that records or maintains records of transactions and events in that county. Sometimes called the county recorder.

Cyberspace: A slang term for the Internet.

Daguerreotype: A type of photograph that required a long exposure time and was taken on silver-plated copper; typically taken between 1839 and 1860.

Database: A collection of structured information that is entered, organized, stored, and used on a computer. Individual pieces of information are stored in fields that become part of a record. One or more records comprise a database.

Death certificate: A legal record stating when and where a person died.

Declaration of intent: A sworn statement by a person who intends to become a naturalized citizen of the United States.

Deed: A document that records the transfer of ownership of a piece of property or land.

Descendant tree: A tree that contains information about an *ancestor* and spouse (or particular spouses if there was more than one), and their children and their spouses, grandchildren and spouses, and so on down the family line; it's usually formatted vertically on a page like a list.

Descendant: A person who descended from a particular *ancestor.*

Dial-up connection: A method of connecting to the Internet wherein your computer uses a telephone line to call in to an *Internet service provider.*

Digital camera: A camera that captures images to memory rather than to film, and then downloads the images to your computer.

Digitized record: A copy or image of a record that has been made using electronic means (typically a *scanner* and computer).

Directory: A collection of information about individuals who live in a particular place.

Download: Getting a file (information or a program) to your computer from another computer.

Electronic mail: Messages that are sent from one person to another electronically over the *Internet.* Also called *e-mail.*

E-mail: Short for *electronic mail.*

Emigrant: A person who leaves or moves away from one country to settle in another country.

Enumeration district: The area assigned to a particular *enumerator* of the *census.*

Enumerator: A person who collects details on individuals during a *census.*

Estate: The assets and liabilities of a person who dies.

Family association site: A Web page that's designed and posted by an organization devoted to researching a particular family.

Family association: An organized group of individuals who are researching the same family.

Family Group Sheet: A summary of a particular family including biographical information about a husband, wife, and their children.

Family history: The written account of a family's existence over time.

Family Outline report: A list of the descendants of a particular *ancestor.*

Family Page: The basic building block for entering and extracting information from the Family Tree Maker program. It contains basic information about vital events in the lives of a family.

FAQ: Acronym for *Frequently Asked Questions.*

Forum: A subject-specific area where members post messages and files.

Fraternal order: A service club or organization of persons.

Frequently Asked Questions: A Web page or message posted to a mailing list or newsgroup that contains answers to the most-asked questions to the particular Web site, mailing list, or newsgroup. Usually serves as a starting point for people new to a site or resource.

Gazetteer: Geographical dictionary that provides information about places.

GEDCOM: Acronym for *Genealogical Data Communication.*

Genealogical Data Communication: The standard file format for exporting and importing information between genealogical *databases;* intended to make data translatable to different genealogical software programs so that you can share your family information easily.

Genealogical society: An organized group that attempts to preserve documents and history for the area in which the society is located; often a genealogical society has a second purpose, which is to help its members research their *ancestors.*

Genealogy: The study of *ancestors, descendants,* and family origins.

Geographic-specific Web site: A Web site that has information pertaining to a particular locality (town, county, state, country, or other area).

Glass plate negative: A type of photograph made from light-sensitive silver bromide immersed in gelatin; typically taken between 1848 and 1930.

Historical society: An organized group that attempts to preserve documents and history for the area in which the society is located.

Home page: The entry point for a *Web site.*

Hourglass tree: A tree that displays both the ancestors and descendants of a particular individual.

HTML: Acronym for *HyperText Markup Language.*

HyperText Markup Language: The programming language of the *World Wide Web.* HTML is a code that's translated into graphical pages by software called a *Web browser.*

Immigrant: A person who moves from one country and settles in another.

Immigration record: A record of a person's entry into a specific country where he or she was not natively born or naturalized.

Index: A list of some sort. An index can be a list of Web sites, types of records, or so on.

Interlibrary loan: A system in which one library loans a book or other material to another library for a person to borrow or use.

Internet service provider: A company or other organization that provides people with access to the Internet through a direct connection or dial-up connection. Also called *ISP.*

Internet: A system of computer networks joined together by high-speed data lines.

Intestate: A person who died without leaving a valid *will.*

ISP: Acronym for *Internet service provider.*

Kinship report: A list of family members and how they relate to one particular individual in your database; kinship reports sometimes include the *Civil Code* and *Canon Code* for the relationship to the individual.

Land grant: Permission to purchase or a gift of land in exchange for military service or other civic service.

Land patent: A document that conveyed the title of a piece of land to a new owner upon that person meeting certain required conditions to own the land.

Land record: A document recording the sale or exchange of land; most land records are maintained at a local level where the property is located.

Lineage-linked databases: Lineage-linked databases are programs that organize information based on the family relationship of individuals.

Lurking: Reading messages that others post to a *mailing list, newsgroup,* or Web site without posting any messages of your own.

Maiden name: A woman's *surname* prior to marriage; sometimes reflected as *née* on records and documents.

Mailing list: An *e-mail* exchange *forum* that consists of a group of people who share common interests. E-mail messages posted to the list come directly to your e-mail; the list consists of the names of everyone who joins the group. When you want to send a message to the group, you post it to a single e-mail address that subsequently delivers the message to everyone on the list.

Manumission papers: Documents granting slaves their freedom.

Marriage banns: A proclamation in front of a church congregation of the intent to marry someone.

Marriage bond: A financial contract guaranteeing that a marriage is going to take place; usually posted by the groom and another person (often the father or brother of the bride).

Marriage certificate: A legal document certifying the union of two individuals.

Marriage license: A document granting permission to marry from a civil or ecclesiastical authority.

Maternal: Relating to the mother's side of the family.

Microfiche: A clear sheet that contains tiny images of documents, records, books, and so on; you must read it with a microfiche reader or other magnifying equipment.

Microfilm: A roll of clear film that contains tiny images of documents, records, books, and so forth; you must read it with a microfilm reader.

Modem: A piece of equipment that allows your computer to talk to other computers through a telephone line; modems can be internal (inside your computer) or external (plugged into one of your computer's serial ports).

Moderator: A person who determines whether a post to a *newsgroup* or *mailing list* is appropriate, and if so, posts it.

Mortgage: Legal agreement to repay money borrowed with real property as collateral.

Muster record: A type of military pay record reflecting who was present with a military unit at a particular time and place.

Naturalization record: The legal document proving someone is a naturalized citizen.

Naturalization: The process of becoming a citizen or subject of a particular country in a manner other than birth in that country.

Netiquette: Simple guidelines for communicating effectively and politely on the *Internet.*

News reader: Software required to read messages posted to a *newsgroup.*

News server: One or more computers that replicate *newsgroups* over the Internet.

Newsgroup: A place to post messages of a particular focus so that groups of people at large can read them online; messages are posted to a *news server* which, in turn, copies the messages to other news servers.

Notebook computer: A compact computer that's portable, often called a laptop.

Obituary: An account of someone's death that usually appears in a newspaper or other type of media.

One-name study: A page on the *World Wide Web* that focuses on research involving one particular *surname* regardless of the geographic location in which it appears.

Online: Gaining access to and using the *Internet;* available through the Internet.

Orphan: An infant or child whose parents are both deceased. In some early times and places, a child was considered an orphan if his or her father had died but the mother was still living.

Outline Descendant tree: A textual report that begins with a particular individual and then lists each descendant on a separate line.

Palmtop: A hand-sized computer that is portable and can contain some of the same programs that are housed on desktop computers.

Passenger list: Listing of the names of passengers who traveled from one country to another on a particular ship.

Paternal: Relating to the father's side of the family.

Pedigree chart: A chart that runs horizontally across a page, identifying a primary person (including that person's name, date and place of birth, date and place of marriage, and date and place of death), his or her parents, and then each of their parents, and so on until the chart runs off the page. Sometimes called an *Ancestor chart.*

Pension record: A type of military record reflecting the amount of a pension the government paid to an individual who served in the military; pension records also showed the amount of pension paid to the widow or orphan(s) of such an individual.

Personal Web page: A page on the *World Wide Web* that was designed and posted by an individual or family.

Petition for land: An application your *ancestor* may have filed for a land grant.

Plat map: A map of lots within a tract of land usually showing the owner's names.

Platinum print: A type of photograph with a matte surface that appeared to be embedded in the paper. Images were often highlighted with artistic chalk, giving the photo a hand-drawn quality; typically taken between 1880 and 1930.

Primary source: A document, oral account, photograph, or any other item that was created at the time a certain event occurred; information for the record was supplied by a witness to the event.

Probate records: Types of court records that deal with the settling of an *estate* upon one's death. Probate records include contested wills and *will* readings; often the file contains testimonies and the ruling.

Probate: Settlement of someone's *estate* after death.

Professional researcher: A person who will research your genealogy — particular family lines — or obtain copies of documents for you for a fee.

Progenitor: The furthest-back *ancestor* you know about in a particular family line.

Query: A research question that you post to a particular Web site, *mailing list,* or *newsgroup* so that other researchers can help you with your genealogical research problems and challenges.

Register form: A standard way of organizing and numbering individuals into a genealogical report. The system was developed for the *New England Historical and Genealogical Register* around 1870.

Robot: A program that travels throughout the *Internet* and collects information about sites and resources that it comes across. Also called a *spider.*

Scanner: A device that captures digital images of photographs and documents into your computer.

Search engine: A program that searches either a large index of information generated by *robots* or a particular Web site.

Secondary source: A document, oral account, or any other record that was created after an event took place or for which information was supplied by someone who was not an eyewitness to the event.

Server: A computer that makes information available for access by other computers.

Service record: A type of military record that chronicles the military career of an individual.

Shareware: Software that you can try before you pay to license and use it permanently; usually you download shareware off the *Internet.*

Signature file: A file you can create and attach to the bottom of your e-mail messages that gives your name, contact information, surnames you're researching, or anything else you want to convey to others.

Site: One or more *Web pages;* also called a *Web site.*

Snail mail: Mail delivered by hand — such as U.S. Mail.

Social Security Death Index: An *index* of those persons for whom Social Security death claims were filed with the United States government.

Sosa-Stradonitz System: See *Ahnentafel.*

Sound card: An internal computer device that enables you to hear any audio that comes on software or audio files that you download off the *Internet.*

Soundex: A system of indexing that places names that sound alike but are spelled differently into groups; the Soundex code for a name includes a letter followed by three numbers.

Source: Any person or material (book, document, record, periodical, and so on) that provides information for your research.

Spider: A program that travels throughout the *Internet* and collects information about sites and resources it comes across. Also called a *robot.*

Stereographic card: A type of photograph that was curved and rendered a three-dimensional effect when used with a viewer; developed in the 1850s.

Surname: A last name or family name.

Survey: Detailed drawing and legal description of the boundaries of a land parcel.

Tax record: A record of any tax paid, including property, inheritance, and church taxes; most taxes were collected at the local level, but the records have now been turned over to government archives.

Telnet: A text-based program that allows you to log in to another computer and view files or documents that are available for public access; you need a Telnet client (software) to use Telnet.

Thread: A group of messages with a common subject on a *newsgroup.*

Tintype: A type of photograph that was made on a metal sheet; the image was often coated with a varnish. Typically taken between 1858 and 1910.

Tract book: A book describing the lots within a township or other geographic area.

Transcribed record: A copy of the content of a record that has been duplicated word for word.

Uniform Resource Locator: A way of addressing resources on the *World Wide Web;* also called *URL.*

URL: Acronym for *Uniform Resource Locator.*

Video-capture board: A device that enables your computer to grab images from your video camera or VCR.

Vital record: Primary record of a vital event in life — birth, death, or marriage; for the most part, originals are kept by local governments. Often called *civil registrations* outside the United States.

Warrant: A certificate to receive land when your *ancestor's* petition for a land grant was approved.

Web browser: Software that enables you to view *HTML* documents on the *Internet.*

Web page: A multimedia document that is created in *HTML* and viewable on the *Internet* with the use of a *Web browser.*

Web site: One or more *Web* pages created by an individual or organization; also called a *site.*

Webmaster: A person responsible for creating and maintaining a particular Web site.

Will: A legal document that explains how a person wants his or her *estate* to be settled or distributed upon death.

Witness: Someone who attests that he or she saw an event.

World Wide Web: A system for viewing and using multimedia documents on the *Internet;* Web documents are created in *HyperText Markup Language (HTML)* and are read by *Web browsers.*

Zip disk: A computer disk that you use with an Iomega Zip drive; stores up to 250MB of data.

Index

• •

• C •

YOUR ONLINE RESOURCE

WWW.DUMMIES.COM

Discover Dummies Online!

The Dummies Web Site is your fun and friendly online resource for the latest information about ...*For Dummies*® books and your favorite topics. The Web site is the place to communicate with us, exchange ideas with other ...*For Dummies* readers, chat with authors, and have fun!

Ten Fun and Useful Things You Can Do at www.dummies.com

1. Win free ...*For Dummies* books and more!
2. Register your book and be entered in a prize drawing.
3. Meet your favorite authors through the IDG Books Author Chat Series.
4. Exchange helpful information with other ...*For Dummies* readers.
5. Discover other great ...*For Dummies* books you must have!
6. Purchase Dummieswear™ exclusively from our Web site.
7. Buy ...*For Dummies* books online.
8. Talk to us. Make comments, ask questions, get answers!
9. Download free software.
10. Find additional useful resources from authors.

Link directly to these ten fun and useful things at **http://www.dummies.com/10useful**

SURF THE NET

WWW.DUMMIES.COM

For other technology titles from IDG Books Worldwide, go to **www.idgbooks.com**

Not on the Web yet? It's easy to get started with *Dummies 101*®: *The Internet For Windows*®*98* or *The Internet For Dummies*®, 6th Edition, at local retailers everywhere.

IDG BOOKS WORLDWIDE

Find other ...*For Dummies* books on these topics:
Business • Career • Databases • Food & Beverage • Games • Gardening • Graphics • Hardware
Health & Fitness • Internet and the World Wide Web • Networking • Office Suites
Operating Systems • Personal Finance • Pets • Programming • Recreation • Sports
Spreadsheets • Teacher Resources • Test Prep • Word Processing

IDG BOOKS WORLDWIDE BOOK REGISTRATION

Register This Book and Win!

We want to hear from you!

Visit **http://my2cents.dummies.com** to register this book and tell us how you liked it!

- Get entered in our monthly prize giveaway.

- Give us feedback about this book — tell us what you like best, what you like least, or maybe what you'd like to ask the author and us to change!

- Let us know any other ...*For Dummies*® topics that interest you.

Your feedback helps us determine what books to publish, tells us what coverage to add as we revise our books, and lets us know whether we're meeting your needs as a ...*For Dummies* reader. You're our most valuable resource, and what you have to say is important to us!

Not on the Web yet? It's easy to get started with *Dummies 101*®: *The Internet For Windows*® *98* or *The Internet For Dummies*®, 6th Edition, at local retailers everywhere.

Or let us know what you think by sending us a letter at the following address:

...*For Dummies* Book Registration
Dummies Press
7260 Shadeland Station, Suite 100
Indianapolis, IN 46256-3917
Fax 317-596-5498

BESTSELLING BOOK SERIES